Racial Minorities
in Multicultural Canada

Edited by
Peter S. Li and B. Singh Bolaria

University of Saskatchewan

Garamond Press
Toronto, Canada

Canadian Cataloguing in Publication Data

Main entry under title:
Racial minorities in multicultural Canada

A selection of papers from the 23rd annual conference of
the Western Association of Sociology and Anthropology,
held at the University of Saskatchewan, Feb. 1982.
Includes bibliographical references.
ISBN 0-920059-00-7

1. Canada - Population - Ethnic groups - Congresses. *
2. Minorities - Canada - Congresses.   3. Multiculturalism
- Canada - Congresses.   I. Li, Peter S.   II. Bolaria,
B. Singh, 1936-   III. Western Association of
Sociology and Anthropology.   Conference (23rd : 1982 :
University of Saskatchewan).

FC104.R32 1983   305.8'071   C83-098858-0
F1035.A1R32 1983

Cover Design: Walter Augustowitsch

Typeset by Moveable Type

Printing by Muskox Press

This publication is supported in part by a grant from the Multiculturalism Directorate, Government of Canada

Garamond Press
163 Neville Park Blvd.,
Toronto, Ontario
M4E 3P7

Preface

In February, 1982, the Department of Sociology, University of Saskatchewan hosted the 23rd annual conference of the Western Association of Sociology and Anthropology (WASA). Of the twenty-nine sessions in the programme, six were in the areas of multiculturalism, race relations, and ethnic institutions. In addition, there were a few papers presented in other sessions bearing tangential relations to the topics. We were the organizers of the programme at that time, and when the conference was over, we saw the possibility of putting together a selection of papers on racial minorities in Canada.

The 23rd WASA conference was funded by a number of sources, including the President's Office, University of Saskatchewan; Protocol Office, Province of Saskatchewan; Secretary of State; and Social Science and Humanities Council of Canada. The grant from the Secretary of State enabled us to organize three additional sessions on multiculturalism and ethnic relations, and to provide travel expenses to some participants. After the conference, we submitted another application to the Multiculturalism Directorate, Secretary of State, and were awarded a grant to publish selected papers on racial minorities from the conference proceedings.

Aside from the major funding from the Secretary of State to publish the monograph, additional financial support was made available to us from the President's Publication Fund, University of Saskatchewan. We wish to thank Dean A. Knight, College of Arts and Science, and Dr. J.A.E. Bardwell, Director of Research, both of the University of Saskatchewan for their support of this project. Mr. George Stushnoff of the Secretary of State, Saskatoon Office, provided helpful comments on the proposal of this manuscript.

The Social Research Unit, located in the Department of Sociology, University of Saskatchewan, agreed to publish this collection in its research monograph series. We appreciate the secretarial and editorial assistance from the department. In particular, we would like to acknowledge Dawn Currie for proofreading the manuscript, and Rhonda Kopp for typing it.

Peter S. Li and B. Singh Bolaria

Introduction

It is over a decade since October 8, 1971, when Prime Minister Trudeau announced in the Canadian parliament the policy of multiculturalism within a bilingual framework. The purpose of the policy, according to the Prime Minister, was "to break down discriminatory attitudes and cultural jealousies... (and) form the base of a society which is based on fair play for all." (House of Commons Debates, October 8, 1971:8545). Despite this intention, there is little indication that racial prejudice has been less prevalent, or ethnic inequality less evident. On the contrary, there are suggestions that racial disharmony is on the rise as the economic recession deepens in the eighties.

The failure of multiculturalism, if it is fair to use such a phrase, is not so much a sound policy mismanaged. Rather, it is a failure to solve non-cultural problems with cultural solutions. Issues of ethnic inequality and racial discrimination have political and economic roots in the history and social institutions of Canada, and their solutions lie beyond what multiculturalism can offer. Some critics of the policy, as for example Brotz (1980), have pointed out the gap between the conceptual muddle of multiculturalism, and the ideological reality of a bourgeois-democratic way of life aspired by all Canadians. Other critics, such as Roberts and Clifton (1982), have argued that most ethnic groups in Canada do not have the structural resources to promote their cultural heritage, and the policy of multiculturalism simply reinforces the concept of "symbolic ethnicity" which provides the appearance of pluralism. Simply put, the irony of multiculturalism is that it furnishes Canadian society with a great hope without having to change the fundamental structures of society. Multiculturalism is the failure of an illusion, not of a policy.

If the eighties is the worst of times since the Great Depression, it is also the best of times, as Trudeau put it in the 1982 Liberal Convention, to re-examine Canadian society. Like other policies, multi-culturalism has to be re-examined in light of the past, and with a view of the future. It is with this intention in mind that we put together this collection. The papers are by no means a solution to a faltering policy, but each in its own way calls to attention aspects of Canadian society from which a better policy may evolve.

This collection has five sections. The first one deals with some official policies in Canada which have implications for race and ethnic relations. Basran's paper on Canadian immigration policy and theories of racism is a critical review of the immigration policy and its implications for racial ideology in Canada. Ubale's paper is a valuable contribution of an administrator's assessments of human rights commissions. The problem for many commissions, as Ubale puts it, is to balance the delicate roles of advocating and regulating racial harmony. The other two papers in this section, by Mazurek, and Dawson, are critical analyses of the school system as a promoter of dominant ideology. The school remains a powerful institution where dominant ideology is maintained and where minority participation is undermined.

The second section of this collection, entitled Minorities and Health Care, examines the important issue of health care participation. Employing the internal colonial thesis, Brady shows that the health care status of treaty Indians has to be understood in a structural and historical perspective. The difference in the quality of life between Indians and non-Indians, as measured by access to psychiatric services, is well documented in the paper by Fritz and D'Arcy. The last paper in this section by New and Watson examines the structural and cultural constraints of health care utilization for Chinese-Canadians.

Section three looks at the ethnic family as a social institution, and addresses the issue of intramarriages. Li's paper on the Chinese-Canadian family suggests that the contemporary form of the Chinese-Canadian family is greatly constrained by historical racism and exclusion, and has little to do with the traditional culture transplanted to Canada. The paper by Abernathy addresses the questions of status integration and ethnic intermarriages, which among other things, have important implications on language maintenance and cultural transmission.

Section four covers the issues of institutional control and ethnic organizations. Ujimoto's paper is a thorough account of the plight of the Japanese-Canadians. His paper addresses the often ignored influence of institutional controls on the social relations of minority members. The paper by Baureis is a successful attempt to typologize various ethnic voluntary associations, using in particular the case of the Chinese.

The last section of this collection deals with some theoretical issues of ethnic studies. Minton's paper is a refreshing approach to minority studies, drawing upon the literature of social psychology and sociology. Bolaria's paper challenges the dominant sociological perspective as applied to non-white minorities, and offers new directions of research in this area.

References

Brotz, Howard
    1980   "Multiculturalism in Canada: A Muddle", **Canadian Public Policy**, VI:1:41-46.
Roberts, Lance and Rodney Clifton
    1982   "Exploring the Ideology of Canadian Multiculturalism", **Canadian Public Policy**, VIII:1:88-94.

TABLE OF CONTENTS

Preface . . . .
Introduction . . . .

1 Racial and Ethnic Policies in Canada

1   Canadian Immigration Policy and Theories of Racism
      G.S. Basran 3

2   Administrative Aspects of Race Relations
    Policies and Programs
      Bhausaheb Ubale 15

3   Multiculturalism and Schools: A Critical Analysis
      K. Mazurek 26

4   Social and Cultural Reproduction
    and the School's Role in Social Mobility
      Don Dawson 31

II Minorities and Health Care

5   The Underdevelopment of the Health Status of Treaty Indians
      Paul Brady 39

6   Pathways to Health Care Among Chinese-Canadians:
    An Exploration
      Peter New and W. Watson 56

7   Comparisons: Indian and Non-Indian Use
    of Psychiatric Services
      Wayne Fritz and Carl D'Arcy 68

III Marriage and Minority Families

8 The Chinese Canadian Family
   Peter S. Li 86

9 Status Integration and Ethnic Intramarriage in Canada
   Thomas J. Abernathy 97

IV Institutional Control and Ethnic Organizations

10 Ethnic Organizational Theory: The Chinese Case
   Gunter Baureis 103

11 Institutional Controls and Their Impact on
   Japanese Canadian Social Relations
   Victor Ujimoto 121

V Theoretical Perspectives of Race Relations

12 Emancipatory Social Psychology as a Paradigm
   for the Study of Minority Groups
   Henry Minton 148

13 Dominant Perspectives and non-White Minorities
   B. Singh Bolaria 157

Part I
Racial and Ethnic Policies in Canada

1

Canadian Immigration Policy and Theories of Racism

Gurcharn S. Basran
   University of Saskatchewan

Introduction

Various efforts have been made by social scientists to explain racism, which is defined as a doctrine holding that there is a connection between racial and cultural traits and that some races are, inherently, superior to others. The main objective of this paper is to review some theories of racism in Canada. Racism in Canada is not the product of the seventies and eighties. It has been practiced systematically by the Canadian government and people in general from the very beginning of Canadian history. It is not an aberration from our way of life, thinking and behaviour. It is a normal, expected and entrenched part of people's behaviour and their attitudes. It has been institutionalized throughout our history. It has been directed mainly against non-white populations in Canada. The chronology of the development of Canadian immigration and ethnic policies is the chronology of the discriminatory policies followed by the Canadian government in relation to non-white populations.

In a way we are all immigrants in Canada, except the Natives. In 1871, when the first census was taken in Canada, ninety-two percent of the three and one-half million people who lived in Canada were either of British (61%) or of French (31%) origin. The British established the first permanent European settlement in the United States in 1607, while the French established the first European settlement in Canada in 1608. Vikings came to Canada in the 1100's, but we do not know much about their settlements and their influence on Canadian history.

Since the earlier settlement days, the Canadian ethnic population has changed significantly. According to the 1971 census, 5.5 million Canadians are in the 'other' category (of neither English nor French origin), that is to say, 26.7 percent of the total population. Approximately 28.7 percent of the present population is of French origin; 44.6 percent is of British origin. This change in itself is a cause for concern on the part of some segments of the white population. More and more new immigrants are now coming from non-traditional (that is, third world and non-white) sources. However, it should be made clear that the traditional sources (British and American) are still dominant in Canadian immigration statistics. The main sources of Canadian immigrants are still the United States and Great Britain (Hawkins, 1971:12). However the relative number of charter members from Europe (English and French) is decreasing.

Not considering the Black settlements in the east, the third world non-white immigration into Canada started around the 1860's. Though this paper does not deal with the Black situation in Canada, it should be pointed out that slavery was practiced in Canada for two centuries and, until around 1850, our forefathers discovered no moral objection to it. (Pentland, 1959:451). Chinese were brought in to work on the construction of the Canadian Pacific line. It was difficult to secure white labour for this purpose. Woodsworth, in his book **Strangers Within Our Gates**, points out:

> "The Chinese, in any number, were first brought in when the Canadian Pacific Railway was being built, in order to work on the construction on that line when it was next to impossible to secure white labour" (Woodsworth, 1909:171).

While discussing the contributions of Chinese labour to the construction of the CPR, John Porter emphasizes:

> "Without Chinese labour the construction and completion of the CPR would have been indefinitely postponed. Not until 1962 were coloured people from Commonwealth countries looked upon as possible immigrants, except for small numbers who were allowed in to work as domestic servants, an entrance status previously held by lower class British and eastern European females" (Porter, 1965:69).

East Indians came to the West Coast of Canada to perform menial jobs on the railroad, in construction and in mining. Some of them had come to Canada after being part of the British Army in India. Canada was viewed as a land of open opportunity.

Non-white immigrants were brought in to serve the economic interests of the Canadian bourgeoisie. The labour was cheap, available, docile, and needed. Moreover, it was possible for the Canadian state to control this immigration according to the racist attitudes of the Canadian population.

The Canadian state, like any other state, serves the interests of the bourgeois class.[1] It facilitates the process of accumulation and profit making by the ruling class. It legitimizes their (the ruling class's) dominant position in the society, as well as their method of control of the system of production and distribution. The state will use physical coercion as a mechanism of social control if other mechanisms of legitimization fail. In Canada, the state plays an important role not only as a government and through its crown corporations, but also through its influence over, and support of, other institutions. Because of its influence in all these areas, it does not have to resort to physical coercion frequently. Members of the society are socialized from day one to accept the given system as legitimate and desirable. Educational institutions and the class media (rather than the mass media) perpetuate it.[2]

To understand racism in Canada, one has to comprehend the nature of capitalism, the role of the Canadian state and the control of the Canadian economy by the United States. Canadian immigration policy has been dictated by these forces.

There are various examples of institutionalized racism in Canada. Students of Canadian history in general, and those responsible for Canadian immigration policy in particular, are well aware of various pieces of legislation, laws and practices that discriminate against the non-white and immigrant population. As soon as CPR construction was completed in 1885, and Chinese labour started entering into other occupations, institutional racism began in various forms (Li, 1979a; Munro, 1974; Palmer, 1970). A head tax of $50.00 was imposed on Chinese in 1885. It was increased to $100.00 in 1900 and $500.00 in 1903. Other Orientals were also subjected to a head tax, while passage assistance was available to the British immigrants. Chinese and East Indians had to pay a head tax in Canada and their immigration was virtually stopped after 1907. Orientals had no voting rights until World War II and were not allowed to practice certain professions in British Columbia. According to the 1906 Immigration Act, important discretionary powers were given to immigration officers, who used them against non-white immigrants in a ruthless and discriminatory manner (Krotki and Matejko, 1977). There were race riots in British Columbia in 1907, in which Orientals were attacked and their properties, businesses and houses destroyed. In 1914 there was the Komagata Maru incident. Four hundred East Indians were not allowed to land in Vancouver on the grounds that the journey from the country of which the immigrants were natives or naturalized citizens was not continuous. The East Indians were travelling on a Japanese ship. This is one of the few times when the Canadian navy went into action to uphold racist laws of the land. In another case in 1923, Chinese were squeezed out of fishing. The Canadians had a gentleman's agreement with the Japanese, limiting Japanese immigration to Canada. In 1907 immigrants from Asia were required to have a minimum of $200.00 in landing money. In 1919 this amount was increased to $250.00. In 1930, section 38 of the Immigration Act prohibited the landing in Canada of immigrants of any Asiatic race. We are familiar with the wartime relocation of Japanese (many of these, Canadian citizens) from the British Columbia coastal areas and virtual confiscation of their property. Their treatment in relocation camps is well documented (Sunahara, 1980; Broadfoot, 1977). In 1946, nearly 4,000 Japanese returned to Japan, many of them disenchanted and disillusioned after their wartime experiences in Canada. It is interesting to note that the U.S. government has made an effort to compensate Japanese-Americans for the loss of their property at the time of the relocation during World War II, but that the Canadian government has been rather quiet about the compensation to Japanese-Canadians. According to 1912 legislation, Saskatchewan made it an offense for an Oriental businessman to hire a white woman. Until 1952 the Japanese immigrants were forbidden to live in Lethbridge by city ordinance. So, the history of non-white immigration in Canada has been based on institutional racism. Canadian immigration policy developed a priority class of immigrants. In 1923, defined by order-in-council 183, British and American immigrants were the most favoured, northern Europeans were relatively well received, and other Europeans were accepted if no one else was available. Non-whites were not welcomed and were actively barred from coming into Canada through various pieces of legislation. This policy was partly justified by immigration officers, as well as government officials, by pointing out the lack of ability of non-white immigrants to assimilate, that is, their inability to adapt to Canada because of their cultural, religious, language and climatic backgrounds,[3] though we do not know of any research to support this myth. Some of the recent studies in the area of race and ethnic relations actually indicate that whites from an Anglo-Saxon Protestant background have a low level of commitment to Canada compared to other ethnic groups (Richmond, 1974:37). If we look at the relative sense of belonging to Canada of various immigrant groups, we find that, compared to immigrants from Britain and the U.S., immigrants from third world countries have a greater sense of belonging. The relative sense of belonging was determined on the basis of the answer to this question: 'Do you now feel that Canada is my "home" country, or do you still feel as if you belong more to your former country?' (Government of Canada, 1974).

After World War II, a large number of third world countries became independent. They started playing an important role in the United Nations. The Non-alignment movement was developed and supported by third world countries. The Cold War between the superpowers (U.S.A. and U.S.S.R.) and their respective allies was a hot issue. Canada experienced rapid economic growth. Canadian immigration policies were changed because of these factors, even though immigration policies remained basically discriminatory against the non-white population. The quota system was introduced, limiting to certain numbers the people allowed into Canada from third world countries. Eventually this system was replaced by the 1967 Immigration Act. Immigrants were allowed to enter Canada in accordance with their desirability as workers and so as to fulfill the growing need of the labour market. The point system was introduced to determine a person's qualifications, ability, training in two official languages (English and French), age, chance of getting a job, education, occupational skills and occupational demands. In 1975, the Canadian government issued the Green Paper and established a parliamentary committee to make recommendations for changing the Canadian Immigration Act. In the Green Paper, Blacks and Asians were seen as agents of social stress and Canadians were congratulated for their 'hospitality in adapting to such novel and distinctive features' (Ellwood, et al., 1975). Various ethnic organizations submitted briefs to this committee and, after visiting major cities in Canada, the committee made its recommendations to the government. The Immigration Act of 1976 was passed on the basis of these recommendations.

This section of the paper has provided a brief history of Canadian immigration policy and of institutional racism against non-white populations in Canada. As racism remains a fact of Canadian life today, as it always has been, the next section will examine some theoretical explanations for racism in Canada.

Theories of Racism

Students of race and ethnic relations are familiar with the theory of assimilation. Students interested in reviewing theories of assimilation should read material by Rebert Park, Louis Wirth, Gordon Milton, Nathan Glaser, Daniel P. Moynihan, Oscar Lewis, and others. As the assimilation theory has been discussed widely as part of race and ethnic relations, I do not intend to discuss it in any detail in this paper. I will provide a brief discussion of the assimilation theory, as it has been dominant, relevant and important in Canadian sociology and is helpful in understanding Canadian immigration policy. This theory proposes the gradual assimilation of ethnic groups into Canadian society. Any difficulties or maladjustments experienced by ethnic groups are primarily explained by references to their culture, beliefs, religious ideas, values and national or geographical background. Assimilation is considered as a gradual and painful process for the ethnic group, but one that is necessary to adapt to the new society.[4] Structural factors such as the nature of the economic system, the role of the state, power relationships, the role of the bourgeoisie, the nature of the institutions, racism, the nature of capitalism, etc., are ignored or are not considered important. This theoretical perspective not only overlooks the nature of the structural arrangements of our society, but it also blames the immigrant groups for not assimilating or not adapting to the Canadian society. This approach ignores the historical reality, as well as the nature of the workings of Canadian society. It must be pointed out that professional social scientists have been used as apologists to justify Canadian immigration policy and the exploitation of the working class (Cappon, 1975).

Marxist Explanation of Racism

From the Marxist perspective, racism is the function of economic inequality, the class system and our system of production and distribution. As the capitalist class has to appropriate profit from the working class and bourgeois existence and survival depends upon the exploitation of labour, racism is used to justify such exploitation. Racism is a mechanism which is used to pay low wages to a certain segment of the population in order to appropriate more surplus value. This population is considered inferior so as to justify their low wages. Racism serves the economic, political and social interests of the ruling class.

Immigration is also used by the ruling class to create a reserve army of labour which can be utilized according to their needs and interests. In Canadian society immigrants are brought in when they are needed and their entry is controlled by economic conditions. Canadian immigration policy has been dictated by the ruling class. Non-white immigrants have been brought in when they were needed to perform some important role in the economy. They have occupied positions which were difficult to fill with a white labour force, or where the white labour force was not willing to do these jobs. When the economic situation has deteriorates, non-white immigrants have been used as scapegoats for the economic ills of the society. They have been used as reasons for unemployment, urban crowding and other problems in the economy.

As immigration is used to create a reserve army of labour, labour unions view non-white immigrants as a reason for the lowering of wages and as having an adverse effect on their bargaining power with the bourgeois class (Casteles and Kosack, 1973). Immigrants sometimes compete with the working class for scarce job opportunities. These factors, as well as socialization, training, education and the mass media, create antagonism between the working class and non-white immigrants. It divides the working class, as many immigrants are also part of this group. Gorz points out that,

> "The absence of immigrant workers would not simply provoke an increase in wages and in political weight, of the national working class, it would detonate a general crisis of capitalist society at every level, by modifying the whole set of historical conditions on the basis of which the price of the labour power and the wage structure is determined." (Gorz, 1973).

So the trade union campaign in Canada, as elsewhere, to stop immigrants from working during a depression, as well as the negative atitudes of the union workers towards immigrants, must be understood in the context of these economic realities (Peterson, 1936:23). Not only the working class, but all Canadians, become opposed to immigration during recession and economic crisis (Wood, 1978:551).

Some Marxists, who follow the split labour market theory, explain ethnic antagonism as the function of the labour market which is split along ethnic lines. According to this perspective, a labour market must contain at least two groups of workers whose price of labour differs for the same work or would differ if they did the same work (Bonacich, 1972). Capitalists want to pay as little as possible and will make use of ethnicity or any other characteristics of the population to justify their low remuneration. Low wages for women and non-white immigrants are explained by Marxists using this perspective (Szymanski, 1976). This systematic exploitation of the working class by the ruling class creates racial discrimination and undermines the solidarity of the working class by focusing on differences along ethnic, colour and sex lines (Szymanski, 1977). Women, coloured and other non-white immigrants are integrated into the work force to keep the wages of the white workers down.

As Nikolinakos points out:

"The sociological, psychological, cultural and geographical aspects of discrimination against racial and ethnic minorities are therefore only the reflection of something deeper: the discrimination of minorities in all its forms aims at facilitating or intensifying exploitation (Nikolinakos, 1973:369)."[5]

In Marxist literature, there is another point of view which emphasizes the positive contributions of landed immigrants and of the immigrant temporary work force in the host societies. Most of the immigrants are young and single and contribute significantly to the productivity of the country into which they immigrate. Immigrants also act to push the local labour force into higher socio-economic and occupational brackets. Moreover, they are not paid as much as the local labour force (Richmond, 1974). As they may be in the country on a temporary basis (as guest workers, temporary work permit holders, seasonal labourers), they usually do not draw unemployment insurance money, disability insurance, social welfare or old age pensions. As these workers are not accompanied by their families, they do not become a burden on institutions or social service agencies. As Samir Amin points out:

"This contribution of labour power of immigrant origin also contributes a hidden transfer of value from the periphery to the center, since the periphery has borne the cost of education and training this labour force" (Amin quoted in Gorz, 1970:29).

People who subscribe to this perspective take the position that the working class in imperialist, western countries benefits from the exploitation of the third world working class in developed countries. Historically speaking, people who were involved in international socialist movements at the end of the nineteenth and the beginning of the twentieth centuries were not much opposed to colonialism and imperialism practiced by western powers in third world countries. The European socialists were skeptical of various liberation movements in third world countries and were more interested in maintaining colonialism. Lenin was one of the few exceptions to those holding this view. Engels discussed the attitude of the British working class and wrote:

"The privileges given to some British workers were possible because of vast profits made by capitalists through domination of the world markets and imperialist exploitation of labour in other countries" (Engels quoted in Casteles and Kosack, 1973:4).

He further states:

"In the long run, wages may grow more in a country which has large scale immigration than that which does not, because of the dynamic effect of increased capital accumulation on productivity" (Engels quoted in Casteles and Kosack, 1973:18).

Some of the western European countries are very much dependent upon the immigrants and guest workers, who play an important role in their economies. By inviting this work force from abroad, the savings for these countries are enormous. According to studies done by Gorz,

"The import of ready-made workers amounts to a saving for the country of immigration, of between £8,000 and £16,000 per immigrant worker, if the social cost of a man of 18 is estimated for west European countries at between five and ten years work. The fact that a large proportion of immigrant workers (90% in Germany and Switzerland) are not accompanied by their families, brings the country of immigration an additional and substantial saving in social capital (housing, schools, hospitals, transport and other infrastructure facilities" (Gorz, 1970:29).

The research in this area is not extensive. Whether the number of immigrant workers and the exploitation of their labour result in an increase or decrease of the wages of the local working class depends upon the power of the labour unions and the social, political and economic arrangements in the host country. Some oil exporting countries in the Middle East (like Saudi Arabia) are also dependent upon a guest labour force from India, Pakistan and some other Asian countries. But exploitation of such a labour force in the Middle East may not necessarily lead to better working conditions and higher wages for the local working class. On the other hand, the exploitation of a guest labour force in West Germany, Switzerland and other European countries may very well result in an improvement in the living conditions of the local labour force. Nevertheless, the important point to keep in mind is that racism and antagonism among the working class are primarily the result of economic forces operating in these countries.

It is not surprising that the Canadian capitalist class, with the support of the Canadian government, depends heavily upon the exploitation of a temporary and seasonal work force. Rather than training the native Indians or other under- and unemployed workers in Canada, it is more profitable for the capitalist to bring people from Latin America, the West Indies and Europe on temporary work permits and to exploit their labour. This type of work force is docile, is paid a low wage and can be sent back when it is not needed. For a capitalist, the labour force is another input in the process of production and can be treated as a commodity. These policies also cause division and racism among the working class.

Another explanation of racism in Marxist literature is based on colonialism. Most of the colonial powers were European. These capitalist countries had to have access to foreign markets and sources of raw material to survive and to expand. Their capitalist economies necessitated the need for colonies. Colonies provided ready-made markets and also were sources from which to draw materials (Hudson, 1972). These colonies were exploited by colonial powers until World War II. Even when these colonies became independent, their economies have been closely tied to the economies of former colonial powers and are still being exploited. Racism, discrimination and exploitation were devised as mechanisms to justify this exploitation. Nikolinakos mentions that, "...during the colonial era racism was used as a tool in exploiting the colonial people through imposing upon them a system of discrimination" (Nikolinakos, 1973:365).

When we study racism in Canada, we realize that it is directed mainly against the non-white population (Henry, 1978; Brown, 1977; Pitman, 1977; Tienhaara, 1974; Li, 1979b; Sunahara, 1980; Mukerjee, 1981).[6] The very fact that the British ruled some countries in the third world and the Anglo-Saxon population is the dominant group in Canada may partly explain the prevalence of this racism in Canada. Baran and Sweezy, when making comments on race prejudice, point out that,

"Race prejudice as it exists in the world today is almost exclusively an atitude of whites and had its origins in the need of European conquerors from the sixteenth century to rationalize and justify the robbery, enslavement and continued exploitation." (Baran and Sweezy, 1966:246).[7]

Conclusion

In conclusion it must be made clear that racism should be understood in the context of the nature of the economy, polity and social structure of Canadian society. Racism is not a random, unique or idiosyncratic behaviour on the part of individuals. It is systematically developed, diffused and used to meet the needs and interests of certain groups in Canadian society. Institutional racism is an important part of Canadian history and is closely related to our system of production, distribution and control of economic resources. Historically, theories of racism were developed to justify colonialism and neo-colonialism. It is used now to support exploitation and imperialism. In other words, racism is an important part of our economic structure and political reality. The Canadian state legitimizes our system of production and distribution and serves the general interest of the bourgeoisie. The general role of the Canadian state is to help the capitalists in the accumulation process and to assist them to increase their profits. The Canadian government's immigration policy is to facilitate this process by providing a cheap labour force as required. During the time of economic crisis, immigrants are used as scapegoats to explain unemployment, urban crowding and other economic ills.

The role of the Canadian state is supported by the mass media, which is controlled and used by a small number of the capitalist class (58% of the daily newspapers in Canada are controlled by Thompson and Southam). The Canadian institutional structure also supports the policies of the economic elite. Social scientists become apologists for government policies which are formulated to protect and enhance the interests of the capitalist class in Canada. As long as the system of capitalism is practised in Canada, Canadian immigration will be tied closely to providing cheap labour for the changing needs of the Canadian economy. Racism will be used to justify the exploitation of the immigrants from third world countries.

Footnotes

1. To understand the role of the state, read Leo Panitch, 'The Role and Nature of the Canadian State' in Leo Panitch (ed.), **The Canadian State: Political Economy and Political Power** (Toronto: University of Toronto Press, 1977).

2. Read an interesting article by Gerald B. Sperling in John A. Fry (ed.), **Economy, Class and Social Reality: Issues in Contemporary Canadian Society** (Toronto: Butterworths, 1979), p. 316.
3. Canadian immigration documents are full of these references. See **Government of Canada, Manpower and Immigration, The Immigration Program** (1932), p. 149; Berry Brewton, **Race and Ethnic Relations** (Boston: Houghton-Mifflin Company, 1958), p. 413; **Canada Year Book** (1955), p. 166; Anthony H. Richmond, **Postwar Immigrants in Canada** (Toronto: University of Toronto Press, 1967), p. 3. Also see a statement of J.P. Guy in **The Canadian India Times**, Ottawa, September 15, 1977, p. 7. David C. Corbett, **Canadian Immigration Policy: A Critique** (Toronto: University of Toronto Press, 1957) pp. 3, 32, 36, 51, 52-54.
4. For a brief review of theories of assimilation and their limitations, see Peter S. Li and B. Singh Bolaria, 'Canadian Immigration Policy and Assimilation Theories' in John A. Fry (ed.) op. cit., p. 411.
5. Also see Tomoko Makabe, 'The Theory of the Split Labour Market: A Comparison of Japanese Experience in Brazil and Canada.' **Social Forces**, Vol. 59, No. 3 (March, 1981), pp. 786-809. Also see Bradley R. Shiller, 'Class Discrimination versus Racial Discrimination', **Review of Economics and Statistics**, Vol. 53, (1971) p. 268.
6. Bharati Mukerjee, 'An Invisible Woman,' **Saturday Night**, March, 1981, p. 36. Supporting this conclusion as well are remarks by Jim Fleming, Federal Minister responsible for Multiculturalism, on a Gallop Poll result according to which one third of more than 2,000 persons polled across the country support the idea of an all-white society for Canada. One of the questions on the poll asked if the respondents would support organizations that work towards preserving Canada for whites only. A startling 31.3 per cent Canadians said they would agree with that more or less, while 15.4 per cent said they agree completely with the all-white concept. Source: **Star Phoenix**, February 27, 1982, Sec. A, p. 8.
7. Also see Robert Blauner, **Racial Oppression in America** (Harper and Row Publishers, 1972).

References

Amin, Samir
 1974   **Accumulation on a World Scale**, New York: Monthly Review.
Baran, Paul A. and Paul M. Sweezy
 1966   **Monopoly Capital: An Essay on the American Economic and Social Order**, London: Penguin Books.
Bonacich, Edna
 1972   "A Theory of Ethnic Antagonism: The Split Labour Market", **American Sociological Review**, 37 (October), 547-559.
Broadfoot, Barry
 1977   **Years of Sorrow, Years of Shame**, Toronto: Doubleday.
Brown, Rose Tanner
 1977   "Racism in Canada: So You Think It's Just a Few Punks in Subway Stations", **The Last Post**, 6(2), p. 29.

Cappon, Paul
  1975 "The Green Paper: Immigration as a Tool of Profit", **Canadian Ethnic Studies Journal**, 7, No. 1, 50-54.
Casteles, Stephen and Coudula Kosack
  1972 "The Function of Labour Immigration in Western European Capitalism", **New Left Review**, 73.
Ellwood, Wayne et al.
  1975 **The Politics of People: The Green Paper on Immigration**, Department of Church in Society, United Church of Canada, No. 9 (May).
Gorz, Andre
  1970 "Immigrant Labour", **New Left Review**, 61.
  1973 "Immigrant Labour", **New Left Review**, 73, p. 28.
Government of Canada
  1974 **Three Years in Canada**, Manpower and Immigration, Information Canada, Ottawa.
Hawkins, Freda
  1972 **Canada and Immigration: Public Policy and Public Concern**, Ottawa: Queen's University Press.
Henry, Frances
  1978 **The Dynamics of Racism in Toronto**, A Report to the Secretary of State, Government of Canada, Ottawa.
Hudson, Michael
  1972 **Super Imperialism: The Economic Strategy of American Empire**, New York: Holt, Rinehart and Winston.
Krotki, Karol J. and Joanna Matejko
  1977 **Chronology in the Development of Canadian Immigration and Ethnic Policies**, An unpublished report, University of Alberta.
Li, Peter S.
  1979a "A Historical Historical Approach to Ethnic Stratification: The Case of the Chinese in Canada, 1858-1920", **Canadian Review of Sociology and Anthropology**. 16, No. 3, 320-332.
  1979b "Prejudice Against Asians in a Canadian City", Canadian Ethnic Studies, 11(2).
Mukerjee, Bharati
  1981 "An Invisible Woman", **Saturday Night**, March.
Munro, John A.
  1974 "British Columbia and the Chinese Evil: Canada's First Anti-Asiatic Immigration Law", **Journal of Canadian Studies**, 6(4): 42-51.
Nikolinako, Marios
  1973 "Notes on an Economic Theory of Racism", **Race**, 14(1972-1973).
Palmer, Howard D.
  1970 "Anti-Oriental Sentiments in Alberta, 1890-1920", **Canadian Ethnic Studies**, Bulletin of Research, Centre for Canadian Ethnic Studies at the University of Calgary, Calgary, Vol. 11 (December).

Peterson, Charles W.
    1936   "Immigration and Its Economic Background", **Farm and Ranch Review**, Calgary.

Pentland, H.C.
    1959   "The Development of a Capitalistic Labour Market in Canada", **Journal of Economics and Political Science**, (25)4.

Pitman, Walter
    1977   **Now Is Not Too Late**, Toronto: Task Force on Human Relations.

Porter, John
    1965   **The Vertical Mosaic: An Analysis of Social Class and Power in Canada**, Toronto: University of Toronto Press.

Richmond, Anthony
    1974   **Aspects of the Absorption and Adaptation of Immigrants**, Canadian Immigration and Population Study, Ottawa: Manpower and Immigration, Information Canada.

Sunahara, Ann Gomer
    1980   **The Politics of Racism: The Uprooting of Japanese Canadians During the Second World War**, Toronto: Lorimer.

Szymanski, Albert
    1976   "Racism and Sexism as Functional Substitute in the Labour Market", **The Sociological Quarterly**, 17(Winter), 65-77.
    1977   "The Effects of Earnings Discrimination Against Women on the Economic Position of Men", **Social Forces**, 56(2).

Tienhaara, Nancy
    1974   **Canadian Views on Immigration and Population: An Analysis of Post-war Gallop Polls**, Ottawa: Department of Manpower and Immigration.

Wood, John R.
    1978   "East Indians and Canada's New Immigration Policy", **Canadian Public Policy**, Autumn.

Woodsworth, James S.
    1909   **Strangers Within Our Gates**, The Missionary Society of the Methodist Church, Canada.

2

Administrative Aspects of Race Relations Policies and Programs

Bhausaheb Ubale
Race Relations Commissioner
for the Province of Ontario

Human Rights and Race Relations

Race relations has been considered as part of the human rights movement both in Canada and the United States. As a result, the legislative provisions concerning race relations have been incorporated in the Human Rights Acts and Civil Rights Acts in both countries. This is a very sound approach to human rights. There is a significant distinction between the Canadian and British approach to race relations. In Britain, the motivation for anti-discriminatory legislation, such as the Race Relations Act 1976, is based on social desirability and not on human rights. In other words, the rationale for the British Race Relations Act implies that it is not *socially desirable* to discriminate against people on the basis of their race. By contrast, the Canadian legislations say that discrimination is against one's *human rights!* Australia and New Zealand had followed the British pattern until quite recently. However, on December 10, 1981, Australia established a Human Rights Commission incorporating a Race Relations Act, and New Zealand did the same in 1978.

Human Rights Legislation is remedial legislation, and, as such, its main thrust is educational and conciliatory. The Human Rights Acts in the various provinces of Canada prohibit discrimination on the grounds of colour, nationality, place of origin, sex, religion, creed, physical handicap, etc. in the area of employment, housing and services. The Acts are administered by the Human Rights Commissions in each province. As race relations is a part of human rights, the entire work concerning race relations is administered by the Commissions.

There are two aspects of race relations work: the advocacy role and the regulatory role. Given the distinctions of these two roles, one might ask whether they can be served best by one agency, i.e. The Human Rights Commission; or by a separate agency within the Commission or the government; or by two separate agencies. Traditionally, the Human Rights Commissions in Canada have performed both the advocacy and regulatory roles, and to some extent have done so very successfully. However, most of these Commissions were established in the sixties when the human rights movement was in its formative stages. Societal responses at that time were more conciliatory toward the complaints filed with the Commissions. This was so, partly because in the sixties the economy was more stable, the population was smaller and there was a shortage of labour. During a healthy economy those who suffer acts of discrimination are more inclined to seek available employment elsewhere instead of spending considerable time exercising their human rights under the code. Consequently, in the sixties, minorities did not file complaints with the Human Rights Commission in large numbers. Moreover, most of the cases that were filed were simple and promptly settled. Therefore, in such formative years, it was both logical and appropriate that the Human Rights Commissions be asked to perform both advocacy and regulatory roles. The complementary impact of both roles remained very strong. With the passage of time, however, both the complainants and respondents have become more aware of their rights and the procedures involved under the Human Rights Code. Increased economic constraints and accelerated competition for jobs have contributed to a lessening of tolerance on the part of complainants and respondents. From the minority community, a host of advocacy groups emerged raising public issues affecting human rights. They naturally sought support from the Human Rights Commissions. These groups expected Human Rights Commissions to assume an advocacy role on behalf of the complainants, both in terms of raising social consciousness, and in exercising vigorous enforcement of the law. It is from this posture that minority groups judge the performance of the Human Rights Commissions. To them the Commissions are their advocates in matters of human rights.

Respondents, on the other hand, especially those from business, trade associations and other institutions, started defending their positions—vigorously. At every successive stage of human rights case investigation they started enlisting legal counsel. They began challenging the advocacy function of the Commissions, and demanded that they perform their quasi-judicial function. In other words, the Commissions should remain impartial while dealing with cases of discrimination. Any advocacy function by the Commissions or their members was seen as a bias act in favour of minorities. This has cast a shadow on the credibility of the Commissions. According to respondents, the Commissions have a regulatory role, and, as such, must follow the procedure set out in the legislation.

In view of this evolutionary pattern, a cleavage has developed between the advocacy and regulatory roles of the Human Rights Commissions. The complementary nature of these roles that existed during the earlier stages of the Commissions' activities has diminished over time. In fact, for all practical purposes, these roles have become incompatible. For example, Commissioners who try to raise public awareness by speaking out on such matters as removal of artificial barriers to employment for minorities, are not viewed as impartial by the employers. An advocacy role requires understanding, assisting and liaising with affected groups. As stated earlier, minority groups expect the Human Rights Commissions to enforce Human Rights legislation vigorously. They measure the success of such enforcement in terms of the success the Commissions have with individual cases. Many cases are dismissed by the Commissions because of insufficient evidence. Once cases are dismissed by the Commissions, there is no appeal system against such decision. As a result, the complainant has no recourse but to drop it. Thwarted by this, the complainants ventilate their protestations about the Commission to community groups and to the media. As a result, a developing perception among community members is that the Commissions are ineffective agencies. This makes it difficult for the staff of the Commissions to establish meaningful working relationships with the community groups. The negativity towards the Human Rights Commissions has been cited as one of the reasons why the minority community did not speak out in Ontario when Bill 7 was attacked by its opponents. In summary, although from an administrative perspective it is very logical and appealing to have the Human Rights Commissions perform these two roles, from a functional point of view, it places enormous constraints on their credibility. The Human Rights Commissions that have tried to perform both advocacy and regulatory functions have not been very successful in doing either. This is especially so in the area of race relations. They have been neither successful in establishing lasting relationships with minority groups in working together to develop a healthy social climate to prevent racism, nor have they been very successful in proving acts of discrimination through their enforcement powers.

Experience in other Countries

Other countries which have enacted anti-discrimination laws appear to have given serious consideration to the problems arising out of entrusting the advocacy and regulatory functions to the same agency, and have therefore created separate agencies to carry out these separate functions.

United Kingdom

In 1965 the then Labour Government in the U.K. enacted The Race Relations Act of 1965. This Act not only put certain discriminatory practices outside of the law, it also provided for a formal system of race law enforcement and some degree of protection for the rights of racial minorities. Under this Act two new agencies were created: the Race Relations Board and the National Committee for Commonwealth Immigrants (NCCI). The former performed the regulatory role of enforcing the Race Relations Act; the latter fulfilled the advocacy role. In 1968 the earlier Act was replaced by tougher legislation, i.e. the Race Relations Act of

1968 which, for the first time, dealt with discrimination in "non-public" areas such as housing and employment. This Act retained the Race Relations Board under the Chairmanship of Sir Geoffrey Wilson, but replaced the National Committee for Commonwealth Immigrants by a new Commission called the Community Relations Commission under the Chairmanship of Mark Bonham-Carter.

The Community Relations Commission, to a large extent, was successful. It was seen to accomplish a great deal, particularly with its program of public education on racial issues. It fostered an extensive library of race and community-oriented literature, and through its liaison with the local Community Relations Councils was widely involved in sponsoring racial tolerance.

In the mid-seventies the Government introduced two Acts: 1) the Sex Discrimination Act 1975 to outlaw discrimination on the grounds of sex and created a new statutory agency called the Equal Opportunity Commission to administer this Act, and 2) a Race Relations Act to replace the old one. Under this Act, the Race Relations Board and the Community Relations Commission were merged into one body called the Commission for Racial Equality (CRE), placing the entire operation under one roof. Several prominent people in the area of race relations, including Mr. Alex Lyon, former labour minister in the Home Office, who was in charge of race relations in Wilson's government, saw more pitfalls than benefits in this approach. Under this Act the CRE dealt with three functions: 1) enforcement of the Act, 2) Community Relations, including funding of local groups (some $8.24 million of a $19.24 million-plus budget goes to local Community Relations Officers and groups) and 3) Research, Public Relations and General Administration.

Regarding its law enforcement role, it is important to point out that the former Race Relations Board had followed more or less the same procedure that is being followed by the Human Rights Commissions in Canada (i.e. case by case approach). That system, and the Board, came under heavy criticism from various groups for its inability to gather sufficient evidence to prove discrimination. Conversely, the Race Relations Act of 1976 gives the right to go before an Industrial Tribunal to those who claim to have been the victims of discrimination in employment, and to county courts in other protected areas. The 1976 Act gives the CRE discretion to aid individual complainants who seek its assistance. Such assistance can be in the form of legal representation, legal advice, advice to procure financial settlement, etc. The new Act gives the Commission for Racial Equality the power to conduct formal investigations in strategic sectors, to tackle indirect discrimination, and to make recommendations.

Here again, there is a division between the regulatory and advocacy functions. The county courts and Industrial Tribunals deal with legal matters leaving all advocacy functions, of which there are three, to be carried out by the CRE:

Firstly—As the Commission does not investigate individual cases or render decisions, the Commission does not perform a regulatory function—instead the complainant goes to civil court under the Race Relations Act.

Secondly—The CRE aids individual complainants to prove his or her case of discrimination. Thus, this function is an advocacy function.

Thirdly—The Commission on its own undertakes formal investigation section by section to uncover the pattern of discrimination.

Once this is done, the Commission makes recommendations. Where appropriate it uses the findings in its investigations as a springboard for publicity and promotional work. The reports on some investigations are major promotional documents. This too is an advocacy function.

Yet the merger of the Race Relations Board and the Community Relations Commission created enormous problems, both from within the CRE itself and from within the community at large. With a staff of about 229 people, the CRE had become a monolithic organization. Moreover, each of its functions requires a particular approach which at times differs substantially with that of the other. These differences lead to frequent ideological clashes between the two divisions. Some Commissioners want to pursue formal investigations vigorously, others fight to devote more resources to community relations. This running feud afflicts both the paid staff and fifteen Commissioners. As a result, the Commission has been criticized continuously for its failure to perform either of its functions effectively, in spite of the fact that both its formal investigative and Community Relations work were designed to promote racial harmony.

As one of CRE's former Commissioners stated to me, the CRE is so preoccupied with its formal investigation that it has neglected its Community Relations responsibility. It was after the creation of CRE that the Notting Hill Carnival erupted even more violently in 1977. Then came Parrick Lane, Southall, Ponstol, Brixton, etc. The Commission's handling of these racial outbursts had a significant turn-off effect among minority groups. They lost considerable trust and faith in the Commission's effectiveness to resolve the racial tensions and conflict. Some people in the U.K. strongly feel that had the Community Relations Commission continued, it would have dealt with racial violence differently.

United States

The administration of race relations is better organized in the United States than it is in the United Kingdom. In the former case, it is organized on a functional basis by establishing separate bodies to carry out the two distinct roles of regulation (as compliance) and advocacy. These bodies are: the Equal Employment Opportunity Commission (EEOC), the Civil Rights Commission (CRC), and the Community Relations Services (CRS). These bodies were all created under the Civil Rights Acts of 1964. The Equal Employment Opportunity Commission was given the responsibility for complaints of discrimination based on grounds of race, colour, sex etc., and following a 1972 amendment to the 1964 Act, was given enforcement power in dealing with such complaints. It operates as an independent agency whose chairman is answerable to the President of the United States and the American people. This arrangement gives the Commission a free hand to deal with problems under its regulatory mandate.

Both the Civil Rights Commission and the Community Relations Services play an advocacy role. The Civil Rights Commission is primarily a fact finding agency created first under the Civil Rights Act of 1957. It investigates sworn affidavits that citizens are being fraudulently deprived of their rights to vote as being denied of such rights due to discrimination based on race, colour, sex, etc. It collects information on legal developments in discrimination, and serves as a natural clearing house for information on discrimination. Like the Equal Employment Opportunity Commission, the Civil Rights Commission is an independent body directly answerable to the President. Its Chairman and six Commissioners appointed by the President with the consensus of the Senate, owe their responsibility ultimately to the American people.

Finally, the Community Relations Services, which is the only Federal agency assigned the specific and distinct task of helping communities "to resolve disputes, disagreements and difficulties relating to discriminatory practices based on race, colour or national origin," has both independence and a broad mandate. Thus, it can respond to a wide range of eventualities, whether to the racial or ethnic disputes resulting from a court order to desegregate a public school or to a minority group's opposition to some corporate action.

Under Title 10 in the Civil Rights Act for the Establishment of Community Relations Service it states:

"There is hereby established in and as a part of the Department of Commerce[1] a Community Relations Service (hereinafter referred to as the "Service"), which shall be headed by a Director who shall be appointed by the President with the advice and consent of the Senate for a term of four years. The Director is authorized to appoint, subject to the civil service laws and regulations, such other personnel as may be necessary to enable the Service to carry out its functions and duties, and to fix their compensation in accordance with the Classification Act of 1949, as amended. The Director is further authorized to procure services as authorized by section 15 of the Act of August 2, 1946 (60 Stat. 810; 5 U.S.C. 55 (a)), but at rates or individuals not in excess of $75 per diem."

Section 106 (a) of the Federal Executive Pay Act of 1956, as amended (5 U.S.C. 2205 (a)), is further amended by adding the following clause thereto:

"Director, Community Relations Service.

It shall be the function of the Service to provide assistance to communities and persons therein in resolving disputes, disagreements or difficulties relating to discriminatory practices based on race, colour, or national origin which impair the rights of persons in such communities under the Constitution or laws of the United States or which affect or may affect interstate commerce. The Service may offer its services in cases of such disputes, disagreements or difficulties whenever, in its judgment, peaceful relations among the citizens of the community involved are threatened thereby, and it may offer its services either upon its own motion or upon the request of an appropriate State or local official or other interested person.

The Service shall, whenever possible, in performing its functions, seek and utilize the cooperation of appropriate State or local, public or private agencies.

The activities of all officers and employees of the Service in providing conciliation assistance shall be conducted in confidence and without publicity, and the Service shall hold confidential any information acquired in the regular performance of its duties upon the understanding that it would be so held. No officer or employee of the Service shall engage in the performance of investigative or prosecuting functions of any department or agency in any litigation arising out of a dispute in which he acted on behalf of the Service. Any officer or other employee of the Service, who shall make public in any manner whatever any information in violation of this subsection, shall be deemed guilty of a misdemeanor and, upon conviction thereof, shall be fined not more than $1,000 or imprisoned not more than one year.

Subject to the provisions of section 205 and 1003 (b) the Director shall, on or before January 31 of each year submit to the Congress a report of the activities of the Service during the preceding fiscal year."

Canada

In Canada, the position is slightly different. In some protected areas under the Human Rights Act, there is a clear distinction between the advocacy role and regulatory role, and in other areas there is none. For example, the Human Rights Act prohibits discrimination on the basis of sex and physical disability as well as race. However, in the case of sex discriminations there is a very explicit division between the advocacy and regulatory roles. The Human Rights Commissions perform a regulatory role,[2] but the governments have created separate agencies to undertake a promotional role on behalf of women. The Status of Women Council tries to raise public consciousness about women's issues; the Women's Bureaus in different ministries across Canada concentrate on promotional work for women in employment mostly in the private sector; and women Crown Employees Offices in some governments monitor employment in the public sector. All these bodies are funded out of public funds and fulfill advocacy roles. Publicly funded agencies, such as the Advisory Council on the Physically Handicapped and the Provincial Handicapped Employment Programs, are also engaged in an advocacy role on behalf of physically handicapped persons.

It is different in the area of racial minorities. The majority of complaints of discrimination filed with the Human Rights Commissions fall mainly into two categories: sex discrimination and race discrimination. Yet, there is no advocacy body created anywhere in this country (with some exceptions in Ontario which I shall return to later in this paper). The entire issue of race relations gets buried somehow in the activities of the Human Rights Commissions. Since the Commissions have to deal with so much reactive work, their efforts in the area of race relations are often postponed or abandoned. Moreover, the importance attached to race relations by the Human Rights Commissions varies from time to time, depending upon the composition of the Commissioners, staff, government policies, etc. As a result of all of these factors race relations has received secondary treatment in a number of provinces in this country. It is simply not logical that an advocacy role in the area of race relations be put together in only one agency, such as the Human Rights Commission, when that agency's major work is a regulatory one in all areas covered by the code.

Realizing this anomaly, and to give more focus on race relations issues, we in Ontario have started a new experiment. The Government of Ontario has established a Cabinet Committee on Race Relations, whose mandate is to formulate and monitor government policy in the area of race relations. Ontario has also established a Race Relations Division and appointed a Race Relations Commissioner to administer the Division. A Race Relations Commissioner and two Commission members form the Division. The Race Relations Commissioner is appointed under statute by the Lieutenant-Governor. Please do not confuse Sub-Committees for the Commission with the Race Relations Division. Sub-Committees are appointed by the Chairman of the Ontario Human Rights Commission, but the Race Relations Division is established under the OHRC Act. The Members of the Division are appointed by the Order-in-Council to serve on the Division. They receive a separate per diem from the Race Relations Commissioner for the work they do for the Division, and a separate per diem for the work they do for the Commission. The Division has been given a separate budget by the Ministry of Labour. It makes its own policy decisions and implements them, reporting to the Commission for information. The main role of the Division is an advocacy one. Thus it has full autonomy in the area of race relations. The regulatory work concerning race relations is done by the full Commission. Since the Race Relations Division Commissioners serve on the Commission, they take part in the Commissioner's deliberations on the cases related to racial discrimination.

In short, the Ontario government has made positive initiatives in making a distinction between the roles of advocacy and regulation in the area of race relations. As with all innovations, some structural problems have emerged in the early stages of our development; however, over time we hope to make corrective inroads toward establishing a fundamentally sound administrative structure for successfully achieving our goals. Ontario has taken a positive and progressive first step toward facilitating effective race relations in its province.

Conclusion

It is imperative that race relations activities be organized under two distinct categories: advocacy and regulatory. There is a great temptation to mix these two roles, but the risk is costly, especially in view of the complexities involved in both activities. It is neither logical nor appropriate to have the proactive activities of race relations encumbered by the reactive activities of the Human Rights Commissions when other issues, such as those of women and the physically handicapped, require separate agencies to effectively fulfill their function. For example, women employees offices in some provinces monitor the employment of women within the various ministries of those provincial governments. Women who feel discriminated against or have job related problems may seek the advice and help of such offices before filing a complaint with the Human Rights Commission. In Ontario and some other provinces the same will be the case for the physically handicapped shortly. There are thousands of minority members employed in the governments who sometimes suffer from double and even triple discrimination, based on race and sex; race and physical handicap; or race, sex and physical handicap. Yet there is no provincial government agency with a purely advocacy role anywhere in Canada to which a racial minority person can go for advice and assistance. Since the office of the Race Relations Commissioner in Ontario is established inside the Human Rights Commission, he/she cannot guide or assist an individual complainant because of a possible conflict of interest. Hence, to such complainants, the role of the Race Relations Commissioner is meaningless. His or her only option at present is to file a formal complaint with a Human Rights Commission. Many minority government employees are very reluctant to file complaints for understandable reasons. During times of high unemployment, people prefer to suffer the humiliation and injustices of discrimination rather than risk their jobs by complaining.

In discussions with a number of employed minority persons, one common problem prevails. In general, senior management expect minority persons to be grateful for being allowed into Canada and for having a job. Many managers believe minority employees should, as a matter of course, start at the lowest levels of employment, irrespective of their qualifications, experience or contributions to the subject area. Whenever a visible minority occupies a position equal to his or her qualifications, it is often with less pay, power and privileges. Yet there is no one they can go to for redress. For reasons already stated, the Human Rights Commission is unsuited to their needs.

To bring all enforcement functions, as well as the advocacy function, under one umbrella runs the additional risk of creating a monolothic organization. Such a set-up may appeal to administrators with an interest in acquiring more power, but it neither serves the interest of society at large, nor makes the work of race relations effective.

Educational or promotional activities require working with minority groups as well as employers. Negative perceptions about the Human Rights Commissions' inability to prove many complaints of racial discrimination overshadows the work of race relations units. As a result, most minority groups feel skeptical and pessimistic about the role of the units. Conversely, because many employers believe that the Human Rights Commissions favour minorities, they are reluctant to form an alliance with the race relations units to institute training programs for their employees. Under this climate of distrust one of society's most effective mechanisms for controlling unnecessary growth of racial tension and conflict would be wasted. The Commissions should be free to concentrate on stamping out racial and other forms of discrimination through enforcement of their legal mandate. After all, the Human Rights Commission is the only agency in each province which has enforcement powers. Even the courts do not have those powers unless complaints are referred to them through Boards of Inquiries. The Commission ought to, therefore, devote all its energy and resources to the role of regulation. There is abounding evidence that when Human Rights Commissions try to perform both the regulatory and advocacy function, they do so with minimal success and maximum criticism.

Under the Ontario Human Rights Act of 1981, new grounds of discrimination have been added which further increase the already overburdened responsibility in the area of enforcement—i.e. contract compliance, affirmative action, physical handicap, etc. In some jurisdictions even the work of enforcement is divided between two separate agencies. Thus, in the United States, in addition to the Equal Opportunity Commission, there is a separate administrative agency to enforce the contract compliance provisions of the Civil Rights Act. What is therefore needed is the development of separate administrative limits on functional lines, for the effective administration of the same act. Thus, in view of the intensity and extensity of racial problems emerging in our society, it is essential that an advocacy unit be established under the Human Rights Act which is separate from the Human Rights Commission.

Assuming there is a willingness to separate the advocacy role from the enforcement role of the Human Rights Commissions, the next question is whether one needs to have a legislation to create an advocacy agency for all areas of discrimination together, i.e. race, sex, physical handicap, etc., or for each area separately. The answer would vary from province to province depending upon the size of its population protected by the code. Firstly, it must be stated that you do not need legislation to create an advocacy agency. An advocacy agency can be established administratively. In the Province of Ontario, the Race Relations Division was established in 1979, long before the amendment to the Human Rights Code in 1981. The Women's Bureau was similarly established without formal legislation. Preventative work needs no formal legislation. The existing legislation is broad enough to allow for a new, separate administrative arrangement for the advocacy function.

The preamble of the Human Rights Code of every province sets out the goal to create a society based on the principles of equality of opportunity, and respect for human dignity irrespective of race, colour, national origin, etc. One can establish a separate advocacy administrative unit to promote the ideals of the preamble—leaving the Commission to administer the Code. By separating these two functions operationally, you maximize their effectiveness and avoid the potential for the kind of bureaucratic in-fighting that exists in the Commission for Racial Equality in the U.K. In this way, the work of one unit will be neither neutralized by, nor antagonistic to, that of the other. In this connection, the U.S. Civil Rights Act offers an example of extreme value.

To those provinces that are thinking of amending their Human Rights Act, I wish to offer the following suggestions:

1) Race Relations must remain an integral part of the Human Rights Act.
2) A clear definition and distinction of the advocacy and regulatory roles must be made in the Human Rights Act, and essential to their success is the establish-

ment of separate administrative units for each role. The U.S. Civil Rights Act provides a good example.

3) As regards law enforcement, all the provisions of the Ontario Human Rights Code 1981 may be adopted with the following additions: a complainant be given the right to prove his or her case in a civil court once the case is dismissed by the Commission.

Under the current procedure, once the Commissions find sufficient evidence to support a complainant's allegations of discrimination, the respondent has an opportunity to disprove said allegations to a Board of Inquiry. At the Board hearing, the respondent is able to examine relevant witnesses and to cross-examine the complainant's witnesses. If the Board of Inquiry is unfavourable to the respondent, he or she can appeal to the civil courts and finally to the Supreme Court of Canada. If, however, the Commissions do not find sufficient evidence to support the complainant's claim of discrimination, the case is closed. In other words, the Human Rights Commissions are the only agencies to terminate the complainant's human rights once his or her case is dismissed. But for the respondent, the Supreme Court of Canada becomes the last agency to terminate his or her human rights. The Commissions' decisions are mainly based on the evidence gathered by the investigating officers. Workers who have knowledge of discrimination at their place of employment are reluctant to support the complainant's claim of discrimination for fear of losing their jobs. But if the complainant has an opportunity to present his or her case before a Board of Inquiry or in court, he or she can subpoena those other relevant witnesses and examine them under oath, as does the respondent. Equally, he or she can cross-examine the witnesses of the respondent. The Commission's present case dismissal practice deprives the complainant of this opportunity. As a result of this perceived inequality on the part of the complainant, the Commission's credibility suffers in the minority community. The provisions as described above would equalize the process of justice for both complainant and respondent.

In summary, race relations issues are likely to dominate national and international discussion in the coming decade because of the emergence of a second generation of minority population in Europe as well as in North America. We therefore cannot afford to adopt a zig-zag approach in responding to the challenges that lie ahead of us. We must be pragmatic. We must provide a sound administrative system that deals effectively and creatively with the prevention and protection of violations against human rights. Given the underlying values that led to the creation of human rights in this country, unlike the social expediency that motivated British initiatives, I am optimistic that changes will occur in the near future to establish appropriate organizational structures to maximize the efficiency and effectiveness of the Commissions' twin roles of advocacy and regulation in the area of race relations.

Footnotes

1. Now under the U.S. Department of Justice.
2. Some Commissioners also speak on this issue.

3

Multiculturalism and Schools:
A Critical Analysis

K. Mazurek,
Dept. of Educational Foundations
University of Alberta

The policy of "multiculturalism within a bilingual framework" has now been a platform of the Canadian federal government for over a decade. A brief change of administration during this period in no way affected the situation. In the interim, four provinces—Ontario, Manitoba, Saskatchewan and Alberta—have also proclaimed their support for the idea (Burnet, 1979:49). In fact, multiculturalism has taken on the vestiges of an official ideology—a set of fundamental assumptions about the nature of Canadian society; a new definition of Canadian identity.

The policy was adopted primarily as a consequence of agitation by non-English/non-French ethnic groups who felt that a policy of bilingualism and bi-culturalism ignored their identities and contributions to Canada. Many of these groups also felt that they were victims of a discrimination that relegated them to low socio-economic status. Multiculturalism would end all of this. Ethnic groups would now be protected from discrimination in jobs and housing by new laws and they would be encouraged to not only retain but to actively foster their cultural heritage.

The school was to play a central role in the achievement of the cultural and economic goals of the new policy. Recognizing that "some of our minorities have been isolated from the arteries of educational progress by social and economic circumstances beyond their control", it was envisioned that strict application of a proposed federal Human Rights Act would protect the economic interests of ethnic groups (First Annual Report, Canadian Consultative Council 1974:15). Correspondingly, a school curriculum revised to include linguistic and sociohistorical cultural dimensions of ethnic groups (taught by teachers appropriately prepared and overseen by ethnically integrated provincial advisory boards) would ensure that the cultural integrity of the ethnic student was protected as he ascended the meritocratic ladder of schooling.

This was, of course, a response to the recognition that school curricula had, in the past, been somehow "biased" against some ethnic groups. Thus, by including ethnic components in the curriculum, all groups would have an equal chance to succeed academically (and thereby, ultimately, economically—especially with the help of the new Human Rights Act which would banish discrimination). In this manner, ethnic groups would not have to choose between their culture and their socio-economic well-being. If the school curriculum reflects ethnic variations and cultural idiosyncrasies, then the student can retain his cultural identity without imperilling his chances for academic success.

What this assumes, of course, is that the curriculum can be "ethnicized" to the point that students of all ethnic backgrounds can have their cultural inheritance and traditional values, behavior and belief systems recognized and rewarded in the classroom. A moment's reflection will show that this would be impossible to attain and, in fact, has not earnestly been attempted.

In reality, the educational manifestations of multiculturalism have seen attempts to include the cultural inheritance of some, but not all, ethnic groups into the classroom. In other words, it is only those immigrant groups who are sufficiently numerous and organized, and who can therefore exert political influence on provincial departments of education and school boards, that have managed to win a place for their language, history, etc., in the curriculum. The federal policy of multiculturalism, then, has not meant recognition for all minority cultures in our educational institutions. Rather it has merely meant a green light for ethnic groups to do battle in the local political arena for the cause of their own languages and cultures.

Some of this agitation has not been without interesting results. For instance, in the province of Alberta the School Act was amended in 1971 to permit instruction through the medium of languages other than English and French. This was at the instigation of politically influential minority leaders and the result has been the proliferation of quite segregated ethnic-specific public schools and ethnic-specific programs within schools, especially in the city of Edmonton (Lupul, 1977:166). At the time of writing these programs are in effect at the elementary level only and operate in a bilingual manner. Half of the day is taught through the medium of the minority language while the other half is in English.

This is probably the most radical example of multicultural education at work. It fosters ethnic segregation in the schools to a far greater degree than the policy adopted by the Toronto Board of Education, for example. That city's contribution to multiculturalism is the Heritage Languages Program which allows for the teaching of minority languages, but only for thirty minutes per day before or after regular school hours, or during an extended day. Either of the two official languages remains as the medium of instruction and ethnic mixing continues in the classroom (Maseman, 1978:41).

The Toronto example is cited merely to highlight the radical nature of the Edmonton experiment. It is certainly true that the long-term consequences of such an experiment are difficult to predict. It is possible, however, to identify certain tendencies already evident. Segregated ethnic programs and schools suggest a move in the direction of a greater degree of "ethnic community closure" and "ethnic institutional completeness" than has hitherto prevailed. This results in limited contact with the broader society and closer and more frequent interpersonal contacts between members of the group.

Such a tendency will undoubtedly foster greater feelings of group cohesion and ethnic pride. But it is improbable that it will do much to build bridges between minorities and the dominant groups. While ethnics may feel better about their ethnicity, they will continue to be victims of discrimination and prejudiced attitudes. It is curious that while Americans are attempting to combat prejudice and discrimination by ethnic and racial integration in their public schools, some Canadian ethnic groups are attempting to move in the opposite direction— segregated schools and school programs!

This is all very fine so long as ethnic groups are aware that there may be a price to be paid for one's ethnicity. That is, there are real, material, educational consequences corresponding to ethnic affiliation. Consider, for example, the findings of Stodolsky and Lesser in the United States and Marjoriebanks in Canada (Stodolsky and Lesser, 1967; Marjoriebanks, 1972). These have cumulated in the now conventional wisdom which recognizes that children's basic cognitive processes such as verbal ability, reasoning, number facility and space conceptualization, as well as attitudes and approaches toward learning, all correlate with ethnic affiliation.

Therefore because, as Marjoriebanks emphasizes, ethnicity influences both the level and pattern of mental abilities it is evident that not all ethnic children have equal advantage in grappling with the school curriculum. Of course, the obvious rebuttal is: change the curriculum. Unfortunately, that hope is probably wholly idealistic. First, in an era of advanced technology and in the climate of the 'back to the basics' movement, it seems rather unlikely that the cornerstone subjects of schools—math, physics, chemistry, English—will be tampered with in any way. Even if we did seek to "ethnicize" these subjects, what could be done? There is no 'German', 'Polish', 'Ukrainian', etc. version of math. All we could do is teach some of these subjects through the medium of an "ethnic language", but that is another matter (and one with its own attendant problems). The point is, the very cognitive strategies and facilities which the basic subjects in our school require are possessed in different degrees by different ethnic groups. The degree to which ethnic consciousness is heightened is the degree to which such differences in mental abilities persist.

One solution to the above problem is to "compensate" disadvantages in one area with advantages in another. Thus, if one grants that some ethnic groups may be at a disadvantage in coping with the so-called "core" subjects, we can redesign old curricula in other subjects and even introduce new subjects. That has, in fact, been done. In particular, social studies has been heavily influenced by the demand to ethnicize the curriculum, and several languages other than French are now recognized as accreditation subjects. Further, school boards are known to favor hiring teachers of ethnic affiliations representative of the community.

In a narrow, technical, sense such measures do indeed make the schools more reflective of their supporters' and clients' needs. For example: The child in a Ukrainian bilingual school, taught by an ethnic Ukrainian teacher, taking Ukrainian as a subject for credit, and studying a social studies curriculum which prominently features the Ukrainians' historical and contemporary contributions to western Canadian society, certainly should feel comfortable in school and can be expected to overcome any (in this case theoretical) disadvantages in the "core" subjects with above average facility in these other areas. However, as Werner et al. emphasize, "bias is inevitable because curriculum development is a social process" and "invariably any curriculum must reflect someone's point of view which embodies biases created by a set of underlying values, beliefs, and experiences" (Werner et al., 1977:9-10).

Therefore, what we have done is substitute one bias with another. In the above example, Ukrainians have been successful in having their own biases replace—or at least compensate for—the biases they (correctly) perceive in the standard public school curriculum which is still weighed with Anglo values. This works out well for groups such as Ukrainians, as this group has a large population in western Canada and a highly developed institutional infrastructure—businessmen's clubs, study institutes, social centers, membership in the economic and political elite, its own press, etc. In other words, Ukrainians in western Canada have both the organization and resources to translate well into educational reality.

However, for every such politically and economically significant group, there are many groups without the resources to so tailor the educational system to their needs. What, realistically, do the numerous small—in terms of numbers, re-sources, etc.—ethnic groups in Canada do to ensure that their "bias" is included in the school? As Porter warned some time ago: Such groups will not have their interests represented because multiculturalism encourages the exercise of group lobbying at the expense of individual interests (Porter, 1975). At the most general level, Porter perceived this to be a threat against the very fabric of the principle of equality of individuals. In the specific, we are warned by Baker that because ethnic groups stand beside each other in "unequal power relationships", they may properly be "conceived of as interest groups" (Baker, 1978:59).

Thus education still remains a "tool" to be used to the advantage of the most powerful interest groups. In this perspective, all multiculturalism does is allow more players into the game: The Anglo and the French interests now have to compete with not just each other but with other significant interest groups. (Viewed in this light, the lukewarm response of Quebec to multiculturalism, on the basis that it may undermine biculturalism, is completely understandable.) The degree to which different ethnic groups are able to manipulate educational institutions in the aforementioned manner is a major contributing factor to attendant socio-economic inequalities between ethnic groups. Thus, beneath the rhetoric and practice of multiculturalism lie very real material inequalities which are all too often obscured.

The preceding dilemmas troubling multicultural policy and practice are genuine problems for the educational community. While the Canadian Consultative Council on Multiculturalism believes that "the only way to create a climate of tolerance and respect for all ethnic groups is through education", we have seen that both the form and process of implementing such a thrust may yield contradictory results (First Annual Report, Canadian Consultative Council, 1974).

References

Canadian Consultative Council on Multiculturalism
    1974   **First Annual Report of the Canadian Consultative Council on Multiculturalism, 14.**
Canadian Consultative Council on Multiculturalism
    1978   **Notes on Multiculturalism,** Minister of Supply and Services, Ottawa.
Baker, Patrick L.
    1978   "Ethnic Analysis of Political Armour: Analytical Problems in the Canadian Mosaic", in Martin L. Kovacs (ed.), **Ethnic Canadians, Vol. 8 of Canadian Plains Studies,** University of Regina, Regina.
Burnet, Jean
    1979   "Myths and Multiculturalism", **Canadian Journal of Education IV(4).**
Lupul, Manoly
    1977   "Multiculturalism and Canadian National Identity: The Alberta Experience", in A Chaiton and N. McDonald (eds.), **Canadian Schools and Canadian Identity,** Gage, Toronto.
Maseman, Vandra
    1978   "Multicultural Programs in Toronto Schools", **Interchange, IX(1).**
Porter, John
    1975   "Ethnic Pluralism in Canadian Perspective", in N. Glazer and D.P. Moynihan (eds.), **Ethnicity: Theory and Practice,** Harvard University Press, Cambridge.
Stodolsky, Susan S. and Gerald Lesser
    1977   "Learning Patterns in the Disadvantaged". **Harvard Educational Review,** 37(4).
Werner, W., B. Connors, T. Aoki, and J. Dahlie
    1977   **Whose Culture? Whose Heritage? Ethnicity Within Canadian Social Studies Curricula,** Center for the Study of Curriculum and Instruction, University of British Columbia.

4

Social and Cultural Reproduction and the Schools' Role in Social Mobility

Don Dawson
University of Alberta

The role of schooling in social mobility has been 'presumed' by functionalists to be that of a meritocratic institution offering opportunities for social mobility through training and the acquisition of specialized knowledge. This role and the nature of 'social mobility' itself will be examined further below. The thesis of cultural reproduction developed here will be that of Pierre Bourdieu. Social reproduction (perhaps economic or class reproduction) is seen as the reproduction of social relations engendered by the capitalist mode of production (Bowles and Gintis, 1976). However, in the discussion below we will argue that such a bifurcation is not necessary in that these theses are indeed parallel and in fact so interdependent that they can be seen as aspects of a single hegemonic reproductive force.

Hence we will first present a structural functionalist view of the 'presumed' role of the school in social mobility followed by a discussion of cultural and social reproduction. Finally, a tentative effort to relate a combined view of reproduction to the role of the school in social mobility will be presented.

Social Mobility and Education: A Functionalist View

In modern capitalist societies 'social mobility' is seen often to be synonymous with 'occupational mobility' (Blaw and Duncan, 1967 among others in the U.S.; Hopper, 1971 for the British case). As one climbs the occupational hierarchy one simultaneously moves up other hierarchies (e.g., class, status, etc.). Although some "incongruence" can occur in one's positions in each of these hierarchies, for the most part individuals share similar hierarchical positions in all societal spheres (Hopper, 1971:26). Some functionalist theorists of social stratification have argued that the hierarchical nature and structural inequality of industrialized nations are inevitable.

> Simply put, the argument is that in a society in which tasks are specialised some will call for qualities which are not widely available amongst the individual members of the society, whilst others will call for qualities which are widely distributed. It is necessary, the argument runs, that the more talented be placed in those occupations which demand their skills. Thus occupations which demand special intellectual, administrative and entrepreneurial skills are vital to the whole society and must be rewarded by great prestige and material returns...
>
> They argue, nevertheless, that there will also be social mobility which will allow the unsuccessful to lose their position, and others possessing special abilities to rise (Bernbaum, 1977:26).

In this argument the talented will be upwardly mobile as they assume 'more frequently important' occupational roles. The less talented offspring of those presently in the important 'talent-scarce' occupations will be inter-generationally downwardly mobile as others more talented and skilled take their places.

In this view society is seen as 'meritocratic' in that individuals achieve an occupational status based upon their skills, talents, and knowledge. In its extreme the functionalist view is expressed in Human Capital theory (Schultz, 1961) which postulates that education is more than merely a consumable but is also an investment in human capital (knowledge and skills). This investment has positive results not only for individuals (private rates of return) but for the entire nation (social rates of return). In this theory individuals benefit from education because "their investment in the acquisition of knowledge and skill has given them ownership of economically valuable capacities" (Karabel and Halsey, 1977:307), and by increasing the efficiency of all workers education contributes on a mass scale towards the growth of the entire economy (Dennison, 1962).

> In its strongest form the meritocratic hypothesis argues that the expansion of schooling should have substantially increased the extent to which occupational status is a function of talent and motivation. As educational qualifications become increasingly important determinants of occupational status, talented and highly motivated children from lower class backgrounds should find it easier than they did in the past to obtain status commensurate with their abilities, while untalented or lazy children of privileged parents should find it more difficult to avoid downward mobility. If we make an assumption that talent and motivation is broadly dispersed throughout all social classes and ethnic groups, the strong version of this argument becomes a proposition about increasing mobility in Western societies in recent decades. Other things being equal, the amount of occupational mobility from generation to generation should increase with educational expansion (Hurn, 1978:90).

It has been shown though that "most social mobility, however, is of a relatively short-range kind and so does not necessarily involve sharp changes" (Parkin, 1971:51). The 'distance' one has moved in the process of being mobile may be very small; social mobility may involve status change but not class change (Levitas, 1974:43), mobility may be horizontal within an occupational "situs" and not involve class or status change (Hopper, 1971:27), and the downwardly mobile tend to be upwardly mobile in the next generation. All in all, that there is little social mobility of consequence in industrial societies is evidenced by the "fairly high degree of *social continuity* in the reward position of family units through the generations" (Parkin, 1971:14). So, despite the enormous expansion of education in North America it has not been demonstrated that there has been substantially increased working class individual upward mobility, nor has expanded schooling made "significant contributions to the more general features of social mobility, and even in raising the productivity, that is the efficiency, of the labour force" (Bernbaum, 1977:44).

Whatever lower class upward mobility which can be attributed to schooling is restricted to infrequent individual mobility (Hurn, 1978:90). Yet as Jencks (1973) reminds us, mobility is not equality. This basic distinction is of fundamental importance to our discussion. The type of individual mobility we have described can be seen as "personal opportunism" (Levitas, 1974:45) which is not necessarily concomitant with widespread lower class upward mobility which would result in a more egalitarian social order. Hopper (1971:304-305) posits that the school must "reject" candidates who are "not sufficiently talented" to benefit from higher learning. In this process of selection the school must systematically "warm-up" those students who will receive further and more specialized training, and "cool-down" those who are to be sent directly into the lower levels of the occupational hierarchy. In his functionalist discussion of the patterns of mobility and non-mobility in industrial societies Hopper (1971) presages the critical theses of social and cultural reproduction of the conflict theorists—"where functionalists have often viewed the educational system as offering opportunities for *mobility for individuals*, conflict theorists have generally stressed the role of education in *maintaining* a system of structured social inequality" (Karabel and Halsey, 1977:35).

In summation, functionalists have 'presumed' that the role of education has been to (1) increase individual mobility, and (2) to at least theoretically promote social equality through mobility. In the performance of these roles the school is seen to meritocratically select the most able students for further education and to educate all students to their highest potential whenever possible.

Social Reproduction—Bowles and Gintis

Bowles and Gintis (1976) see the educational system in the capitalist economy as a key element in the reproduction of the social division of labour. They posit that schooling in 'capitalist America' perpetuates the "class relations of the production process, and thus serves to perpetuate the social, political, and economic conditions through which a portion of the product of labour is expropriated in the form of profits" (Bowles and Gintis, 1976:11). The school does this as a consequence of a "straightforward correspondence principle: For the past century at least, schooling has contributed to the reproduction of the social relations of production largely through the correspondence between school and class structure" (Bowles and Gintis, 1976:130).

In capitalist society the social relations of production reflect by and large a "hierarchical division of labour" with control from the top down. According to the ownership of the means of production there are "rigid patterns of dominance and subordinacy" (Bowles and Gintis, 1976:46) which are reproduced in the school system as it performs its integrative function. Bowles and Gintis (1976:47) believe that schooling performs an essential "integrative function—through its reproduction of a stratified labour force for the capitalist enterprise". Hence, "the main role of education is the production of an adequate labour force in a hierarchically-controlled and class-stratified production system" (Sarup, 1978:167).

To accomplish this 'integration of youth into the economic system' the social relationships of the school—between administrators, teachers, students, and their work—replicate the hierarchical, alienated, and fragmented division of labour of the work place. "By attuning young people to a set of social relationships similar to those of the work place, schooling attempts to gear the development of personal needs to its (the work place's) requirements" (Bowles and Gintis, 1976:131). When this is done values, beliefs, and behaviours are transformed and reproduced "bringing the individual in line with the needs of capital accumulation and the extension of the wage-labour system" (Bowles and Gintis, 1976:47).

In Bowles and Gintis' interpretation of social reproduction the educational system does not promote working class social mobility in any form, but rather is structured in order to reproduce the social relations of production towards the end of teaching working class individuals to be "properly subordinate and to render them sufficiently fragmented in consciousness to preclude their getting together to shape their own material existence" (Bowles and Gintis, 1976:310). Therefore the school must socialize the social classes differently to reinforce the production-based social inequalities.

> Although all schools must repress and coerce students to secure a comp-liant and efficient adult labor force, different schools accomplish this function in different ways. The values and qualities required by an efficient manual worker on the production line are different from the values and qualities needed by an executive of a large corporation. While the manual worker must be taught punctuality, the ability to follow instructions, and some degree of respect for his superiors, the executive needs some degree of flexibility, an ability to tolerate ambiguity and favorable attitudes towards change and innovation (Hurn, 1978:50).

Thus working class schools, the schools of ethnic, racial, and other minorities emphasize behavioral control and rule-following, coercive authority structures and minimal chance for successful advancement. The school roles then "mirror the characteristics of inferior job situations" (Bowles and Gintis, 1976:132). Conversely, schools of the capitalist classes (in well-to-do suburbs, etc.) stress participation, indirect supervision, and internalized standards of control.

Therefore, "schools which treat students of varying social origins differently, reinforce those class-based personality traits that, much more than cognitive differences, explain why the children of the privileged tend to occupy the higher points in the social division of labour" (Karabel and Halsey, 1977:34). Bowles and Gintis reject the educational meritocracy as a "facade" which is used to cover up the reproduction of economic relations" (2976:103). Social reproduction is economic and class reproduction—the social relations engendered by the economic division of labour of the capitalist mode of production are reproduced, and social classes are thus reproduced. Working class students are socialized into working class roles, and are not given an opportunity for social mobility. That some minimal mobility is allowed as a "safety-valve" to help maintain stability (Parkin, 1971) does not negate the social reproduction thesis.

Cultural Reproduction—Pierre Bourdieu

When Pierre Bourdieu writes of cultural reproduction he is not referring to the reproduction of the Durkheimian notion of 'consensus on values' (Bourdieu, 1977:488; Kennett, 1973:239), but he is referring to reproduction of the culture of the dominant classes of society (Bourdieu and de Saint-Martin, 1974:354).

> In a stratified social order, dominant groups and classes control the most socially valued and legitimate cultural meanings. When inculcated through education, these meanings tend to elicit assent and encourage respect by subordinate groups for the social order. Thus, symbolic meanings mediate power relations among social groups and classes; culture, at its most fundamental level, is not devoid of political content but is an expression of it (Swartz, 1977:547).

Indeed, exclusion of lower classes or "popular" culture from the "academic" culture of the school can be seen as a political act (Bourdieu, 1971:200-201).

The key concept in Bourdieu's analysis is the notion of "cultural capital". This cultural capital consists of "literature, science, religion, art, language and all symbolic systems falling within the widest interpretation of the term" (Kennett, 1973:239) and is comparable to economic capital in that it is transmitted by inheritance and in 'invested' in order to be cultivated (Bourdieu, 1977). Linguistic and cultural 'competence' are aspects of cultural capital that facilitate academic achievement for individuals. Simply put, Bourdieu's thesis states that the educational system discriminates in favour of those who are the inheritors of cultural capital.

Specifically, Bourdieu and de Saint-Martin (1974:357) state that "the cultural capital inherited from the family... can be simply measured by the scholastic level reached by ancestors two generations back". Whatever means are used to specify the amount of inherited cultural capital it is apparent that social elites are generally well endowed in this regard be they highly educated or not:

The culture of the elite is so near to that of the school that children from the lower middle class (and *a fortiori* from the agricultural and industrial working class) can only acquire with great effort something which is *given* to the children of the cultivated classes—style, taste, wit—in short, those attitudes and aptitudes which seem natural in members of the cultivated classes and naturally expected of them precisely because (in the ethnological sense) they are the *culture* of that class (Bourdieu, 1974:39).

Due to their lack of this cultural capital the lower class have much less chance in school than those who have "scholarly culture as their maternal culture" (Bourdieu and de Saint-Martin, 1974:354). Bourdieu is proposing that schooling's reproduction of the structure of the distribution of cultural capital along class lines is a vicious circle wherein cultural capital builds upon cultural capital— "level of education is nothing more than the accumulation of the effects of training acquired within the family and the academic apprenticeships which themselves presuppose this previous training" (1977:493).

In addition to the working class students' poverty of cultural capital there exists also a working class "ethos" (Bourdieu, 1974:32) which works to shape attitudes towards educational institutions. The working class ethos leads to "self-elimination" (Swartz, 1977:539) in that within this ethos the students' "subjective hopes" are very low for scholastic achievement because their "objective chances" are minimal (Bourdieu, 1974:34).

The reproduction of social hierarchies is legitimized by the school because it converts "social hierarchy into academic hierarchy" and conceals this reproduction "beneath a cloak of a perfectly democratic method of selection" (Bourdieu, 1977:496 and 497).

In other words, by treating all pupils, however unequal they may be in reality, as equal in rights and duties, the educational system is led to give its *de facto* sanction to initial cultural inequalities...our own pedagogical tradition is in fact, despite external appearances of irreproachable equality and universality, only there for the benefit of pupils who are in the *particular position* of possessing a cultural heritage conforming to that demanded by the school (Bourdieu, 1974:38).

Hence, although formally equitable the school selection procedure as envisioned by Bourdieu both perpetuates and legitimizes social inequalities as it reproduces the hierarchical distribution of cultural capital along class lines. Bourdieu (1974:43) further claims that the myth of 'perfect mobility' (i.e., equal chances for mobility) is in reality an impossibility. And finally, "the exceptional success of those few individuals who escape the collective fate of their class apparently justifies educational selection and gives credence to the myth of the school as a liberating force among those who have been eliminated, by giving the impression that success is exclusively a matter of gifts and work" (Bourdieu, 1974:42).

A Combined Reproduction Thesis

As we have seen, both Bowles and Gintis and Pierre Bourdieu in their social and

cultural reproduction theses respectively do not 'presume' (as do many functionalist interpretations) that the school is a meritocratic mechanism promoting social
mobility. Both these postulate that the schools reproduce the existing hierarchy of
social inequality.

We propose that although Bourdieu acknowledges 'that the holders of
economic power have more chances than those who are deprived of it also to
possess cultural capital" (1977:507), his treatment of cultural reproduction is
made to appear too distinct a process from that of economic social reproduction.
On the other hand, the social reproduction thesis as expressed by Bowles and
Gintis, because of its reliance on the correspondence principle, tends to treat
schools as 'black boxes' and misses the dynamics of cultural capital and its
reproduction. If we recognize the dialectical nature of the relationship between
culture and economy we must deal with cultural and social reproduction together.
"In short, anything less than analyzing the nexus of relationships between
economic and cultural capital fails to catch the interpenetration of cultural and
economic reproduction" (Apple, 1978:407).

To accomplish this combined analysis we can make use of the crucial Marxist
concept of 'hegemonic' as developed by Gramsci. The traditional use of the term
emphasized political and economic domination while Gramsci "stressed the role
of consciousness, culture, and ideology in the maintenance of unequal social and
economic systems" (Apple, 1978:406). In analyzing this concept Williams
(1976:304) explains that "hegemony supposes the existence of something which is
truly total... which is lived". Hegemony is defined then as "the central, effective
and dominant system of meanings and values, which are not merely abstract but
are organized and lived" (Williams, 1976:205). While in this sense hegemony
takes on a more cultural meaning, if we do not neglect its basis in politico-
economic domination, hegemony relations are developed and reproduced.
Hegemony acts as a "reproductive force" for those who "control cultural capital as
well as economic capital" (Apple, 1979:154). Within an analysis of the nature of
hegemony educational researchers and educators must hold up their day-to-day
activities to "political and economic scrutiny, to see school as part of a system of
mechanisms for cultural and economic reproduction" (Apple, 1979:11).

In summation, then, through the reproductive force of the dominant
hegemony schooling serves to reproduce concomitantly the cultural as well as
social (economic) relations of capitalist society, and thus to prevent or severely
limit social mobility. We believe this composite view has more explanatory power
than does either the cultural or social reproduction theses alone.

References

Apple, Michael W.
1978 "The New Sociology of Education: Analyzing Cultural and Economic Reproduction", **Harvard Educational Review**, 48(4).
1979 **Ideology and Curriculum**, London: Routledge and Kegan Paul.

Berbaum, Gerald
   1977   **Knowledge and Ideology in the Sociology of Education**, London: Macmillan.
Blau, P.M. and O.D. Duncan
   1967   **The American Occupational Structure**, New York: Wiley & Sons.
Bourdieu, Pierre
   1971   "Systems of Education and Systems of Thought", in Young (ed.), **Knowledge and Control.**
   1974   "The School as a Conservative Force: Scholastic and Cultural Inequalities", in Eggleston (ed.), **Contemporary Research in the Sociology of Education.**
   1977   "Cultural Reproduction and Social Reproduction", in Karabel and Halsey (eds.), **Power and Ideology in Education.**
Bourdieu, Pierre and Monique de Saint-Martin
   1974   "Scholastic Excellence and the Values of the Educational System", in Eggleston (ed.), **Contemporary Research in the Sociology of Education.**
Bowles, Samuel and Herbet Gintis
   1976   **Schooling in Capitalist America**, New York: Basic Books.
Denison, Edward F.
   1969   "The Contribution of Education to the Quality of Labor: Comment", **American Economic Review**, 59.
Hopper, Earl
   1971   **Readings in the Theory of Educational Systems**, London: Hutchinson.
Hurn, Christopher J.
   1978   **The Limits and Possibilities of Schooling**, Boston: Allyn and Bacon.
Jencks, Christopher, et al.
   1972   **Inequality: A Reassessment of the Effect of Family and Schooling in America**, New York: Basic Books.
Karabel, J. and Halsey, A.H.
   1977   **Power and Ideology in Education**, New York: Oxford Press.
Kennett, John
   1973   "The Sociology of Pierre Bourdies", **Educational Review**, 25(3).
Levitas, Maurice
         Marxist Perspectives in the Sociology of Education, London: Routledge and Kegan Paul.
Parkin, Frank
         Class Inequality and Political Order, London: MacGibbon and Kee.
Sarup, Madan
   1978   **Marxism and Education**, London: Routledge and Kegan Paul.
Schultz, Theodore W.
   1961   "Investment in Human Capital", **American Economic Review**, 2(1).
Swartz, David
   1977   "Pierre Bourdieu: The Cultural Transmission of Social Inequality", **Harvard Educational Review**, 47(4).
Williams, Raymond
   1976   "Base and Superstructure in Marxist Cultural Theory", in R. Dale et al. (eds.), **Schooling and Capitalism**, London: Routledge and Kegan Paul.

Part II
Minorities and Health Care

5

The Underdevelopment of the Health
Status of Treaty Indians

Paul D. Brady
University of Saskatchewan

Introduction

This paper is intended to provide an understanding of the underdevelopment of
the health status of the registered Indian population of Saskatchewan. To accomplish this goal it is necessary to employ both a structural and historical perspective.
The underdevelopment of registered Indian health status will therefore be viewed
as a major consequence and contradiction of the development of capitalism in
Canada. Specifically this phenomena will be explained within the context of the
imposed social, political, and economic structures of internal colonialism.

Internal Colonial Model

The following is a brief historical outline of the development of capitalism in
Canada as it affected Canadian Indians.

Both Marx (1906) and Lenin (1973) have shown that the inherent contradictions of capitalist production forced its outward expansion and determined the
colonialist era of world history. Previous to European contact, the North American Indian enjoyed excellent health status and had a knowledge of herbal remedies
and medical techniques which were advanced in comparison to their European
counterparts (Vogel, 1970).

The arrival of Europeans in North America coincided with the decline of
feudalism and the growth of mercantile capitalism in Europe. The mercantile
capitalist period was characterized by the unilateral transfers of wealth from

hinterlands to the developing capitalist centers in Europe. This primitive accumulation of capital took place by means of plunder or highly unequal trade practices on the part of Europeans (Marx, 1906; Baran, 1957). In Canada the primitive accumulation of capital took place largely through the fur trade.

Initially, Canadian Indians were vital to the fur trade and as military allies to either the French or British traders (Patterson, 1972). As the quintessence of the fur trading system, the Indians constituted a vital and necessary labour force during the mercantile capitalist period. By 1821, the Hudson Bay Company had established a monopoly over the fur trade in Canada. In the interim, Indians had become dependent on European goods—tools, steel knives, firearms, food—obtained through the fur trade, and were being separated from their traditional means of subsistence (Stanley, 1961; Patterson, 1972). Indian dependence on European goods, and thus the colonial system, coupled with the monopoly position of the Hudson Bay Company, allowed their maximum exploitation with Bay profits reaching 20,000,000 Sterling by 1857 (Meyers, 1972).

At the same time, the introduction of European infectious diseases such as smallpox, tuberculosis, typhoid, whooping cough, measles, and venereal disease, severely decimated the Indian population (Rea, 1968; Parnell, 1976; Vogel, 1970; Crowe, 1974).

> Cree expansion westward and northward in the nineteenth century was not stopped by a series of smallpox epidemics which struck them twice in the eighteenth century and again in the early nineteenth century. It is asserted that their numbers declined in the mid-nineteenth century from approximately 4,000 to about 1,000 though their territorial span remained unchanged...The decimation of the Assiniboines, due also to epidemics, may have aided Cree expansion into areas formerly occupied by the Assiniboines in Southern Manitoba and Saskatchewan. A smallpox epidemic in 1836 is estimated to have killed 4,000 or more Assiniboines of Canada (Patterson, 1972:95).

With the exception of the North, the fur trading era in Canada ended with the transfer of the Hudson Bay Company's monopoly over Rupert's Land to the Dominion government in 1868 (Cummings and Mickenberg, 1970). Within the same period emergent monopoly capitalism in Europe necessitated a tightening of the relationship with the colonies to facilitate the export of capital and the appropriation of markets and raw materials (Lenin, 1973). British imperialism required that the Canadian colony serve these demands and in addition, absorb a large percentage of surplus British population. In other words, these dictates required implementation of a settler agricultural economy and the termination of Indian land title. At this juncture in Canadian history Indians no longer constituted a vital and indispensable labour force, but rather were forced to become an economically redundant population group. The expulsion of Indians from the production process highlights a fundamental contradiction in the capitalist mode of production. Marx (1906) has explained how the creation of relative surplus population is inherent in the development of capitalism.

It is capitalist accumulation itself that constantly produces, and produces in direct ratio of its own energy and extent, a relatively redundant population of labourers... The labouring population, therefore, produces along with the accumulation of capital produced by it, the means by which itself is made relatively superfluous, is turned into a relatively surplus population, and it does this to an always increasing extent... This surplus population becomes... a condition of existence of the capitalist mode of production (Marx, 1906:691-693).

The expulsion of Indians from the production process is the point in history that marks their forced transformation into a problem population within the proletariat class. The most distinguishing characteristic of this population is the fact that their behaviour, personal qualities, or position threatens the social relations of production in capitalist societies. Specifically, problem populations threaten, hinder, or question the following:

1. Capitalist modes of appropriating the product of human labour.
2. The social conditions under which capitalist production takes place.
3. Patterns of distribution and consumption in capitalist societies.
4. The process of socialization for productive and non-productive roles.
5. The ideology which supports the functioning of capitalist society (Spitzer, 1975:642-643).

Indian resistance to the implementation of a settler agricultural economy, and their economic obsolescence as a labour force, made them obstacles to the development of capitalism in Canada. The reaction to this obstruction called for the forced negotiation of treaties. Between 1871 and 1923, eleven treaties were signed extinguishing Indian title in Manitoba, Saskatchewan, Alberta and the North West Territories. These famous treaties were not negotiated between equal parties, but rather the Indians were forced to sign under duress (Stanley, 1952). In settlement of the treaties, it was made plain by the Dominion authorities that the settlers would take the Indians' land regardless of whether they accepted the treaty (Cummings and Mickenberg, 1970). The treaties culminated in the appropriation of Indian lands, resulting in their alienation from traditional means of production, and their internment on reserves.

The reserves were initially regarded as temporary training centers in which the Indians would be taught European culture followed by enfranchisement and assimilation into the dominant society. This notion of the reserves originated with the 1830 British Colonial Office adoption of the assimilation policy (Upton, 1973; Surtees, 1969). The policy was passed on to the Dominion government in 1867 and has been retained to the present day. The view expressed in the assimilation policy was that Indians were lost savages who should be saved and civilized (Surtees, 1969). In reality the assimilation policy was only an ideological tool; for in practice the British always maintained a rigid non-assimilation policy in their colonies (Kennedy, 1945).

On the reserves Indians were to take up an agricultural existence, one completely foreign to their traditional nomadic lifestyle. The ideological basis of the assimilation policy was readily revealed by official actions. The government often withheld food rations causing starvation (Andrews, 1975; Stanley, 1961) and

treaty (Patterson, 1972). Hildebrandt (1970:322) reports that in 1877-78 the
entire Indian population of Saskatchewan received only 2 ploughs, 2 harrows, 13
spades, 18 axes, 41 hoes, 4 oxen, 1 bull, 1 cow, 32 bushels of barley seed, 4 of oats
and 616 potatoes. The disastrous effects of reservation life on the health status of
prairie Indians was largely due to official acts which severely hindered their
adjustment. Starvation and malnutrition made Indians much more susceptible to
infectious European diseases.

> Even more destructive was the epidemic that ran riot among Indians of
> the Qu'Appelle Valley Reservation in Western Canada. The tuberculosis
> mortality rate among them reached a fantastic figure corresponding to
> 9,000 per 100,000—the highest on record anywhere at any time. This
> was barely three decades after these Indians had to abandon their free way
> of life on the prairies (Dubos and Dubos, 1952, p. 191).

The legislating of the assimilation policy was the first step towards institutionalized racism in Canada. The United States Center for Racial Justice gives
the following definitions of institutional racism:

- The patterns in the life and practice of an institution that perpetuate
  inequalities in the treatment of and relationships between persons functioning in and affected by that structure.

- A set of rules, either conscious or unconscious, that creates a powerless group
  and a powerful group, which leads to exploitation of one group over another
  on the basis of race.

- A group or organization that, because of its rules, regulations and mode of
  operation, systematically excludes any ethnic group by not allowing them
  the opportunities, privileges and rights of others.

  (Canadian Welfare, 1974:23).

Numerous authors have established the origins of racism in colonial regimes.
Racism functions as a justification for, and at the same time, a means by which
colonizers exploit indigenous people. This exploitation facilitates capitalist accumulation (Little, 1958; Boggs, 1970; Baran and Sweezy, 1966; Casanova,
1965; Cox, 1948; Blauner, 1969; Willhelm, 1969; Nikolinakas, 1973;
Balandier, 1966; Kennedy, 1945). In the present case, racism was used to justify
the appropriation of Indian land and their confinement on reserves.

The British North America Act, Section 91, Subsection 24, gave to the federal
government exclusive authority to legislate for Indians, and land reserved for
Indians (Cummings and Mickenberg, 1970). The passage of the Indian Act,
which remains in effect to the present day, manifests the classic characteristics of
colonial legislation (Kennedy, 1945; Casonova, 1965; Tabb, 1970). For example,
the Act gives the federal government complete economic and political control
over Canada's Registered Indians. It allows the central government power to
control virtually everything that is done on Indian reserves. The Act has been used
to destroy Indian culture by outlawing many of the most powerful Indian
customs. Indian gift giving ceremonies, traditional dances, and festivals were
made illegal. Indians could not appear in any public show in aboriginal costume
without the consent of the Superintendent of Indian Affairs. Not until 1951 were

these restrictions lifted. Not until 1960 were Indians given the right to vote in federal elections (Soonias, 1978; Frideres, 1974; Melling; 1966; Zlotkin and Colborn, 1977).

The Indian Act is a separate set of laws used to govern Indian Canadians. These laws do not apply to non-Indians. The Act itself, which contains one hundred and twenty-four sections, provides extensive controls, prohibitions and restrictions which effectively strip Indians of the power to control their own affairs. More importantly, the passage of the Indian Act established a dependent colonial relationship between the Indians and the dominant Canadian society, which serves to perpetuate Indians as a problem population within the proletariat class. Indian reserves became internal colonies which are exploited by the dominant society. The exploitation centers on the appropriation of raw materials from the reserves. Indians receive only marginal employment and profit from the extraction by non-Indians of reserve resources such as oil, timber, water, and minerals (Frideres, 1974:157-181; Zlotkin and Colborn, 1977; Hildebrandt, 1970).

According to the Hawthorne Report (1966:368):

> ...Indian administration was a version of colonialism. The Branch was a quasi-colonial government dealing with almost the entire life of a culturally different people who were systematically deprived of opportunities to influence government, a people isolated on special pockets of land and who were subject to separate laws.

Similarly, Carstens (1971:129) states:

> The Indians of Canada who are under the Indian Act and live within the economic, social, and territorial confines of reserves are not wards of the Government as some have argued; they are members of little colonies within the borders of the dominating nation.

Frideres (1974:157) outlines seven aspects of colonialism and finds them all applicable to Indians in Canada. These are:

1. The forced entry of the colonizer
2. The destruction of the aboriginal system of life (political, economic, kinship structure, value system)
3. External political domination
4. Native economic dependence
5. Low standards of social services provided
6. Racism
7. Establishment of a color line

To summarize, the internal colonial approach to the development of capitalism in Canada has indicated the class position of registered Indians. Employing this framework registered Indians are seen to constitute a problem population within the proletariat class. The maintenance and perpetuation of registered Indians as a problem population is due to the establishment of a colonial relationship between the Indians (colonized) and the dominant society (colonizers). A major consequence of the colonial relationship has been to produce the overall social, political and economic subordination of registered Indians in Canadian society.

Social Status

In order to pursue an understanding of the health status of Saskatchewan's registered Indians, it is necessary to provide a further and specific discussion of their position as a problem population within the proletariat class. This will be accomplished by discussing in detail their socioeconomic status through the use of indicators of income, occupation, education, social welfare and housing.

Income

Although data on the income level of registered Indians is limited, it has been well established that they rank among the poorest of the poor throughout Canada (Economic Council of Canada, 1968:121-124).

Data shows that in the early 1960's over 45% of Indian families on reserves earned $1,000 per year or less, and that 75% earned $2,000 or less (McEwen, 1964:103). The Hawthorne Survey (1966:45) found that total earnings of registered Indians in Canada amounted to $300 per capita, as compared to the Canadian average of $1,400. A similar contrast was found in comparing the average yearly earnings per worker. For registered Indians the figure was $1,361, while for non-Indians it was $4,000 (1966:95-96).

It has been estimated that in 1970, 62% of employed registered Indians earned less than $2,000 (Department of Indian Affairs and Northern Development, 1980:62). Less dated information indicates that the income level of registered Indians has not changed substantially. Frideres (1974:26) reports that only 20% of the total registered Indian population make more than $3,000 per annum, with nearly one-half earning less than $1,000 per annum. Data from the 1971 and 1976 Census indicates that the average income of registered Indians is well below the national level (Department of Indian Affairs and Northern Development, 1980:62). Using the standard set by the federal government, over 80% of registered Indians in Canada are living below the poverty line (Frideres, 1974:24).

The income level of Saskatchewan's registered Indians conforms closely with the national picture. That is, the income level of Saskatchewan's registered Indians can best be described as meager. Out of the total reserve population of 26,000, only 6,000 had a cash income in 1969. Of this number, only 11% earned $3,000, while over 60% earned less than $1,000 (Dosman, 1972:39). Statistics indicate that the income of registered Indians saw only a marginal increase in the following six years. In 1975 the average wage earnings for Indian people on Saskatchewan reserves amounted to approximately $1,500. This compares very poorly with the provincial average of $10,000 for non-Indians (Federation of Saskatchewan Indians, 1978:6). Clearly, the wages and income of registered Indians are much lower than those of the vast majority of non-Indian Canadians.

Occupation

As occupation and income are closely related, it is not surprising that Indian reserves offer little to almost no opportunity for employment. Studies show that more than 70 percent of working age registered Indians are employed for less than nine months per year. (Department of Indian Affairs and Northern Development, 1980:46). Federal government statistics show that a mere 6% of the total Saskatchewan on-reserve working age registered Indian population had full time employment in 1969. It has been estimated that the registered Indian population experience an unemployment rate in the range of 40 to 90 percent (Siggner, 1979:33; Department of Indian Affairs and Northern Development, 1977:15).

The lack of full-time employment for registered Indians is due in part to their position in the occupational hierarchy. Throughout Canada Indians are over-represented in unskilled or semi-skilled occupations, having almost no presence among the white collar ranks (Statistics Canada, 1980:174.) Furthermore, predictions indicate that their employment situation will deteriorate as mechanization eliminates jobs previously available to unskilled workers.

Statistics show that on Saskatchewan reserves the unemployment rate for registered Indians is rising. In 1971, 75.5 percent of working age reserve Indians were unemployed, whereas by 1975 this figure had reached 79% (Saskatchewan Indian Cultural College, 1975:2). The fact that registered Indians, in common with other colonized people, do not have access to the full range of available employment is one important reason for their present and continuing poverty.

Education

There are a number of studies available in the literature which document the failure of the educational system to meet the needs of registered Indian students. These studies have shown repeatedly that the great majority of Indian students do not continue through the educational system. The Hawthorne Survey (1966:130) found that for the twelve year school cycle between 1951 and 1962, 94% of Indian students did not graduate. Recent government statistics indicate that school completion for registered Indian students has improved only modestly. In 1965, only 10% of Indian students remained to grade 12 from grade 2, while by 1975 this figure had increased to 20% (Department of Indian Affairs and Northern Development, 1980:49). Nevertheless, this compares very poorly with the retention rate for the total population of 75% in 1975 (Siggner, 1979:28).

Viewing these figures, it is easy to conclude that registered Indian students are at a disadvantage compared with their non-Indian counterparts. Data shows that in 1975 over 60% of reserve Indian students in Saskatchewan were behind in grades, with those over ten years of age behind an average of 2.3 years (Saskatchewan Indian Cultural College, 1975:13). Other figures show that over 79% of Saskatchewan's reserve Indians have less than grade nine education, while 2.3% have grade twelve and only .2% of those between the ages of twenty-five and thirty-four years have a university degree (Saskatchewan Indian Cultural College, 1976: Appendix C).

Studies in search of explanations for the high Indian attrition rates find agreement with those showing that educational achievement is strongly related to the social class background of the student (Coleman, 1966; Rist, 1970). The present educational system in Canada caters to urban, middle income, non-Indian students. For this reason it is both irrelevant and alien when placed within the context of Indian reserves (Frideres, 1974:47). In addition, other studies have shown that the content of education serves to provide a cultural insult to Indians by presenting material which depicts them in derogatory terms and interprets history from the viewpoint of the colonizer Europeans (Manitoba Indian Brotherhood, 1974). Taken together, these studies suggest that the present educational system serves to promote feelings of self-doubt, failure and inferiority in Indian students. A number of authors have traced the embedding of this type of psychological inferiority, or what is more generally referred to as a colonized personality, to the dominant colonial institutions (Memmi, 1965:79-118; Puxley, 1977:103-119; Kennedy, 1945:311; Fanon, 1968:250).

Social Welfare

Indian reserves throughout Canada have previously been described as acting as internal colonies whose resources are exploited by the dominant society. One of the immediate consequences of this process has been to produce the extreme economic dependency of the registered Indian population. Indicative of this dependency is the dramatically increasing registered Indian reliance on social assistance. In 1966, 36% of registered Indians living on reserves in Canada received social assistance, compared to the national rate of 3.6%. In this same year, the use of social assistance by registered Indians on a per capita basis was twenty-two times higher than for the non-Indian population (Department of Indian Affairs and Northern Development, 1980:28). By 1974, the rate of social assistance for on-reserve registered Indians in Canada had risen to 55%. This represents a 52% increase from the 1966 rate. Once again, this rate compares very unfavorably with the national rate which was only 6% in the same year (1980:28).

In 1972, over 61% of on-reserve Saskatchewan Indians were dependent on social assistance for support (Statistics Canada, 1974:252). This figure grew to 72% by 1975, an increase of over 18% (Federation of Saskatchewan Indians, 1978:6). Although these figures can be interpreted to encourage the commonly held view of Indians as inherently lazy collectors of unlimited welfare dollars, statistics clearly disprove this ideology. In terms of actual dollars, the total cost of the social assistance program for on-reserve Indians in Saskatchewan amounted to over $9 million in the fiscal year 1973-1974 (Statistics Canada, 1977:291). Though this appears an exhorbitant amount, the annual asistance per person was only $541, or slightly higher than $45 per person per month. Furthermore, other data clearly shows that historically nearly one half of all welfare expenditures for registered Indians have been in the form of cash payments, with little directed towards preventative services (Department of Indian Affairs and Northern Development, 1980:27). This strongly suggests that the welfare expenditures function primarily for social control purposes by fostering and perpetuating registered Indian dependency.

With regard to the actual welfare services provided for registered Indians, a number of studies have pointed out that these are substandard in comparison to those available to non-Indian Canadians (Frideres, 1974:16). In the past, Indians were excluded from a variety of programs including supplementary allowances, and old age and blind person benefits. They have also not been equally able to take advantage of subsidized university and technical training, nor government cultural and recreational expenditures on parks, libraries, community centers and so forth (Hawthorne et al., 1966:321). For these reasons, the federal government has actually pocketed considerable amounts of money through reduced spending on registered Indians. This becomes apparent in comparing government expenditures on registered Indians and non-Indians in Canada. For example, the total budget for the Department of Indian Affairs was approximately $360 million in 1974. Nearly one-half of this money was consumed by the department in administrative expenses. Another quarter went for various support services, while only the remaining quarter went directly to Indian reserves in the form of loans, grants and programs. This amounts to an average spending of approximately $360 per Indian. In contrast the federal government spent an average of $6,500 on each resident of Prince Edward Island in 1972 (Parnell, 1976:115). Evidently, the standard of social assistance, as measured in dollars and services, is much lower for registered Indians than for other Canadians.

Housing

The present housing conditions for on-reserve Indians are among the worst in Canada. A recent federal government survey found that 26% of reserve families were either doubling or tripling up with another family to obtain shelter, or were occupying houses unfit for human habitation. In addition it was also found that 25% of Indian families were living in houses which needed major repairs to meet minimum health and safety standards. Overall, 40% of reserve houses needed either replacement or major repairs (Department of Indian Affairs and Northern development, 1977:8; Siggner, 1979:39).

In addition to the above, reserve houses also lack the general facilities that were long ago taken for granted in non-Indian homes. Across Canada, only 50% of reserve houses have potable water and only 45% have sewer disposal and indoor plumbing (Siggner, 1979:40). On Saskatchewan reserves only 4% of reserve houses have sewer, 3.6% running water, 2.2% indoor toilet, 1.7% indoor bath, and 3% telephone (Saskatchewan Indian Cultural College, 1975:4-10)).

The substandard housing and overcrowding are extremely detrimental to the health status of Indian people. These conditions are directly related to the heightened incidence of disease among registered Indians as compared with the general population. These include a greater incidence of respiratory diseases such as bronchitis, pneumonia, emphysema and acute respiratory infections especially prevalent among Indian children. (C.A.R. Denis et al., 1977). The heightened incidence of infectious and parasitic diseases such as gastroenteritis, tuberculosis, scabies, middle ear infections and other skin diseases are also related to the poor housing and overcrowded living conditions (Department of National Health and Welfare, 1979:8). Furthermore the dilapidated housing and lack of facilities greatly contribute to the high rate of fires and fire deaths on Indian reserves. Statistics show that the on-reserve death rate due to fires is nine times the national average. In 1978, 186 homes were destroyed by fire resulting in the deaths of fifty-five Indian people (Department of Indian Affairs and Northern Development, 1977:9).

In summary, the socioeconomic status of Canada's registered Indians has been described in order to provide a more comprehensive picture of their class position. The socioeconomic indicators employed show that registered Indians suffer a subsistence level income, high rates of unemployment, low occupational status, intensive welfare dependence, dilapidated housing and a general standard of living closely resembling that found in underdeveloped third world countries.

Health Status

The above indicates that registered Indians in Saskatchewan have an extremely low socioeconomic status. This fact has immediate consequences for their health status. Numerous studies have shown that low socioeconomic status is strongly related to a heightened mortality level. The studies have consistently shown that the highest infant and general mortality rates occur among the lowest socioeconomic status groups (Antonovsky, 1967; Stockwell et al., 1978; Morris and Heady, 1955; Kitagawa and Hauser, 1973; Adamchak, 1979; Markides and Barnes, 1977).

In the following, comparative mortality data will be used to assess the relative health status of the registered Indian population of Saskatchewan. The use of mortality data to assess health status is a basic and standard convention (Wylie, 1970:102). In comparing two populations, the one with the greater mortality rate would be assigned a lower ranked health status.

Crude Mortality Rates

Table 5-1 shows the crude mortality rates of the registered Indian and non-Indian populations of Saskatchewan. Despite the yearly fluctuations, the registered Indian rates as a whole have decreased from a high of 10.7 per 1,000 in 1960 to 7.7 in 1978. The non-Indian crude mortality rates, on the other hand, have shown a general increase from 7.7 per 1,000 in 1959 to 8.2 in 1978.

Comparing the two populations, from 1959 to 1969 the registered Indian rates were higher than those of the non-Indian population, while from 1970 to 1978 the Indian rates were lower.

Employing crude mortality rates to indicate health status, the lower crude mortality rates of the registered Indians indicates a higher ranked health status. In other words, the registered Indian population has a better health status than the non-Indian population of Saskatchewan.

Although federal government agencies consistently use crude mortality rates to compare the overall health status of registered Indians and non-Indians, crude mortality rates are not designed for comparative purposes (Statistics Canada, 1974:241; 1977:283; 1980:177). When used in this manner, crude rates are misleading and give a false impression of relative health status (Shryock and Siegel et al., 1976:241).

Table 5-1

**Crude Mortality Rates per 1,000 for the Registered Indian
and Non-Indian Populations of Saskatchewan
1959 to 1978**

Year	Registered Indians	Non-Indians
1959	9.7	7.7
1960	10.7	7.4
1961	10.2	7.6
1962	9.7	7.5
1963	10.2	7.9
1964	8.2	7.8
1965	9.7	7.8
1966	9.1	7.8
1967	9.2	7.7
1968	8.9	7.8
1969	8.1	7.8
1970	7.1	8.0
1971	6.7	8.0
1972	6.2	8.3
1973	5.5	8.5
1974	6.8	8.7
1975	6.7	8.5
1976	5.7	8.6
1977	6.7	8.2
1978	7.7	8.2

Derived from Department of National Health and Welfare, "Vital Statistics for the Registered Indian Population of Saskatchewan, 1972-1978; Saskatchewan Health, **Vital Statistics, 1959-1978**.

Standardized Mortality Rates

To obtain a precise and accurate assessment of the comparative health status of registered Indians it is necessary to compute standardized mortality rates. These are superior to crude rates because they are designed specifically for comparing the mortality levels of different populations. Table 5-2 shows the standardized mortality rates for the registered Indian and non-Indian populations of Saskatchewan from 1966 to 1978. Evident from this table is the overall rise in Indian mortality (9.9 per 1,000 in 1966 to 11.5 in 1978) compared to the overall decline

Table 5-2

Standardized Mortality Rates for the Registered Indian and Non-Indian Populations of Saskatchewan, 1966 to 1978

Year	Registered Indians	Non-Indian	Percent Excess Registered Indian Rates: Non-Indian Rates
1966	9.9	6.6	50%
1968	10.3	6.5	58%
1970	10.7	6.4	67%
1972	10.3	6.3	63%
1974	10.0	6.4	56%
1976	8.7	6.2	40%
1978	11.5	5.9	95%

1) Standardized to the 1956 Saskatchewan Census population; rates per 1,000 population.
2) Source: Derived from Saskatchewan Department of Public Health, **Vital Statistics (1959-1973)**; Saskatchewan Health **Vital Statistics (1974-1976)**; Department of National Health and Welfare, **Vital Statistics for the Registered Indian Population of Saskatchewan (1973-1978)**; Department of Indian Affairs and Northern Development, **Registered Indian Population by Age, Sex, and Residence Saskatchewan Region**, (1966-1978).

in non-Indian mortality (6.6 in 1966 to 5.9 in 1978). More importantly, it is also evident that the registered Indian population suffers from an overwhelmingly higher mortality rate than the non-Indian population. In 1966 the registered Indian mortality rate was 50% greater than the non-Indian rate, 67% greater in 1970, 56% greater in 1974, and 95% greater in 1978. Quite clearly, the standardized death rates indicate that the health status of registered Indians ranks substantially lower than that of the non-Indian population.

Further investigation of the relative health status of registered Indians requires analysis of the impact of specific causes of death on their population. For this purpose, the death rates for the leading causes of death from 1959 to 1978 among the registered Indian population were compared with the death rates for these causes among the non-Indian population. It was found that the average death rate for accidents among registered Indians was 3.6 times higher than the non-Indian population; suicide and self-inflicted injury 3 times higher, homicide 1.8 times higher, congenital anomalies 1.4 times higher, certain causes of perinatal mortality 3.2 times higher, pneumonia 3.3 times higher and tuberculosis 9.4 times higher (Brady, 1981: Chapter 6).

Further analysis revealed that there were distinct differences in the leading causes of death which affect the Registered Indian and non-Indian populations. From 1959 to 1978, homicide, tuberculosis, infectious diseases, and gastro-enteritis and colitis were leading causes of death unique among the registered Indian population. Clearly, the registered Indian population suffers from a larger number of leading causes of death associated with non-disease and infectious causes. These causes are considered to be largely preventable. By way of contrast, among the non-Indian population, infectious diseases ceased to be among the leading causes of death over four decades ago (Saskatchewan Department of Public Health, 1960:28).

As well as differences in the leading causes of death, it was also found that there were marked differences between the two populations in the average ranking of the leading causes of death. Among the non-Indian population, diseases associated with degenerative causes including heart diseases, malignant neoplasms (cancer), cerebrovascular disease, diabetes mellitus, diseases of the arteries, arterioles and capillaries had comparatively higher ranks.

In contrast, the leading causes of death associated with infancy, (pneumonia, congenital anomalies, certain causes of perinatal mortality) and infectious causes (tuberculosis, gastro-enteritis and colitis, infectious diseases) and non-disease causes (accidents, homicide, suicide and self-inflicted injury) had average ranks which were comparatively higher among the registered Indian population (Brady, 1981: Chapter 6). The higher average ranks of these causes clearly indicates their increased importance upon mortality among registered Indians. Furthermore, the higher average ranking of these causes is a major difference in the mortality patterns between the two populations.

The difference in the mortality patterns must be viewed as having the most negative consequences for the registered Indian population. They continue to be subjected to leading causes of death which were long ago eliminated as leading causes among the non-Indian population. They also suffer greater mortality from causes associated with infancy and non-disease and infectious causes than do the non-Indian population. Indeed the average age at death for registered Indians in Canada was 44 years in 1976, compared to an average age in the general population of 67 years (Siggner, 1979:6). This situation is due mainly to structural, not individual, factors. It is directly related to the unequal and disadvantaged conditions of life forced upon registered Indians in Canadian society.

Summary

This paper has sought to provide an understanding of the underdevelopment of the health status of Saskatchewan's registered Indians. For this purpose the internal colonial model has been employed to explain the health status of registered Indians within the context of the imposed social, political and economic structures of internal colonialism. The model emphasizes that the underdevelopment of registered Indian health status is a major consequence and contradiction of the development of capitalism in Canada.

References

Adamchak, Donald
  1979   "Emerging Trends in the Relationship Between Infant Mortality and Socioeconomic Status", **Social Biology**, 26, 16-29.
Antonovsky, Aaron
  1967   "Social Class, Life Expectancy and Overall Mortality", **Milbank Memorial Fund Quarterly**, 45:31-73.
Balandier, G.
  1966   "The Colonial Situation: A Theoretical Approach", in I. Wallerstein (ed.) **Social Change, the Colonial Situation**, New York: John Wiley & Sons, Inc.
Baldus, Bernd
  1975   "The Study of Power: Suggestions for an Alternative", **Canadian Journal of Sociology**, 1:179-201.
Baran, Paul and Paul Sweezy
  1966   **Monopoly Capital**. New York: Modern Readers Paperbacks.
Baran, Paul
  1957   **The Political Economy of Growth**. New York: Modern Readers Paperbacks.
Blauner, Robert
  1969   "Internal Colonialism and Ghetto Revolt", **Social Problems**, 16:393-408.
Boggs, James
  1970   **Racism and the Class Struggle**. New York: Monthly Review Press.
Brady, Paul
  1981   "The Health Status of the Registered Indian Population of Saskatchewan: 1959-1978." M.A. Diss., Saskatoon: Department of Sociology, University of Saskatchewan.
Canada, Department of Indian and Northern Affairs
  1966-   "Registered Indian Population by Age, Sex and Residence: Saskatchewan
  1978   Region." Ottawa: Program Reference Centre.
  1970   **Survey of Indian Bands and Reserves**, Ottawa.
  1977   **Indian on Reserve Housing Program**, Ottawa.
  1980   **Indian Conditions:** A Survey, Ottawa.
Canada, Department of National Health and Welfare
  1973-   "Vital Statistics for the Registered Indian Population of Saskatchewan."
  1978   Regina.
  1979   "Indian Health: Discussion Paper." Ottawa (Mimeographed).
Canada, Statistics Canada
  1980   "The Indians and Metis of Canada," in **Perspectives Canada III**, Ottawa.
  1977   "Native Peoples", in **Perspectives Canada II**, Ottawa.
  1974   "Native Peoples", in **Perspectives Canada I**, Ottawa.
Canadian Welfare
  1974   "News and Comment", Canadian Welfare, 50:23.
Carstens, Peter
  1971   "Coercion and Change", in R. Ossenberg (ed.) **Canadian Society**, Scarborough, Ontario: Prentice-Hall of Canada Ltd.

Casanova, Pablo
    1965   "Internal Colonialism and National Development", **Studies in Comparative International Development**, 1:27-37.
Coleman, James et al.
    1966   **Equality of Educational Opportunity**, Washington, D.C.: Government Printing Office.
Cox, Oliver
    1948   **Caste, Class, and Race**, New York: Modern Reader Paperbacks.
Crowe, Keith
    1974   **A History of the Original Peoples of Northern Canada**, Montreal: Queen's University Press.
Cummings, Peter and Neil Mickenberg
    1970   **Native Rights in Canada**, Toronto: The Indian and Eskimo Association of Canada.
Denis, C.A.R., S. Drope and D. Matz
    1977   **Medicare Data: Its Use in Defining the Effects of the Environment on Health**. Ottawa: National Research Council.
Economic Council of Canada
    1968   "Indians, Eskimoes, and Metis", in **The Challenge of Growth and Change: Fifth Annual Report**, Ottawa: Queen's Printer.
Fanon, Frantz
    1968   **The Wretched of the Earth**, New York: Grove Press, Inc.
Frideres, James
    1974   **Canada's Indians: Contemporary Conflicts**, Scarborough, Ontario: Prentice-Hall of Canada.
Hawthorne, H.B. (ed.)
    1966   **A Survey of the Contemporary Indians of Canada**, Ottawa: Indian Affairs Branch.
Hildebrandt, Heather
    1970   "People Farms", in W.E. Mann (ed.) **Poverty and Social Policy in Canada**, Toronto: Copp Clark Publishing Company.
Kabwegyere, Tarsis
    1972   "The Dynamics of Colonial Violence: The Inductive System in Uganda", **Journal of Peace Research**, 4:303-314.
Kennedy, Raymond
    1945   "The Colonial Crisis and the Future", in R. Linton (ed.) **The Science of Man in the World Crisis**, New York: Columbia University Press.
Kitagawa, E.M. and P.M. Hauser
    1973   **Differential Mortality in the United States: A Study in Socioeconomic Epidemiology**, Cambridge, Massachusetts: Harvard University Press.
Lenin, V.I.
    1973   **Imperialism, the Highest Stage of Capitalism**, Peking: Foreign Language Press.

Little, Kenneth
1958   **Race and Society**, Paris: UNESCO.
Manitoba Indian Brotherhood
1974   **The Shocking Truth about Indians in Textbooks**; Winnipeg, Manitoba: Manitoba Indian Brotherhood.
Markides, K.S. and D. Barnes
1977   "A Methodological Note on the Relationship Between Infant Mortality and Socioeconomic Status with Evidence from San Antonio, Texas", **Social Biology**, 24:38-44.
Marx, Karl
1906   **Capital**, Vol. I, New York: The Modern Library.
McEwen, E.R.
1964   "Equality of Opportunity", **Human Relations**, 5:1-3.
Melling, J.
1966   "Recent Developments in Official Policy Towards Canadian Indians and Eskimos", **Race**, VII, 378-398.
Memmi, Albert
1965   **The Colonizer and the Colonized**, Boston: Beacon Press.
Meyers, Gustavus
1972   **A History of Canadian Wealth**, Toronto: James Lewis & Samuel.
Morris, J.N. and J.A. Heady
1955   "Mortality in Relation to Father's Occupation: 1911-1959", **The Lancet**, 1:554-559.
Nikolinakos, Marios
1973   "Notes on an Economic Theory of Racism", **Race**, 14:365-381.
Parnell, Ted
1976   **Disposable Native**, Alberta Human Rights and Civil Liberties Association, Edmonton.
Patterson, E. Palmer
1972   **The Canadian Indian: A History Since 1500**, Don Mills, Ontario: Collier-MacMillan Canada Ltd.
Puxley, Peter
1977   "The Colonial Experience", in Mel Watkins (ed.) **Dene Nation: The Colony within**, Toronto: University of Toronto Press.
Rea, K.J.
1968   **The Political Economy of the Canadian North**, Toronto: University of Toronto Press.
Rist, Ray
1970   "Student Social Class and Teacher Expectations: The Self-Fulfilling Prophecy in Ghetto Education", **Harvard Educational Review**, 40:411-451.
Ryan, William
1971   **Blaming the Victim**, New York: Pantheon.
Saskatchewan, Saskatchewan Department of Public Health
1959-   **Vital Statistics for the Province of Saskatchewan**, Regina:
1973   Government of Saskatchewan.

Saskatchewan, Saskatchewan Health
  1959- **Vital Statistics for the Province of Saskatchewan**, Regina
  1978   (Mimeographed).
Saskatchewan Indian Cultural College
  1976   "Reserve Economies and Reserve Development." Saskatoon (Mimeographed).
  1975   "A Socio-Economic Profile of Saskatchewan Indians and Indian Reserves." A
          Brief presented to the Federation of Saskatchewan Indians Annual Conference,
          Saskatoon (Mimeographed).
Siggner, Andrew
  1979   "An Overview of Demographic Social and Economic Conditions among
          Canada's Registered Indian Population", Ottawa: Indian and Inuit Affairs
          Program.
Shrylock, H. and S. Siegel et al.
  1976   **The Methods and Material of Demography**, New York: Academic Press.
Soonias, Rodney
  1978   "History of the Indian Act", **Saskatchewan Indian**, 8: No. 2, 4-5; No. 4,
          20-21; No. 5, 19-21.
Spitzer, Steven
  1975   "Towards a Marxist Theory of Deviance", **Social Problems**, 22:638-651.
Stanley, George
  1952   "The Indian Background of Canadian History", **Canadian Historical Associ-
          ation Annual Reports**, 14-21.
  1961   **The Birth of Western Canada**, Toronto: University of Toronto Press.
Stockwell, Edward, J. Wicks and D. Adamchak
  1978   "Research Needed on Socioeconomic Differenntials in U.S. Mortality", Public
          Health Reports, 93:667-672.
Surtees, R.J.
  1969   "The Development of an Indian Reserve Policy in Canada", **Ontario History**,
          LXI:87-98.
Tabb, W.K.
  1970   **The Political Economy of the Black Ghetto**, New York: W.W. Norton and
          Company.
Union of B.C. Indian Chiefs
  1975   **The Indian Act and What It Means**, Vancouver: Union of B.C. Indian
          Chiefs.
Upton, L.F.S.
  1973   "The Origins of Canadian Indian Policy", **Journal of Canadian Studies**,
          8:51-61.
Vogel, Virgil
  1970   **American Indian Medicine**, New York: Ballantine Books.
Wylie, Charles M.
  1970   "The Definition and Measurement of Health and Disease", **Public Health
          Reports**, 85.
Willhelm, Sidney
  1969   "Black Man, Red Man, and White America: The Constitutional Approach to
          Genocide", **Catalyst**, 4:1-62.
Zlotkin, Norman and Donald Colborn
  1977   "Internal Canadian Imperialism and Native People", in J. Saul and Cheron
          (eds.) **Imperialism, Nationalism and Canada**, Toronto: New Hogtown
          Press.

6

Pathways to Health Care Among Chinese-Canadians: An Exploration*

Peter Kong-ming New   *and*   *Walter Watson*
    University of South Florida   *Brock University*

Introduction

The work of scholars concerned with ethnicity and its associated concepts is dominated by a series of debates between two groups, those approaching 'ethnicity' from a macro perspective (societal or structural) and those dealing with the micro level (group processes or culture). Current work shows a decided shift in focus from processes within ethnic groups such as assimilation and acculturation (c.f. Montero, 1979, 1980, 1981), to the more structural issues of opportunity, economic development, immigration policies, discrimination, and the like (e.g., Thomspon, 1979; Chan and Cheung, 1982; Hawkins, 1974; Kuo, 1979; Li, 1979a, 1979b; Wickberg, 1981; Johnson, forthcoming).

---

* The authors wish to thank Peter S. Li for the oppoprtunity of exploring some of the ideas in this paper with various colleagues. They also wish to thank the various Chinese community leaders in St. Catharines, Winnipeg and Vancouver who met with them during February and May, 1982. We are also grateful to Dr. Yuet Wah Cheung, Lingnan College, Hong Kong, who made some suggestions on the earlier draft.

One of the major reasons for the dominance of structural analysts in recent ethnic studies is that they argue fairly convincingly that the larger society plays a major role in the lives of immigrants, e.g. various political and social forces prevent immigrants from receiving *all* the benefits and opportunities available to the native born. Thus, the earlier sociologists, such as Siu (1964), who advanced the notions of the 'sojourner', do not take into consideration the larger societal structures, nor do they provide a complete picture of the factors influencing the lives of immigrants.

With historical and structural factors dominating ethnic inquiries, fewer researchers are paying attention to individuals and the reasons they behave as they do. There remains the ongoing puzzles as to why ethnic groups survive and why certain cultural traits persist (Reitz, 1980). The authors of this paper wish to explore several aspects of these cultural and structural perspectives as they relate to the investigation of the 'pathways' (Hesler et al., 1975) used by Chinese-Canadians to obtain health care. The concept 'pathway' is defined as those sets of activities, both cognitive (decisions, feelings) and behavioural (discussions), that lead an individual to a particular action (seeking help).

Some may consider this a spurious issue. Illness is more immediate than language or the arts and a person, if sick in Canada, would immediately seek appropriate help from a physician or medical institution. Furthermore, since most people are reimbursed, at least for all major expenses, and there are numerous medical facilities, cultural or structural factors would have little to do with health care (Coburn et al., 1981). At least one major Ontario study of health service utilization would appear to confirm this position (Marr, 1976).

However, we would argue that, among Chinese-Canadians, the paths they take (or delay in taking) can be affected by the cultural beliefs of health and illness, perception of guilt and shame; and, further, these paths can be altered by the structure which the larger society places on them. Examination of the types of health care the Chinese utilize—western or Chinese trained physicians, herbalists, accupuncturists, bone setters, traditional (family) cures or (Chinese) patent medicines—may indicate that cultural and structural forces play a more significant role that even we suspect (see New, 1977; Hessler et al., 1975; Twaddle and Hessler, 1977: 139-159). Anecdotally, there is a fair bit of evidence that not only ethnics, but also non-ethnics often go to great lengths to seek out faith healers—some travelling to foreign countries (**Toronto Globe and Mail**, 1982; **Canadian Family Physician**, 1981; Lechky, 1980).

At present, the authors of this paper are planning a research project to examine the pathways which the Chinese-Canadians take to obtain health care. This will, of necessity, include obtaining systematic data on the use of traditional Chinese or alternative medical care. Thus, they have made some preliminary inquiries regarding Chinese health care in St. Catharines, Winnipeg, and Vancouver. In the remainder of the paper, the efficacy of the cultural and structural perspectives will be examined in some detail in the light of the information we have gathered thus far.

Ethnicity and Health Care

In most studies which have dealt with ethnicity and health care, one of the guiding assumptions has been that ethnic groups 'bring' with them the prevailing ideologies and health practices of their 'homeland'. The concepts of health and illness of the ethnics, usually fairly complex and with some scientific bases, would dictate the healing and therapies chosen, even when they are transposed into another culture (see for example Leslie, 1976).

Recent studies in the Vancouver area by Tsung-yi Lin, M.D., a psychiatrist, and his colleagues would certainly bear this out. They studied the Chinese who had serious mental illness. Not only did they maintain their cultural beliefs about health and illness, but they also added another layer of belief regarding guilt and shame (Lina and Lin, 1980). They beliefs held them back from seeking psychiatric help, quite readily available in the Vancouver Chinatown area (Lin and Lin, 1978; Lin et al., 1978).

Aside from the cultural beliefs, language barriers may create a structural problem. For instance, in our pilot study of health care among the Chinese in St. Catharines, Ontario, we found that the Chinese health care seeker would prefer going to a Chinese physician who could communicate in the patient's dialect and where certain Chinese expressions of symptoms (hot fire rising in the liver) would, hopefully, be understood (New and Watson, personal interviews).

Furthermore, both languages and beliefs interact. If the Chinese medical or social workers does not share these beliefs, even though they may be able to speak a particular dialect, their inability to 'understand' the symptom (e.g. 'fright') would continue to place the patient at a disadvantage (Wong, 1978).

A second assumption utilized by those studying ethnic health is that through time, as the ethnic individual becomes assimilated and adopts the prevailing health practices of the dominant society, former beliefs and practices are leavened and even fall by the wayside. When one considers that here in Canada, as in many other countries, medicare would reimburse practically all health care costs incurred in the 'mainstream' health care system, there are no economic barriers to assimilation. Furthermore, as one must pay for non 'mainstream' care there are strong economic incentives to override the cultural orientations toward traditional health care.

The results of a recent study by Kuprowsky (1981) in Vancouver show that many Chinese have clearly delimited the capabilities of Chinese herbal medicine and western medicine. Personal interviews by the authors with western-trained Chinese health care providers reveal that indeed Chinese continue to differentiate the use of both resources for different symptoms and stages of illness, e.g. 'winter soup' to prevent illness (New and Watson, personal interviews). One could argue that the use of Chinese herbal medicines is due to their relative inexpensiveness. This is far from the case—in Vancouver some single ginseng roots are selling for as much as $1,400 per root.

A third assumption is that with each successive generation, ethnics become "less ethnic" leaving behind "cultural baggage" such as traditional healers and medicine. There is, of course, good evidence that the third or fourth generation are becoming more like those in the dominant society (see Montero, 1980). However, in Canada, where there is a strong sentiment to preserve the ways of many cultures (Reitz, 1980: 38-50), it may be easier to retain one's own language and culture. The preservation and, in some areas expansion of the ethnic economic, business and professional communities, greatly facilitates this retention of culture by providing a 'complete' ethnic community within the majority culture (Reitz, 1980; Chan and Cheung, 1982; Li, 1979a). In both Vancouver and Toronto, the Chinatowns appear to contain all the essential business, professional and social services necessary for an individual to live a full, rich 'Chinese' life within Canada.

The only area where this ethnic lifestyle may be weak is health care. There are western-trained Chinese physicians and dentists who practice in the Chinatowns of Vancouver and Toronto, and herbal stores abound. There is less certainty about the availability of other traditional treatments and personnel (e.g. Chinese physicians) and, there is no systematic data about the use of these various options. Although traditional anthropological studies of health beliefs and practices among different cultural groups *in situ* are numerous (see Landy, 1977; Logan and Hunt, 1978; Kleinman et al., 1975), they do not give us any information about how these practices fare when moved into another country.

A recent publication, edited by Alan Harwood (1981), has detailed some of the practices and health beliefs among ethnic Americans. Seven ethnic groups are covered: the U.S. Blacks, Chinese, Haitians, Italians, Mexicans, Navajos and Puerto Ricans who have migrated to the U.S. mainland. As one may expect, although there is strong impressionistic evidence that each ethnic group continues these traditional practices, there does not seem to be any common underlying reasons for the persistence in the use of traditional medicine.

Cultural and Structural Constraints

The vague and unsatisfactory answers regarding this problem have encouraged us to propose our study. In our reasoning, we feel that both the cultural and structural factors are at work (interact) and, more important, one other factor has been overlooked; W.I. Thomas' old dictum, the definition of the situation (McHugh, 1968). Often, the pathways or moves which the ethnics take depend on their perception of health and illness and, possibly even more critically, their perception of the meaning of the health care institution. For instance, is the hospital a place where they will be cured or is it a 'death house' where they will be left unattended? Current work along the same line is exemplified by Kleinman (1980) who discusses the cultural context of health and illness in a much more definitive manner by examining the way persons in other cultures explain their symptoms. One may well argue that in health care, Thomas and Klkeinman's concepts may be more central than the cultural-structural reasoning of ethnic studies.

The following are some of the concerns which have led to this suggestion:

First, is the selection of medical service: the reasons individuals use various traditional healers or medicines. Having migrated from one culture into another, the original health beliefs may continue to be at work, particularly if the traditional healers and medicine sources are available and can be used. Possibly the most important factor at work here is the structural aspect of language. If the healers and herbal store owner can communicate with the ethnic person in his language, then the use of that mode of healing is much easier. One should add that in Toronto and Vancouver, possibly other Canadian cities as well, the healers and herbal sources are steadily growing.

A mitigating factor, again structural, is that some western-trained ethnic practitioners are locating in Chinatown areas. Thus, in Canada, there may be some repetition of the phenomonon noted by Lieberson in Chicago; deliberate selection of ethnic neighborhoods as the site of professional practices by ethnic physicians in the 1950's (Lieberson, 1958). Given this, one might expect that the Chinese patient may gravitate to these physicians (where various insurance programs will reimburse most patient costs), located in an ethnic neighborhood, who can communicate with the patient in his primary dialect.

However, recently, increasing numbers of Chinese are immigrating from different parts of China, plus Southeast Asia, the Carribean, Africa and South America, and new dialects are in use. Many Chinese businessmen and professionals now speak the 'northern' or 'pu-t'ung hua' dialects of the People's Republic of China, as well as the more traditional Cantonese and Toisan. Increasingly, health professionals will have to be able to converse in a number of dialects. If they do so and *yet* the Chinese continue to use a traditional healer, this would be indicative of the dominance of cultural over structural (language barriers) factors in the selection of health care (**Toronto Globe and Mail**, 1982).

Second, any research on health care utilization would have to pay some attention to the structure of the Canadian health care system and the 'place' of the ethnic health practitioner within this system. Most researchers look at the 'patient-doctor' relationship as a dyadic relationship. But, as we know only too well, when the patient enters into the health care system, the process involves much more (Coburn et al., 1981). For any minor ailments, the 'patient-doctor' relationship circumscribes care adequately. However, for any major illness, one would have to extend this relationship to include the health institution (hospital), payment mechanism (insurance), government (public health), and many other parts of the system such as services (laboratories and ambulances). If an ethnic physician does not have access to a hospital or hospital affiliations, or is not part of the health system, then that ethnic patient he cares for will be at a disadvantage. What we suggest is that medical 'gatekeepers' may prevent the ethnic physician from obtaining specialized training and certification, becoming affiliated in a specialized hospital or association, and obtaining full access to the system. This can also mean that technical advances in medicine may not be within reach of the ethnic physician. The end result is that the dissatisfied ethnic patient may leave the system, and continue (or return to) seeing traditional healers and medicines.

In Vancouver, just the reverse is the case. In 1907, at the request of the Bishop of Vancouver, the Missionary Sisters of Immaculate Conception (based in Montreal) established a small clinic to care for Chinese immigrants. Through the years, this clinic developed into an 18 bed hospital—Mount Saint Joseph—which, after World War II, has grown to 320 beds. About forty of the one hundred and twenty staff physicians are Chinese and many of the nursing and other health professionals are also Chinese (Mt. St. Joseph Hospital 1971 and 1981). In addition, the hospital employs Chinese cooks so that its staff and patients may have Chinese meals in the cafeteria. Although now British Columbia health legislation no longer permits private, restricted, hospitals and only 40% of its present patients are Chinese, this hospital is still widely known as the "Chinese Hospital" (New and Watson, personal interviews).

Third, western medicine and its health care system have their own culture. The studies of Hall (1944), Solomon (1952), Merton et al. (1957), and Becker et al. (1961), illustrate how medical students and physicians, alike, have to learn and be socialized into this unique culture. What this implies, of course, is that the 'successful' patient is one who has also learned this culture and can play the appropriate 'sick role' in order to receive optimal benefits. For the ordinary person or physician learning this culture is a difficult task; for an ethnic patient or physician, this may be impossible.

Fourth, the many ethnic studies, which have been done on commercial and business enterprises (Bonanich, 1973; Light, 1972, 1980; Chan and Cheung, 1982), suggest that the probability of ethnic survival is heightened when it is accompanied by a range of institutions and services which meet all the needs of a particular ethnic group. In the Canadian urban centers the authors visited, the Chinese community leaders were very aware of the need for a 'healthy' Chinatown that is not just a tourist center but also provides for the needs of its residents as well as the larger metropolitan Chinese community (New and Watson, personal interviews). Traditionally, Chinatowns across North America have been dominated by a Chinese Benevolent Association, normally made up of a small group of older businessmen, politically tied to the Guomindang (KMT) Party (New and Watson, personal interviews). Chinatowns have generally been a 'first stop' for immigrants with the more successful immigrant and successive generations leaving as soon as possible. More recently, however, young professionals and businessmen have challenged the "old line" leaders. They have returned to Chinatown and set up a variety of businesses and professional offices. Chinatowns such as Vancouver's have become a general shopping, business, cultural and entertainment center for all the Chinese in the Vancouver area. In Vancouver, these younger leaders have wrested control of the Chinese Benevolent Association from the "old line" leaders and in the process developed a variety of new cultural and social services to provide for all the needs of the community (New and Watson, personal interviews). The authors sense this same type of development in other Chinatowns in Canada. The effect of these developments on the ethnic health delivery system, composed of herbal or traditional medicine stores, healers, western-trained physicians, as well as ethnic clinics, may very well be to enhance the use of traditional medical practices. China itself has a long history of dual medical systems, traditional and western, operating both side-by-side and interactively (New, 1977).

Finally, one should pay attention to the historical forces at work in the community, particularly immigration policy (Hawkins, 1974; Li, 1979b, 1980). Persistence in the use of traditional medicine, it may be hypothesized, would be related to periods when immigration is encouraged or closed. Culturally, ethnic identity may gradually disappear if immigration flow stops, thus cutting off all sources of renewal (Montero, 1981). Ethnic concentrations evaporate and ethnic enterprises may disappear. When the reverse happens, which seems to be the case in Canada at present (Immigration and Manpower, 1980a; Statistics Canada, 1980 and 1981), ethnic concentrations may foster the growth of traditional medical services. Not only that, but the new waves of immigrants may bring new uses for traditional medicines or new therapies. The continued 'ties' with the old country become a bridge between the old and the new. It is not so much a matter of persistence, in this situation, as continuity.

Historical discrimination against Asians (c.f. Hawkins, 1974; Johnson, I.P.; and Li, 1979a, 1979b, 1980) has also played a major role in medical care. As an example prior to 1947, in British Columbia, it was against the law for Chinese to engage in many professions including law and dentistry. Chinese could, however, become doctors. Not only would this affect the ability of the Chinese community to provide a full range of professional and business services, it would mean that western-trained physicians were one of the few professional services available. In addition, as one of the few professionals available in the community, doctors would be likely to have significant leadership roles, thus affecting the visibility and perception of medicine.

Of particular historical and medical significance has been the immigration of Vietnamese refugess, many of whom consider themselves to be ethnic Chinese. In 1979, the first year, almost 18,000 were admitted to Canada (Employment and Immigration, 1980a). They undoubtedly bring with them yet another mixture of ideologies, health beliefs and practices, some of which are tempered by the fact that they lived under French rule for many years. However, of more importance is the fact that many Vietnamese were involved in special medical programs that identified them to local public health authorities. Many of these authorities initiated medical screening, innoculation and health information programs (Employment and Immigration, 1980b; New and Watson, personal interviews). All immediate health problems were treated and the programs often included introducing them to private physicians and dentists. These special programs, unique in Canada's medical history, may allow the Vietnamese to move into 'mainstream' health care faster and more completely than the typical Chinese immigrants for whom health programs were not available.

Discussion

The issues raised in this paper suggest that a more "holistic" view than that used in most ethnic studies is required when examining health care utilization among Chinese-Canadians. Health care begins when a person decides that they are sick and takes some action to relieve or cure the illness. It ends when the person decides they are recovering or cured. In examining the various contingencies that may affect how a person enters and moves through their 'pathway' to health care, we show that structural, cultural and perceptual factors all play important roles.

The historical circumstances which led to changes in immigration policies and discriminatory laws had much to do with how the Chinese would congregate or disperse within Canadian society, and the structure and 'health' of their communities. These would influence the growth, decline or revitalization of Chinese communities, hence the ability to obtain services as well as access to services, particularly for those who do not speak English. Also, within flourishing Chinese communities, herbal and other traditional medicines or practices could carry on and the Chinese who wish these services can easily avail themselves.

Chinese community structure is particularly relevant to its medical and social services. In Vancouver, the (S) United Chinese Community Enrichment Service Society (S.U.C.C.E.S.S.) now has over 150 volunteers, a budget of $200,000 per year and serves approximately 14,000 clients per year. The Chinese Cultural Centre in Vancouver is yet another organization which performs multiple social service functions. Both these organizations are or have been headed by prominent Chinese dentists. In Winnipeg, a physician is deeply involved in the Chinese community social services and also works among the Vietnamese population. In these instances, their health professional expertise would undoubtedly enhance the visibility of health care needs of the Chinese. In addition, the 'Chinese Hospital', Mount Saint Joseph in Vancouver, makes every effort to cater specifically to the Chinese patients.

These are just some of the structural elements in the Chinese community which would affect the Chinese-Canadian's entry into the 'mainstream' health care system. The beliefs in health and illness, of course, are cultural "barriers" (if one views these beliefs as antagonistic forces) to the Canadian health care system. At the same time, as Kleinman, Lin, and others are suggesting, the health care professionals must understand these prevalent beliefs which are at work among the Chinese. If these beliefs are ignored, the health professionals, in effect, have sest up barriers of their own, cutting off potential points of contact with the Chinese patients and delaying the provision of health care.

How do these forces work? What are the cultural and structural constraints? How do the pathways conform to some of these cultural and structural factors when a Chinese seeks health care? In this paper, we have only begun to suggest that these questions must be systematically examined. This, we hope to do soon.

References

Becker, H.S., Geer, Hughes, and Strauss
1961   **Boys in White: Student Culture in Medical School,** University of Chicago Press, Chicago.

Bonacich, E.
   1973   "A Theory of Middleman Minorities", **American Sociological Review**, 38:583-594.
Breton, R.
   1978   "The Structure of Relationships Between Ethnic Collectives" Driedger (ed.), in **The Canadian Mosaic: A Question of Identity**, McClelland and Stewart, Toronto, 55-73.
   1979   "Ethnic Stratification Viewed from Three Sociological Perspectives", Curtis and Scott (eds.), **Social Stratification: Canada**, Prentice-Hall, Scarborough, Ontario: 270-294.
Canadian Family Physician
   1981   "Immigrants' Use of Faith Healers Said Not a Threat to Medicine", **Canadian Family Physician**, 27:1892-1893.
Chan, J.B.L. and Cheung, Y.W.
   1981   "Ethnic Resources and Business Enterprise: A Study of Chinese Businesses in Toronto", American Sociological Association, Toronto.
Chow, W.S.
   1981   **A Chinese Community in a Prairie City: A Holistic Perspective of Its Class and Ethnic Relations**, unpublished Ph.D. Thesis, Michigan State University (Dept. of Anthropology).
Coburn, D., C. D'Arcy, P.K. New, and G. Torrance
   1981   **Health and Canadian Society; Sociological Perspectives**, Fitzhenry and Whiteside, Toronto.
Darroch, A.G.
   1979   "Another Look at Ethnicity, Stratification and Social Mobility in Canada", **Canadian Journal of Sociology**, 4:1-25.
   1981   "Urban Ethnicity in Canada: Personal Assimilation and Political Communities", **Canadian Review of Sociology and Anthropology**, 18:93-100.
Employment and Immigration
   1980a Immigration Statistics (1979), Immigration and Demographic Policy Group, ISSN 0576-2288, Cat. No. WH-5-006, Ottawa.
   1980b South east asian refugee newsletter: Special Edition **Health Care**, Facts for Sponsors of Indochinese Refugees, Vol. 11, No. 3 (March 6, 1980), Public Affairs Division.
Hall, O.
   1944   **The Informal Organization of Medical Practice in an American City**, Unpublished Ph.D. Thesis, University of Chicago.
Harwood, A. (ed.)
   1981   **Ethnicity and Medical Care**, Harvard University Press, Cambridge, Mass.
Hawkins, F.
   1974   "Canadian Immigration Policy and Management", **International Migration Review**, 8:141-153.
Hessler, R.M., M.F. Nolan, B. Ogbru, and P.K. New
   1975   "Intraethnic Diversity: Health Care of the Chinese-Americans", **Human Organization**, 34:253-262.

Johnson, G.E.
  1983   "New Wine in Old Bottles? Chinese Canadians in the 1970's", in J.E. Elliot
         (ed.) **Two Nations, Many Cultures,** 2nd Ed., Prentice-Hall Canada,
         Scarborough.
Kelner, M., O. Hall and I. Coulter
  1980   **Chiropractors: Do They Help?,** Fitzhenry and Whiteside, Toronto.
Kleinman, A.
  1980   **Patients and Healers in the Context of Culture: An Exploration of the
         Borderland Between Anthropology, Medicine and Psychiatry,** Uni-
         versity of California Press, Berkeley.
Kleinman, A., P. Kunstadter, E.R. Alexander, and J.L. Gale (eds.)
  1975   **Medicine in Chinese Cultures: Comparative Studies in Health Care in
         Chinese and Other Societies,** U.S. Government Printing Office, Washing-
         ton, D.C.
Kuo, W.H.
  1979   "On the Study of Asian-Americans: Its Current State and Agenda", **The
         Sociological Quarterly,** 20:279-290.
Landy, D. (ed.)
  1977   **Culture, Disease and Healing: Studies in Medical Anthropology,**
         Macmillan Publishing, New York.
Lechky, O.
  1980   "Keeping the Faith Means Big Money", **The Medical Post** (Toronto), 16:70.
Leslie, C. (ed.)
  1976   **Asian Medical Systems: A Comparative Study,** University of California
         Press, Berkeley.
Li, P.S.
  1979a "Prejudice Against Asians in a Canadian City", **Canadian Ethnic Studies,**
         11:70-77.
  1979b "A Historical Approach to Ethnic Stratification: The Case of the Chinese in
         Canada, 1858-1930", **The Canadian Review of Sociology and Anthropol-
         ogy,** 16:320-332.
  1980   "Immigration Laws and Family Patterns: Some Demographic Changes Among
         Chinese in Canada, 1885-1971", **Canadian Ethnic Studies,** 13:58-73.
Lieberson, S.
  1958   "Ethnic Groups and the Practice of Medicine", **American Sociological
         Review,** 23:542-549.
Light, I.
  1972   **Ethnic Enterprise in America,** University of California Press, Berkeley.
  1980   "Asian Enterprise in America: Chinese, Japanese, and Koreans in Small
         Business", in S. Cummings (ed.), **Self-Help in Urban America: Patterns of
         Minority Business Enterprise,** Kennikat Press, Port Washington, N.Y.
Lin, T.Y. and M.C. Lin
  1978   "Service Delivery Issues in Asian-North American Communities", **American
         Journal of Psychiatry,** 135:454-456.
  1980   "Love, Denial and Rejection: Responses of Chinese Families to Mental Ill-
         ness", in A. Kleinman and T.Y. Lin (eds.) **Normal and Abnormal Behavior
         in Chinese Culture,** D. Reidel Pub., Dordrecht; 387-401.

Lin, T.Y., K. Tardiff, G. Donetx and W. Goresky
  1978   "Ethnicity and Patterns of Help-Seeking", **Culture, Medicine and Psychiatry**, 2:3-13.

Logan, M.H. and E.E. Hunt Jr.
  1978   **Health and the Human Condition: Perspectives in Medical Anthropology**, Duxbury Press, North Situate, Mass.

Marr, W.L.
  1976   "Labour Market and Other Implications of Immigration Policy for Ontario"; Working paper # 1/76, Ontario Economic Council, Toronto.

Merton, R.K. et al.
  1957   **The Student-Physician**, Harvard University Press, Cambridge.

McHugh, P.
  1968   **Defining the Situation: The Social Organization of Meaning in Social Interaction**, Bobbs-Merrill Co., Indianapolis.

Montero, D.
  1979   **Vietnamese Americans: Patterns of Resettlement and Socioeconomic Adaptation to the United States**, Westview Press, Boulder, Colorado.
  1980   **Japanese Americans: Changing Patterns of Ethnic Affiliation Over Three Generations**, Westview Press, Boulder, Colo.
  1981   "The Japanese Americans: Changing Patterns of Assimilation Over Three Generations", **American Sociological Review**, 46:829-839.

Montero, D. and R. Tsukashima
  1977   "Assimilation and Educational Achievement: The Case of the Second Generation Japanese-Americans", **The Sociological Quarterly**, 18:490-503.

Mount Saint Joseph Hospital
  1971   **50th Anniversary of the Arrival in Vancouver of the Missionary Sisters of the Immaculate Conception**, Mount Saint Joseph Hospital, Vancouver.
  1981   **Annual Report**, 1981-82, Mount Saint Joseph Hospital, Vancouver.

New, P.K.
  1977   "Traditional and Modern Health Care: An Appraisal of Complementarity", **International Social Science Journal**, 29:483-495.

New, P.K. and W. Watson
  1982   Personal Interviews with various Chinese community leaders: St. Catharines, Ontario; Winnipeg, Manitoba; and Vancouver, British Columbia.

Reitz, J.G.
  1980   **The Survival of Ethnic Groups**, McGraw-Hill Ryerson, Toronto.

Siu, Paul C.P.
  1964   "The Isolation of the Chinese Laundryman", Burgess & Bogue (ed.) **Contributions to Urban Sociology**, University of Chicago Press, Chicago.

Solomon, D.N.
  1952   **Career Contingencies of Chicago Physicians**, Unpublished Ph.D. Thesis, University of Chicago.

Statistics Canada
  1980/1 **Canadian Statistical Quarterly**, Statistics Canada, November, Ottawa.

Thompson, R.H.
  1979 "Ethnicity Versus Class: An Analysis of Conflict in a North American Chinese Community", **Ethnicity**, 6:306-326.
Toronto Globe and Mail
  1982 "Eleven Canadians Die in Fiery Philippine Crash on Visit to Faith Healer", January 28:1.
Twaddle, A.C. and R.M. Hessler
  1977 **A Sociology of Health**, C.V. Mosby Co., St. Louis.
United Chinese Community Enrichment Services Society
  1982 **SUCCESS, ANNUAL REPORT**, 1981-1982, S.U.C.C.E.S.S., Vancouver.
Wickberg, E.
  1981 "Chinese Organizations and the Canadian Political Process: Two Case Studies" in J. Dahlie and T. Fernando (eds.), **Ethnicity, Power and Politics in Canada**, Methuen, Toronto.
Wiley, R.
  1967 "The Ethnic Mobility Trap and Stratification Theory", **Social Problems**, 15:147-159.

7

Comparisons: Indian and non-Indian Use of Psychiatric Services*

Wayne Fritz and Carl D'Arcy
  Psychiatric Reserach Division
  University Hospital
  Saskatoon

Introduction

Little is known in Canada about Indian use of psychiatric treatment services (Hylton et al., 1980; Jilek-Aall, 1976; Martens, 1973). This is unfortunate since it hinders any comparative assessment of the mental health services that are provided to Indian people and impedes the development of services directed to meet unique needs of Indian communities. The absence of basic utilization data is probably due to the fact that few provincial health agencies routinely identify and record the Indian status of patients who make use of their mental health services. Saskatchewan is one of the few exceptions in this regard. Perhaps because it has a relatively high proportion of Indian people in its population, Saskatchewan Health has consistently identified status Indian use of provincially funded health services. Consequently, it is possible to make use of Saskatchewan Health data bases to compare both longitudinal and current Indian and non-Indian use of provincial psychiatric treatment services.

---

* The financial support of the Psychiatric Research Division, Saskatchewan Health and the support of a National Health Scholar Award for Carl D'Arcy are gratefully acknowledged.

The purpose of this paper is three-fold:

1) to briefly examine selected demographic, cultural and socioeconomic characteristics of the Saskatchewan Indian and non-Indian populations;

2) to review Saskatchewan studies comparing the prevalence of psychiatric disorders among Indian and non-Indian populations;

3) to compare trends in the rates of treatment, mix of services and types of psychiatric diagnoses assigned to Saskatchewan Indian and non-Indian patients in the public and private treatment sectors.

Indian and Non-Indian Populations In Saskatchewan

The Saskatchewan Indian and non-Indian populations differ in a number of important characteristics and life circumstances. Indian people constitute approximately 5% of the Saskatchewan population (Saskatchewan Indian Cultural College, 1975). The rate of natural increase among the Indian population is more than double that of the non-Indian population (Department of Health, 1978; Department of Indian and Northern Affairs, 1980a, 1980b). Unlike the non-Indian population which is widely dispersed throughout central and southern Saskatchewan, the Indian population is geographically concentrated in rural reservations located along a 200-mile diagonal corridor where the precambrian shield and great plains meet. During the past decade, an increasing number of Indian people have migrated from rural reservations to urban centers (F.S.I., 1978). Approximately two-thirds of the Indian population still live on reserves or crown land while almost one-half of the non-Indian population reside in urban areas (Department of Indian and Northern Affairs, 1980a; F.S.I., 1978).

Some theorists have suggested that a population's underlying cultural values will influence their use of available health services (Foucault, 1973; Zola, 1966). Unfortunately, little systematic research has been conducted examining Saskatchewan Indian and non-Indian differences in cultural values. Frideres claims that Indian people are more collaborative and less individualistic; more spiritually and less activity oriented than the surrounding non-Indian population (Frideres, 1974). Spence suggests that Indian people differ from non-Indians in that they value consensual rather than adversarial decision-making and personal rather than formal relationships (Zborowski, 1952). However, Nagler in a survey of Indian and non-Indian students in a small Alberta town (similar to many Saskatchewan towns) found that Indian adolescents endorsed cultural values of rationality, calculation and personal reserve more frequently and uniformly than their non-Indian peers (Roy, 1970). Hylton et al. note that cultural values among Saskatchewan Indians are changing, particularly among young Indian people who are placing greater value on individualism, material success and male-female equality than their parents do (Hylton, 1980). Better information about the nature, distribution and expression of Indian and non-Indian cultural differences would be useful when trying to assess how cultural value differences may influence Indian and non-Indian use of psychiatric treatment services.

There is no question that Saskatchewan Indians, like most Canadian Indian people, have a significantly lower standard of material life than the non-Indian population. Over 80% of employable Saskatchewan Indian people are unemployed and living in poverty, usually on social welfare payments (F.S.I., 1978; Hylton, 1980; Department of Indian and Northern Affairs, 1980b). They are less educated, more poorly housed, more frequently have a variety of childhood diseases and have a shorter life expectancy than non-Indian people in Saskatchewan (Department of Health, 1978; Department of Indian and Northern Affairs, 1980a & 1980b). Saskatchewan Indian people are more frequently incarcerated in provincial jails for non-payment of legal offences. They more frequently have their children apprehended by child welfare authorities and are more likely to experience personal injury through accidental cause than non-Indian people in Saskatchewan (Hylton, 1980; Department of Indian and Northern Affairs, 1980b). From an etiological perspective, Indian people in Saskatchewan are more subject to chronic life stresses associated with poverty and traumatic life events than are non-Indian people.

Saskatchewan Prevalence Studies

Two Saskatchewan studies have attempted to compare the prevalence of psychiatric disorders among Indian and non-Indian populations. Table 7-1 summarizes their major findings. In 1970, Roy et al. surveyed the prevalence of psychiatric disorders in ten Indian reservations and 18 rural municipalities in the North Battleford area (Saskatchewan Health, 1980). Disorders were identified on the reservations through an active case finding survey in collaboration with public health nurses and in the rural municipalities through a search of local medical records. The overall prevalence rate of psychiatric disorders among the Indian population was found to be 273/10,000 population—80% higher than the prevalence rate of 152/10,000 among the non-Indian population. The Indian population had a higher prevalence rate than the non-Indian population for every major category of psychiatric disorder. The largest relative differences between populations were in the prevalence of mental retardation, followed by psychoses, neuroses and alcoholism. Of the psychoses, schizophrenic disorders were found to be four times more prevalent among Indians than non-Indians; other functional psychoses were slightly less prevalent among the Indian population.

Another Saskatchewan study, by Martens in 1972, compared the prevalence of anxiety among a randomly selected sample of Indian people in eight Indian reservations with that of non-Indian people in 17 rural municipalities (Nagler, 1972). The study, carried out in the North Battleford area, was a replication of a World Health Organization study examining health status and utilization of medical services. One of the measures of health status used was a ten-item "manifestation of anxiety" scale adapted from the Cornell Medical Index. The scale included items dealing with tension, tiredness, headaches and feelings of inadequacy and depression. Affirmative answers were considered indicators of emotional disturbance. Scale scores were collapsed to differentiate between those with no anxiety symptoms and those manifesting some level of anxiety. Sixty-five percent of the Indian sample indicated that they had one or more anxiety symptoms compared to only 50% of the non-Indian sample.

The limitations of these two studies are evident. Both were based on populations from one rural area of the province. Roy et al. used a different data collection method for the Indian and non-Indian populations, while Martens' "measure of anxiety" may be as much a reflection of poor physical health or general life stress as it is of a psychiatric disorder. Nonetheless since these studies provide the only comparative prevalence data on Indian and non-Indian populations, one has little choice but to consider them in light of provincial utilization data.

Public and Private Treatment Sectors

Two distinct treatment sectors—a public and a private sector—have evolved to meet the psychiatric treatment needs of the Saskatchewan population. These two sectors differ in organization, provision of services, historical development and current size.

TABLE 7-1

Prevalence Rates per 10,000 Population
(Roy et al., 1970)

	Indian (N=4,723)	Non-Indian (N=28,096)
Psychoses	91	57
Schizophrenia	57	16
Functional (other)	34	30
Organic	----	11
Neuroses	82	57
Alcoholism	13	6
Mental Retardation	66	23
Other Disorders	21	9
TOTALS	273	152

Manifestation of
Anxiety Symptoms
(E. Martens, 1972)

	Indian (N=1,105)	Non-Indian (N=823)
Yes	65%	50%
No	35%	50%

The "private treatment sector" consists of both specialist and non-specialist physicians providing psychiatric treatment services on a fee-for-service basis. Clinical practices are organized primarily on a group basis although there are still some solo practitioners. Outpatient psychiatric services are provided in physicians' clinics or offices while voluntary inpatient treatment services are provided in general wards of general hospitals under the supervision of private physicians (D'Arcy). The number of privately practising physicians has more than doubled from 448 in 1969 to 926 by 1978 (Spence, 1973). Along with this increase in numbers, general practitioners have also been increasingly located in smaller cities and towns throughout the province. A recent government study on rural medical services estimates that only 3% of the provincial population live more than 25 miles away from a general practitioner and at least minimum hospital services (Saskatchewan Hospital Services Plan, 1978). Private specialist psychiatric care has rarely been provided outside of Regina and Saskatoon, the province's two largest cities. Decisions about the provision of services to Indian and non-Indian patients are made on an individual basis by the treating physician.

The term "public treatment sector" is used to refer to the Saskatchewan Psychiatric Services Branch, and the Department of Psychiatry, University Hospital in Saskatoon. (The Department of Psychiatry, University Hospital is generally considered part of the public treatment sector because of its close ties with the Psychiatric Services Branch, its regional service approach and its role as a clinical teaching centre.) Psychiatric Services Branch (PSB) staff are salaried civil servants. In each of the province's eight health regions, inpatient treatment services are provided through a psychiatric ward or inpatient centre which is designated under the Mental Health Act to permit voluntary *and* involuntary admissions. Outpatient treatment services are provided by a mixture of psychiatrists, psychiatric nurses, psychologists and social workers through the use of regional clinics and home visits. In rural areas, smaller geographic catchment areas have been established with multi-disciplinary mental health teams being assigned responsibility *and* travel resources to provide treatment services in that area. The Branch has attempted to make specialist psychiatric care more accessible in rural areas through its use of travelling mental health teams despite a decrease in staff from 1,173 in 1969 to 889 in 1978 (Department of Health, 1978). Decisions about the provision of services to Indian patients are made by regional clinicians as no branch-wide policies have been developed concerning special treatment services to Indian people.

General Utilization Trends

The utilization data to be presented come from the public and private treatment sectors from two overlapping time periods. Data on psychiatric services provided by the private treatment sector were obtained from the Saskatchewan Medical Care Insurance Commission and the Saskatchewan Hospital Services Plan for the years 1969-1974. The data were merged to create a research file of persons who had received inpatient or outpatient services from a private sector physician for a reason explicitly diagnosed as being psychiatric in nature (D'Arcy, 1976). Data on psychiatric services provided by the public treatment sector were obtained from the annual statistical reports and the case register of the Psychiatric Services Branch for the years 1967-1978 (Department of Health, 1978).

Both services (event) and patient (individual) data are presented. The service data consists of: (a) the number of admissions to or separations from an inpatient facility; and (b) the number of reported contacts or billed services provided to outpatients. The patient data consists of: (a) the number of patients who received some form of outpatient treatment; and (b) the diagnosis assigned to a patient when they received either inpatient or outpatient service. Indian patients and services to Indian patients were identified by a unique alphanumeric character in the health service card numbers issued by the provincial health department to all Saskatchewan Status Indians.[1] To facilitate Indian and non-Indian population comparisons while controlling for differences in population sizes, both service and patient data are presented as rates per 10,000 population.

On the basis of the comparative prevalence and stressful life event indicators available, one would expect the Indian population to have higher rates of treatment than the non-Indian population for all major categories of psychiatric disorder. However, the utilization data suggest that Indian status, psychiatric diagnosis and treatment sector have an interactive causal influence on volumes and types of treatment services received by the Indian and non-Indian populations.

Inpatient Admission/Separation Rates

Graph 7-1 displays the standardized psychiatric admission/separation rates for the Saskatchewan Indian and non-Indian populations in both the public and private treatment sectors. In both sectors, since 1972, the Indian population has had higher admission rates for psychiatric care than the non-Indian population. Both the Indian and non-Indian populations were more frequently admitted for psychiatric care in general wards of general hospitals than they were in designated psychiatric inpatient facilities. The 1974 Indian separation rate in the private sector was 176/10,000 population, 62% *higher* than the non-Indian separation rate of 109/10,000. In the public sector, the Indian population had a 1978 admission rate of 40/10,000, 11% *higher* than the non-Indian admission rate of 36/10,000.

For both populations, the largest increases in admission/separation rates occurred in the private treatment sector. However, in both sectors, the Indian population had the largest increases. Between 1969 and 1974, the Indian population's private sector separation rate increased an average of 13.6% per year compared to an average increase of only 4.8% among the non-Indian population. In the public sector, between 1967 and 1978, the Indian population had an average admission increase of 16.9% per year compared to an average increase of only .8% among the non-Indian population.

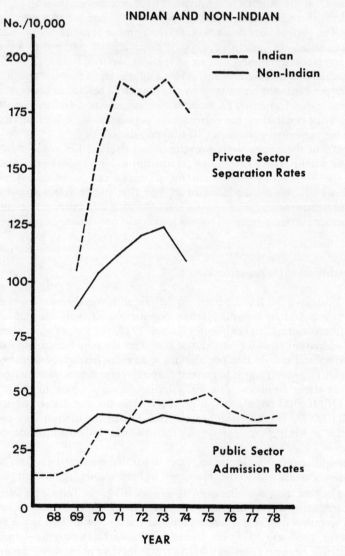

Graph 7-1

NUMBER OF PSYCHIATRIC ADMISSIONS/SEPARATIONS
PER 10,000 POPULATION:

INDIAN AND NON-INDIAN

Graph 7-2

NUMBER OF PSYCHIATRIC OUTPATIENTS PER 10,000 POPULATION: INDIAN AND NON-INDIAN

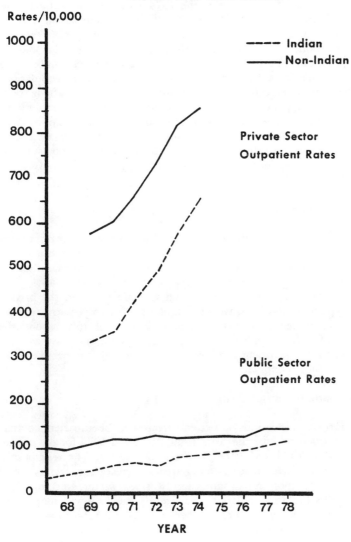

Rates/10,000

---- Indian
—— Non-Indian

Private Sector
Outpatient Rates

Public Sector
Outpatient Rates

YEAR

Outpatient Treatment Rates

Graph 7-2 compares the standardized rates at which the Indian and non-Indian populations received outpatient psychiatric treatment. In both sectors, the Indian population's outpatient treatment rate was much lower than that of the non-Indian population. In the private sector, the 1974 Indian outpatient rate was 660/10,000 population, 23% *lower* than the non-Indian outpatient rate of 855/10,000 population. In the public sector, the 1978 Indian outpatient rate was 115/10,000 population, 20% *lower* than the non-Indian outpatient rate of 144/10,000 population. The private treatment sector treated the bulk of all psychiatric outpatients from both populations. Although both populations showed significant increases in the rate at which they received outpatient treatment services, the Indian population's outpatient rate increased most rapidly. In the private sector, between 1969 and 1974, the Indian population's outpatient rate had an average increase of 19% per year, compared to a 9.6% increase among the non-Indian population. In the public sector, the Indian population's outpatient rate showed an average increase of 19.9% per year, compared to only 3.7% among the non-Indian population.

Outpatient Service Rates

Graph 7-3 compares the standardized rates at which private sector physicians billed for outpatient psychiatric treatment services and for which public sector clinicians reported service contacts with psychiatric patients or their families. In both sectors, the Indian population consistently received at least 40% *fewer* outpatient services per capita than the non-Indian population. In the private sector, the Indian population had an average rate of increase in psychiatric services of 25% per year compared to an average annual increase of 16% among the non-Indian population. In the public sector, the Indian population's average rate of increase in psychiatric treatment services was 24% per year, compared to only 6% among the non-Indian population.

Admission: Outpatient Service Ratios

Standardized ratios of admissions:outpatients treated and of outpatients:outpatient services were calculated for the years 1969, 1972 and 1974 for the private sector, and for 1967, 1974 and 1978 for the public sector. The relationship between the use of psychiatric inpatient and outpatient treatment services varied significantly depending upon Indian status and treatment sector. In comparison to non-Indians, the Indian population consistently had a lower number of outpatients per admission and a lower number of outpatient services per outpatient, irrespective of treatment sector. In the public sector, the Indian population averaged 52% *fewer* outpatients per admission and 118% *fewer* outpatients per separation and 30% *fewer* services per outpatient than the non-Indian population. The private sector has increasingly treated a larger number of Indian outpatients

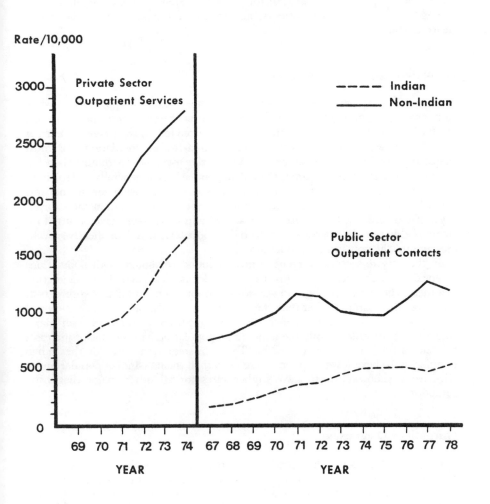

Graph 7-3

NUMBER OF PSYCHIATRIC OUTPATIENT SERVICES/CONTACTS
PER 10,000 POPULATION:

INDIAN AND NON-INDIAN

per admission but provided fewer services per Indian outpatient than the public sector.[2]

Diagnostic Trends

Comparative diagnostic data is presented for the years 1967, 1972 and 1978 for the public sector and for the years 1969, 1972 and 1974 for the private sector. Analysis of the rates of treatment for major categories of psychiatric diagnoses reveal substantial differences between Indian and non-Indian populations in both the public and private treatment sectors. These differences were more pronounced among outpatients than inpatients, and in the private rather than the public treatment sector.

Admission/Separation Diagnoses

Graph 7-4 displays standardized admission rates for the two populations when compared by major diagnostic category and treatment sector. In the public sector, the Indian population was most frequently admitted for the treatment of neuroses and alcohol/addiction disorders, while the non-Indian population was most frequently admitted for schizophrenic and affective psychoses. Although there has been some fluctuation over time, the Indian population has generally had substantially higher admission rates than the non-Indian population for alcoholism, neuroses, character and behaviour disorders, but lower admission rates for all psychotic disorders. The greatest increases in admission rates have occurred for alcohol/addiction disorders among the Indian population, and for affective psychoses among the non-Indian population.

In the private sector, different trends are found. Although both populations received inpatient treatment most frequently for neuroses and alcohol/addiction disorders, the Indian population was admitted for alcohol/addiction disorders at rates over three times higher than the non-Indian population. Between 1969 and 1974, the Indian population increased their inpatient care rates for all major categories of disorders while the non-Indian population had significant increases for only alcohol/addiction disorders. The consistent trend was for the Indian population to have lower inpatient care rates than the non-Indian population for affective psychoses but to have higher rates for all other major diagnostic categories.

Outpatient Diagnoses

Graph 7-5 displays the standardized rates at which the two populations received outpatient treatment for major types of psychiatric disorders. In both sectors the Indian population had lower average outpatient rates than the non-Indian population for every major diagnostic category *except* alcohol/addiction

Graph 7-4

NUMBER OF PSYCHIATRIC ADMISSIONS/SEPARATIONS PER 10,000 POPULATION
COMPARED BY MAJOR DIAGNOSTIC CATEGORY, TREATMENT SECTOR AND INDIAN STATUS

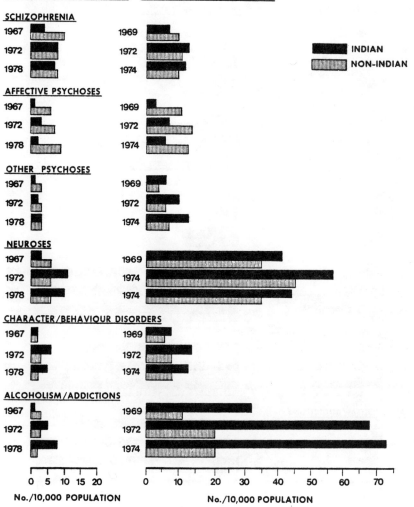

Graph 7-5

NUMBER OF PSYCHIATRIC OUTPATIENTS PER 10,000 POPULATION COMPARED
BY MAJOR DIAGNOSTIC CATEGORY, TREATMENT SECTOR AND INDIAN STATUS

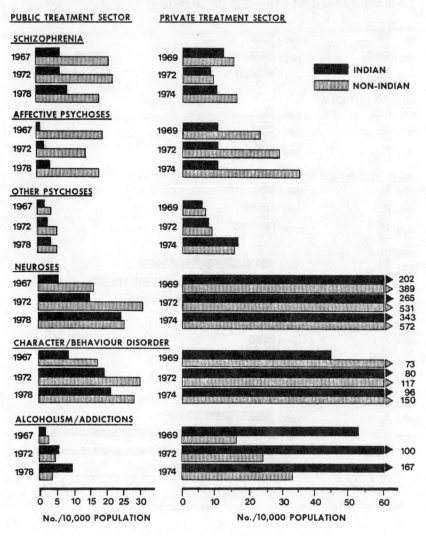

disorders. The largest Indian/non-Indian diagnostic differences in the public sector were in their treatment rates for schizophrenic and affective psychoses, while the largest differences in the private sector were in their treatment rates for neuroses and alcohol/addiction disorders. The non-Indian population showed consistent increases in their outpatient treatment for all major diagnostic categories in both the public and private treatment sectors. The Indian population showed increases in their outpatient treatment rate for all major diagnostic categories except schizophrenic and affective psychoses in the private treatment sector.

Admission: Outpatient Diagnostic Ratios

Standardized ratios of admissions:outpatients for the two populations were calculated for each major diagnostic category. In both the public and private treatment sectors, there were significant differences in the mix of inpatient to outpatient services provided to the two populations. In both sectors, the Indian population averaged fewer outpatients per psychiatric hospitalization for every major diagnostic category except alcohol/addiction disorders. The greatest absolute differences between the two populations occurred for the treatment of character and behaviour disorders, as the non-Indian population averaged at least 140% more outpatients per admission than the Indian population. In both sectors, the mix of inpatient to outpatient services provided to the two populations was most similar for psychotic disorders and most dissimilar for non-psychotic disorders.[2]

Summary and Discussion

To conclude, the data presented indicate that there are major differences between Saskatchewan Indian and non-Indian populations in regard to the prevalence of different psychiatric disorders, their rates of treatment, and the mix of inpatient and outpatient services they receive. Moreover, the interplay between Indian status, psychiatric diagnosis and treatment rate also varies between the public and private treatment sectors. The data raise a number of fundamental questions as to why these differences exist. The answers may lie in biological and cultural factors that influence the formation of psychiatric disorders and in attitudinal and organizational factors which influence the use of treatment services. Although definitive answers cannot be currently provided, one can speculate about the possible contribution of such factors to the major differences in Indian and non-Indian use of psychiatric treatment services.

The overall trend has been for the Indian population to increase its use of treatment services more rapidly than the non-Indian population. The faster rates of increase in Indian treatment rates may be attributable to a higher prevalence of psychiatric disorders among the Indian population combined with the increasing accessibility of treatment services for both populations. In the private sector, where treatment rates increased most rapidly for both populations, increases in the number of practising physicians made services more accessible. In the public sector, treatment services were made more accessible, particularly in rural areas, by the development of regionalized outpatient service programs. In both sectors the non-Indian population has shown utilization trends very similar to those of the Indian population but had lower absolute increases as they probably always had greater accessibility to psychiatric treatment services.

Striking differences occur between the Indian and non-Indian populations in regard to the mix of inpatient and outpatient treatment services they receive. The Indian population had significantly higher admission rates but lower outpatient treatment rates than the non-Indian population. Moreover, the private sector has increasingly treated a larger number of Indian outpatients per psychiatric admission but provided fewer services per Indian patient than the public sector. These differences may be attributable to a mixture of cultural, attitudinal and organizational factors. Hendrie and Hanson have suggested that professional treatment staff view their Indian patients as being victimized members of a cultural minority group living in a social environment conducive to psychiatric disorders (Hendrie, 1970). Consequently, physicians believing that outpatient treatment would likely be ineffective in such an environment might readily hospitalize Indian patients to remove them from this environment, but may not be as forceful in providing follow-up outpatient care. Clinicians who perceive that there are cultural or class-based communication difficulties between themselves and their Indian patients might be inclined to use behavioural or chemotherapy forms of treatment rather than psychotherapy which depends upon the development of a personal relationship and effective communication. Indian patients who value personal rather than formal relationships and anticipate spiritual rather than behavioural or chemotherapy forms of treatment may find their relationship with professional treatment staff to be quite dissatisfying. Under such circumstances, although Indian patients might seek inpatient or outpatient assistance during a crisis situation, they might be less likely to continue with outpatient care than non-Indian patients with similar psychiatric disorders.

Differences between the public and private treatment sectors in regard to the mix of services provided to Indian people may be attributable to the different ways in which the two sectors provide outpatient care. Private practices are generally organized so that outpatients travel to the physician's clinic to receive services. The onus is on the patient to appear at the office to receive treatment services. The public treatment sector is organized so that clinicians routinely travel to rural areas, including Indian reservations, to provide patient services in the patient's home. Although both sectors provide fewer outpatient services to Indian than non-Indian patients, the public sector may provide the most services to Indian outpatients because it is organized to take services to clients rather than rely solely on patient compliance in returning for treatment.

Both continuities and discontinuities are found between the community epidemiological data available and the utilization data examined. Neuroses and alcohol/addiction disorders were found by Martens and Roy et al. to be substantially more prevalent among their Indian than their non-Indian population samples. In both treatment sectors, the Indian population has had higher admission rates for neuroses and higher admission and outpatient treatment rates for alcohol/addiction disorders than the non-Indian population. It would appear that the mental health system is appropriately responding, at least for inpatient treatment, to a higher prevalence of such disorders among the Indian population. However, a more ambiguous situation exists for psychotic disorders. Roy et al. found functional and particularly schizophrenic psychoses to be more prevalent among their Indian than their non-Indian sample. But, in both sectors the Indian population has lower admission and outpatient rates for such disorders than the non-Indian population. This suggests three possibilities. First, Roy et al's. findings may be atypical for Saskatchewan Indian population. Schizophrenic and affective psychoses may be less prevalent among the Indian population and the utilization trends may simply reflect this fact. Second, schizophrenic and affective psychoses may be more prevalent among the Indian population but Indian patients for unknown reasons are particularly unlikely to seek or receive psychiatric treatment services for these disorders. Third, clinicians may consistently misdiagnose or fail to identify functional or schizophrenic psychoses among their Indian patients. Of these three alternatives, the first currently appears most plausible although comparative epidemiological and help-seeking studies would be required to resolve the issue.

It is probable that the Indian population's use of psychiatric treatment services in Saskatchewan will continue to increase more rapidly than it will for the non-Indian population. The Indian population is still growing more rapidly than the non-Indian population. To the extent that chronic poverty and associated life stresses contribute to neuroses and alcohol/addiction disorders, there is little reason to anticipate any major reduction in the prevalence of such disorders among Saskatchewan Indian communities. Moreover, continued urban emigration by Indian people will also bring increasing numbers of Indian patients to those centres where treatment services are most accessible. It is not clear how the mental health system will adapt to increasing use of treatment services by Indian people. Because of its organizational structure, the public treatment sector is most potentially capable of responding to such demands by development of specialized staff and service programs for Indian patients. However, unless the public sector reverses its decline in staff resources, it is probable that the bulk of treatment services will still continue to be provided by private physicians in outpatient settings. It is a moot question whether private physicians will have the motivation, time or resources to provide more intensive outpatient services to their Indian psychiatric patients.

From a practical treatment perspective, it would be useful to more clearly understand how the expression of Indian cultural values influences the treatment behaviour of Indian patients and how non-Indian clinicians can recognize and effectively use those cultural values in their treatment activities. In the longer term, it is essential that clinicians, health planners and Indian leaders begin to seriously think about the primary prevention of psychiatric disorders among Indian communities. There has recently been much discussion in the mental health literature about various ways to improve mental health by environmental modification and strengthening individual coping skills (Hamm, 1979). The application of such ideas in Indian communities might be,at least as fruitful as continuing to increase the provision of psychiatric treatment services.

Footnotes

1. All persons in Saskatchewan with the legal status of Treaty Indian are assigned a special "R" character in their SHSP number. Consequently, the presence or absence of this "R" character can be used to determine Indian and non-Indian status.
2. Space limitations prevent inclusion of the supporting tables in the manuscript but these can be obtained from the author on request.

References

D'Arcy, C., J.A. Schmitz, and G. Bold
    Patterns in the Delivery of Psychiatric Care, Applied Research Unit, University Hospital, Saskatoon.
D'Arcy, C., M. Vanden Hamm, and S. Goldie
    1976   "The Development of a Comprehensive Psychiatric Service Utilization Data File", Canadian Journal of Public Health, 67:237-248.
Department of Health
    1978   Department of Health Annual Report, Queen's Printer, Regina.
Department of Indian and Northern Affairs
    1980a   Registered Indian Population and Annual Growth Rate for Canada and Regions for Selected Years: 1947-1978, Ottawa.
    1980b   Indian Conditions: A Survey, Ottawa.
Federation of Saskatchewan Indians
    1978   Survey of Off-Reserve Band Members, Prince Albert.
Faucault, M.
    1973   Madness and Civilization: A History of Insanity in the Age of Reason, Vintage Books, New York, New York.
Frideres, J.S.
    1974   Canada's Indians: Contemporary Conflicts, Prentice-Hall of Canada Ltd., Scarborough, Ontario.
Fritz, W.B.
    1976   "Psychiatric Disorders Among Natives, and Non-natives in Saskatchewan", Canadian Psychiatric Association Journal 21(6):393-400.
Hamm, C.A.
    1979   Annotations from the Literature on Prevention and Intervention in Mental Health, Applied Research Unit, University Hospital, Saskatoon.
Hylton, J., W. Fritz, J. King, and O. Brass
    1980   Fostering the Mental Health of Persons of Indian Ancestry in Saskatchewan, Mental Health Saskatchewan, Regina.

Jilek-Aall, L.
    1976   "The Western Psychiatrist and His Non-Western Clientele", **Canadian Psychiatric Association Journal**, 21(6):353-359.

Hendrie, H.D. and D. Hanson
    1970   "A Comparative Study of the Psychiatric Care of Indian and Metis", **American Journal of Orthopsychiatry**, 42(3).

Leon, R.L.
    1968   "Some Implications for a Preventive Program for American Indians", **American Journal of Psychiatry**, 125(2).

Margetts, E.L.
    1974   "Symposium—Canada's Native People—Methodology and Topics of Research", **Canadian Psychiatric Association Journal**, 19(4):329-330.

Martens, E.
    1973   "Utilization of Medical Care by Saskatchewan Indians in the North Battleford Area", A thesis submitted to the Department of Social and Preventative Medicine, University of Saskatchewan, Saskatoon.

Nagler, M. (ed.)
    1972   **Perspectives on the North American Indians**, McClelland and Stewart Ltd., Toronto.

Roy, C., A. Choudhuri and D. Irvine
    1970   "The Prevalence of Psychiatric Disorders Among Saskatchewan Indians", **Journal of Cross-Cultural Psychiatry**, 1(4).

Saskatchewan Health
    1980   **Report of the Thrust Group Task Force on Rural Health Policy**, Regina.

Saskatchewan Hospital Services Plan
    1978   **Saskatchewan Hospital Services Plan Covered Population**, Queen's Printer, Regina.

Saskatchewan Indian Cultural College
    1975   **Saskatchewan Indians and Indian Reserves: A Socio-Economic Profile**.

Saskatchewan Medical Care Insurance Commission
    1978   **Saskatchewan Medical Care Insurance Commission Annual Report**, Queen's Printer, Regina.

Spence, A.
    1973   "Indian Culture" in D.B. Sealey and V.J. Kirkness (eds.) **Indians Without Tipis: A Resource Book by Indians and Metis**, William Clair (Manitoba) Limited, Winnipeg.

Zborowski, M.
    1952   "Cultural Components in Responses to Pain", **Journal of Social Issues**, 8.

Zola, I.K.
    1966   "Culture and Symptoms—An Analysis of Patients Presenting Symptoms", **American Sociological Review**, 31.

Part III
Marriage and Minority Families

8

The Chinese-Canadian Family

Peter S. Li
University of Saskatchewan

Despite the popular belief that the traditional Chinese family is large and complex, there is no evidence to indicate that the Chinese-Canadian family resembles the popular image of the traditional Chinese family. In fact, it is doubtful if extended familism ever existed on a large scale in China, let alone overseas. The historical facts about the Chinese in Canada show that except in isolated cases, the Chinese-Canadian family did not emerge until after the Second World War, despite the arrival of Chinese in Canada as early as 1858. For reasons which were beyond their control, most Chinese immigrants in Canada before the war were denied a conjugal family life, and were forced to live in a predominantly married-bachelor society. The post-war changes, notably the removal of legislative exclusion of Chinese immigration to Canada, enabled the reunion of some Chinese family members. Subsequent amendments in the Immigration Act gradually allowed the immigration of Chinese families to Canada.

The empirical case of the Chinese-Canadian family challenges some basic assumptions purported in the assimilationist and pluralist views of ethnicity. In essence, the former sees the demise of ethnicity in a basically Anglo-Saxon Society, while the latter stresses ethnic persistence in the formation of a multicultural mosaic. Despite a difference in emphasis, both views share a narrow theoretical orientation towards immigrant lives (Li and Bolaria, 1979). The assumptions of these views basically assert that immigrants, coming from cultural origins different from the dominant culture, have brought with them to North America distinctive organizations which are unique to their cultural heritages. Over time, as some immigrants are assimilated into host society, these heritages begin to fade. In other cases, immigrants manage to resist assimilation, and are able to preserve some elements of their culture. Immigrant families, accordingly, are seen as transplanted institutions through which linguistic and other cultural traits are transmitted from one generation to the next, albeit diluted in the process.

The assimilationist and pluralist biases tend to perpetuate a misconception of immigrant societies as mere extensions of old world cultures. Changes in ethnic lives and organizations in the host society are interpreted as forces to retain or to give up transplanted heritages. The end result is a failure to see immigrant societies as taking on a route of their own, often independent of old world cultures, but constantly subjected to the economic and other factors of the host society.

In this paper, I argue that traditional Chinese familism has little to do with the development of the Chinese-Canadian family. The emergence of institutional racism against the Chinese in Canada resulted in legal control and exclusion of the Chinese, which in turn, delayed the growth of the Chinese-Canadian family. The anti-oriental policy of the Canadian government over an extended period of time produced other ramifications on the demographic and familial structures of the Chinese community, the effects of which were evident even long after the restrictive measures were removed. Largely as a result of more Chinese being permitted to enter Canada after the war, the Chinese-Canadian family began to emerge. The 1971 Census of Canada indicated that the Chinese-Canadian family was similar to the Canadian family, when comparisons were made along a number of available characteristics. These findings should be interpreted in light of the demographic changes among the Chinese community in the post-war era, and not as a result of the decline of traditional Chinese families in the process of so-called assimilation.

The Myth and Reality of the Traditional Chinese Family

The common view of the traditional Chinese family is that of a large patriarchal system characterized by a complex structure that involved a few generations living under the same roof. Such a structure is believed to have been economically viable and popular in mainland China at least until the nineteenth century and possibly until the early part of the twentieth century. Kinship ties are seen as the fundamental relationships in Chinese society, the prevalence of which was supported by the pseudo-religious precepts of Confucianism. Such a view of the traditional Chinese family is basically false (see, for example, Freedman, 1961-62; Ho, 1965; Levy, 1949).

The misconception of the traditional Chinese family is largely due to confusions at a number of conceptual levels. First, there is a profound difference between the ideals of traditional familism, as incorporated in the ethical precepts of neo-Confucianism, versus the actual form of the Chinese family as an empirical reality. The Confucian ethics on filial piety, domestic harmony, and ancestral worship represented a political view which facilitated the social control of the state (Freedman, 1961-62). The proponents of Confucianism came from the aristocracy

(Ho, 1965). Although over time the family-oriented values were disseminated among the Chinese mass, China remained a land of small families since the collapse of the feudal system in the fourth century B.C. (Ho, 1965). Second, the Chinese family varied in form according to regions and social origins. The vast territory of rural hinterlands means that the majority of the population belonged to the peasantry, in contrast to the minority of gentry which was mainly based on urban centres. Between the two regions and social origins lies the difference of the high-status and low-status families. Third, a distinction should be drawn between the natural family and the organized clan, the latter being at best marginal to the economic life of the Chinese since its emergence in the eleventh century in China (Ho, 1965).

Since a large and complex family requires a certain level of material affluence to support, historically such a structure was only possible among the Chinese gentry (Fei, 1946). In terms of population, the gentry as a social class would rule out over ninety percent of the country, the majority of which belonged to the peasantry. The family unit at this level was numerically small and structurally simple (Freedman, 1961-62; Ho, 1965). Economic necessity compelled both the husband and the wife to participate actively and jointly in agricultural production. The ideology of patriarchy operated much more weakly at this level of familial organization, in contrast to its stronger manifestation among the high-status families.

That the traditional Chinese family was small in size is supported by substantial empirical evidence. Ho (1965), for example, reports the average size of the Chinese households as 5.96 in A.D. 755, 5.68 in AD 1393, 5.33 in A.D. 1812, and about 5 for the first half of the twentieth century. These statistics suggest that the economic conditions of life in China limited the family size to one which is familiar to the nuclear family of the industrial nations of the twentieth century. They further suggest that extended familism was at best an ideal of neo-Confucianism that might have been realized only among a few of gentry origin.

Historical Background of Chinese Immigration to Canada

Chinese immigration to Canada began around 1858 when gold was discovered in Fraser Valley, British Columbia. The initial wave of Chinese immigrants came from the United States where they had been working in gold mines along the West Coast. Subsequently Chinese immigrants came from China, partly in response to the labour shortage in British Columbia, but more so to escape the economic hardship of life in their homeland, which had been devastated by imperialist invasions and peasant revolts (Li, 1979).

The Chinese who came to Canada in the nineteenth century were mostly of peasant background, originating from the coastal provinces of Kwangtung (Lai, 1975). Although there were independent merchants, miners, workers, and students who immigrated to Canada, many Chinese were recruited as contract labourers to be employed in various labour-intensive industries. Between 1876 and 1880, the number of Chinese arriving at Victoria by ship was 2,326; and the number rose to 13,245 for the period 1881 to 1883, when the construction of the

Canadian Pacific Railway was underway (Li, 1979).

At the outset, the Chinese were not considered by the Canadian general public as a permanent part of Canadian society. They were recruited to fill a vacuum created by the shortage of white labourers. As long as the shortage was maintained, the Chinese were tolerated in various labour-intensive industries such as mining, railroad construction and forest clearing. But as soon as the initial developments had been completed, and white labourers became more available, the Chinese were viewed as competitors taking away Canadian jobs and depressing wages. The Dominion Government of Canada passed its first anti-Chinese bill in 1885, the year the Canadian Pacific Railway was completed. Prior to that year, Prime Minister MacDonald was unwilling to restrict Chinese immigration for fear of labour shortage in completing the transcontinental railroad (Li, 1979). Henceforth, for over sixty years, Canada maintained an explicit policy aimed at restricting and later excluding the Chinese from entering Canada.

The Chinese Immigration Act of 1885 (S.C. 1885, c. 71) imposed a head tax of $50 on practically every Chinese entering Canada. The head tax was increased to $100 in 1900 (S.C. 1900, c. 32), and $500 in 1903 (S.C. 1903, c. 8). The Chinese Immigration Act of 1923 excluded all Chinese from entering Canada (S.C. 1923, c. 38). The Act was maintained for twenty-five years until its repeal in 1947 (S.C. 1947, c. 19). In addition to these federal acts, various provinces passed numerous bills to restrict the civil and political rights of the Chinese. The Chinese in British Columbia, for example, were disfranchised as early as 1875. They were barred from owning crown lands, taking employment on public works, owning a liquor license or a hand-logger's license, to mention just a few. By the outbreak of the First World War, the Chinese in Canada, particularly those on the West Coast, were virtually reduced to second class citizens.

The Chinese Canadian Family: Historical Patterns

Very few of the Chinese who came to Canada during the nineteenth century brought their families with them. With the exception of perhaps some Chinese merchants who could afford to do so, the majority of the Chinese were young adult males who came singly. Before the end of the Second World War, conjugal family life among the Chinese-Canadians was rare, and the Chinese community consisted predominantly of married-bachelors who maintained financial contacts with their families in China (Hoe, 1976).

It is sometimes argued that immigrants are unwilling to identify with the host society because of a sojourner orientation (see for example, Siu, 1952; Li, 1976), which would also, according to the argument, explain their reluctance to immigrate with their families. In the case of the Chinese in Canada, there is little basis to support this explanation. Economic hardship and social hostility deterred many Chinese from bringing their wives and children in the period before the Chinese Immigration Act of 1923, when it was still legally possible for them to sponsor their relatives to come to Canada. The very same economic factor which compelled many of them to leave China in the first place also prevented them from being able to pay for the passage of their family members. The cost of bringing a family member increased substantially after 1885 when a head tax of $50 was imposed on practically every Chinese entering Canada. This cost was increased to $100 in 1900, and $500 in 1903 as the head tax was raised. Most Chinese probably had difficulty raising the money for their own entry, let alone the tax for their family members.

Aside from the financial cost involved, there were social costs which tended to discourage the Chinese from bringing their families. Hostility and discrimination against the Chinese often led to abuses and attacks. The Chinese quarters and enclaves were frequent targets of racial harassments. Among the more serious incidents were the anti-Oriental riots of 1887 and 1907 in Vancouver (Roy, 1976; Morton, 1974). The latter riot brought such damage to the Chinese and Japanese communities that the federal government had to appoint a Royal Commission to investigate the incident and to compensate for the losses of the victims (King, 1980). The apprehension of the Chinese was well summarized by a witness who testified before a Royal Commission in 1902.

"A large proportion of them would bring their families here were it not for the unfriendly reception they got here during recent years, which creates an unsettled feeling" (Royal Commission, 1902:2326, cited in Li, 1980a).

The Chinese Immigration Act of 1923 excluded all Chinese from immigrating to Canada. Until its repeal in 1947, it was legally impossible for many Chinese wives in China to unite with their husbands in Canada. This legal barrier further reinforced the sex imbalance among the Chinese-Canadian community, which remained the highest among the ethnic groups in Canada (Li, 1980a). Table 8-1 shows for example, the number of males per 100 females was 2,790 in 1911, 1,533 in 1921, 1,241 in 1931. Despite a general decline in the unbalanced sex ration, it remained at a high level of 785 in 1941, and 374 in 1951. In fact, it was not until the sixties that the ratio began to approach an equilibrium. For the period between 1921 and 1951, the improvement towards a more balanced sex ratio might have been due partly to a decline in the male population as many left Canada, and partly to a modest increase of the native-born Chinese-Canadians.

The absence of Chinese women also meant that the growth of a second-generation of Chinese-Canadians was severely hampered. Although the native-born among the Chinese increased from 7 percent in 1921 to 12 percent in 1931, and to 20 percent in 1941, the majority of the Chinese in Canada remained foreign-born as late as 1971. Undoubtedly, this delay of the second generation had a lot to do with the policy of exclusion towards the Chinese. In contrast, the native-born population among the adult Japanese-Canadians in the Canadian labour force in 1971 was 76 percent, as compared to a corresponding figure of 20 percent among Chinese-Canadians (Li, 1980b). The Canadian immigration policy permitted the Japanese to bring their wives to Canada since 1908 (see Adachi, 1976).

During the period of legislative exclusion between 1923 and 1947, many married Chinese men in Canada had to live separate from their wives in China. Married life was just as transient as the marriage, which often took place during a hasty trip to China. After the marriage, these married-bachelors would return to

Canada until the next time they could afford another trip home (see Hoe, 1976). For many, it meant a long period of separation from their families. The ultimate dream for them remained to save enough money through years of hard work, and eventually to retire in China to join their families. Given that most Chinese had only menial jobs, it is doubtful if many could have had their dream realized. Many of these married-bachelors maintained periodic contacts with their families through letters and remittances. The long period of separation resulted in many families members remaining strangers to each other (Hoe, 1976).

Table 8-2 provides some evidence to illustrate the pattern of marriage and the family among the Chinese before and after the war. The figures from 1941 show that the male population was over twelve times that of the female population. Among those who were married, the sex ratio was 2,001 Chinese men to 100 Chinese women. This high ratio gives some support to the life of the Chinese married-bachelors in Canada.

Table 8-1

Sex, Ratio and Nativity of Chinese in Canada, 1881—1971*

Year	Total Number of Chinese in Canada	Males per 100 Females	Percent Native Born
1881	4,383	------	0
1891	9,129	------	0
1901	17,312	------	---
1911	27,831	2,790	3
1921	39,587	1,533	7
1931	46,519	1,241	12
1941	34,627	785	20
1951	32,528	374	31
1961	58,197	163	40
1971	118,815	112	38

* Source: Censuses of Canada, 1911, Special Report on the Foreign-Born Population, Table 22, p. 50; 1911, Volume II, Table XII, pp. 368-9; 1921, Volume I, Population, Table 29, pp. 560-3; 1931, Volume XIII, Racial Origins and Nativity of the Canadian People, W. Burton Hurd, Table 16, p. 768; 1931, Volume I, Summary, Inserted Table, between pp. 234-235; 1941, Volume I, General Review and Summary Tables, Tables 35-36, pp. 694-7; 1951, Volume I, Population, General Characteristics, Table 31, pp. 31-1; 1951, Volume II, Population, Table 37, pp. 37-1; 1961, Volume I, Part 2, Series 1.2, Bulletin 1.2-5, Population, Ethnic Groups, Table 35, pp. 35-1—35-2; 1961, Volume II, Part I, Bulletin 7.1-6, Origins of the Canadian Population, Table XVII, p. 6-38; 1971, Volume I, Part 2, Bulletin 1.3-2, Population, Ethnic Groups, Table 3, pp. 3-1—3-2; 1971, Public Use Sample Tape, Individual File, special computation.

Table 8-2

MARITAL STATUS BY SEX, FOR CHINESE IN CANADA
FIFTEEN YEARS OF AGE AND OVER, 1941-1971*

	1941 N	1941 %	1951 N	1951 %	1961 N	1961 %	1971 N	1971 %
MALE								
Single	4,186	14.4	4,739	20.7	7,398	27.5	15,610	35.6
Married	23,556	81.1	17,155	75.1	18,013	67.0	26,285	59.9
Widowed or divorced	1,291	4.4	954	4.2	1,458	5.4	1,975	4.5
Total	29,033	99.9	22,848	100.0	26,869	99.9	43,870	100.0
FEMALE								
Single	992	42.4	1,455	31.8	2,019	14.2	9,390	24.6
Married	1,177	50.4	2,842	62.1	11,275	79.4	24,350	63.7
Widowed or divorced	168	7.2	281	6.1	906	6.4	4,460	11.7
Total	2,337	100.0	4,578	100.0	14,200	100.0	38,200	100.0
MALES PER 100 FEMALES								
Single	422	---	326	---	366	---	166	---
Married	2,001	---	604	---	160	---	108	---
Widowed or divorced	769	---	340	---	161	---	44	---
Total	1,242	---	499	---	189	---	115	---

* Source: Censuses of Canada, 1941, Volume 1, Table 37, pp. 698-699; 1951, Volume II, Table 31, pp. 31-1 to 31-2; 1961, Volume 1, Part 3, Bulletin 1.3-7, Table 106, pp. 106-1 to 106-12; 1971, Volume 1, Part 4, Bulletin 1.4-6, Table 14.

Table 8-3

Some Characteristics of Chinese-Canadian Families As Compared to All Canadian Families, 1971

	Canada		Chinese in Canada	
	N	**%**	**N**	**%**
Individuals belonging to a:				
Census Family[1]	18,707,700	87.4	103,500	83.1
Economic Family[2]	683,700	3.2	8,100	6.5
Non-Family[3]	2,010,500	9.4	13,000	10.4
Total Individuals	21,401,900	100.0	124,600	100.0
Average number of persons in the Census Family	4.50		4.63	
Average number of children born to women 15 years of age and over, ever married	2.77		2.63	

1. Defined in 1971 Census of Canada as: "consists of a husband and wife (with or without children who have never been married, regardless of age) or a parent with one or more children never married, living in the same dwelling" Statistics Canada (1972:6).
2. The Economic Family includes those not classified in the Census Family, and all members of a group living together who are related to each other by blood, marriage or adoption. For example, parents living with their married son and daughter-in-law is classified as an Economic Family.
3. Includes those not classified in the Census Family or Economic Family.

Source: Compiled from Public Sample Tape, Individual File, 1971 Census of Canada. Prince Edward Island, Yukon and Northwest Territories are not included in the Public Use Sample Tapes.

The Chinese-Canadian Family: Post-War Changes

With the repeal of the Chinese Immigration Act in 1947, Chinese were permitted to enter Canada on a limited basis. The admission of Chinese was first restricted to wives and unmarried children under eighteen years of age (P.C. 1930-2115), and later expanded to include sponsored relatives (P.C. 1956-785). It was not until 1962, however, that Chinese could apply as independent immigrants to Canada.

The change in the immigration policy towards the Chinese in the post-war era greatly altered the demographic composition of the Chinese-Canadian community. Between 1947 and 1962, 21,877 Chinese entered Canada; the sex ratio among these immigrants was 98 men to 100 women. In the five years after the change of the Immigration Act in 1962, 18,716 Chinese immigrated to Canada, the majority of whom were female. The sex ratio for this period was 72 men to 100 women. From 1968 to 1976, 91,490 Chinese immigrants were admitted, sith a sex ratio of 98 men to 100 women.

These statistics indicate a more balanced sex ratio of the post-war Chinese immigrants entering Canada. These immigrants gradually changed the demographic structure of the Chinese community. By 1971, the sex ratio among Chinese-Canadians was restored to a more balanced level of 112 men to 100 women (see Table 8-1). Undoubtedly, the wave of post-war immigration and the subsequent growth in the second-generation had much to do with this change.

Some of the post-war Chinese immigrants were wives and children who were long separated from their husbands and fathers in Canada. The change in the immigration policy made it possible for some families to reunite. The post-war years also witnessed a period of family migration to Canada for the Chinese, as opposed to the pattern of predominantly male immigrants before 1923. Table 8-2 shows some of these changes. As the overall unbalanced sex ratio began to decline in the post-war years, the sex ratio among the married men and women dropped from 604 in 1951 to 160 in 1961, and to 108 in 1971. These figures reflect in part the demise of the married-bachelor society as conjugal family life emerged in the Chinese-Canadian community.

In contrast to the rural background of the early Chinese immigrants, the newcomers after the war were mainly urban-dwellers who had spent some time in Hong Kong or Taiwan prior to their immigration to Canada. They also came from a more diversified occupational background, with a large percentage in the professional and technical fields. These changes would suggest that the post-war Chinese-Canadian family might resemble more the families of an industrial society than the structure implied in the highly dramatized traditional Chinese family.

Table 8-3 provides some comparisons of the Chinese-Canadian families with all Canadian families, based on the 1971 Census of Canada. The figures show that 83.1 percent of Chinese-Canadians belonged to a census family, which is similar to a nuclear family, as compared to 87.4 percent Canadians belonging to the same category. The percentage of Chinese-Canadian in an economic family tends to be higher (6.5 percent) as compared to that of all Canadians (3.2 percent).

With regard to the average family size, Table 8-3 shows that the average number of persons in the census family was 4.63 for Chinese-Canadians and 4.50 for all Canadians. The average number of children born to Chinese women, 15 years of age and over, who ever married was 2.63, as compared to 2.77 among all Canadian women of the same category. These statistics suggest that the Chinese-Canadian family in 1971 was quite similar to the average Canadian family with respect to family size and fertility rate of married women.

Summary and Conclusions

Two misconceptions might have distorted the understanding of the Chinese-

Canadian family. The first pertains to the theeoretical biases of the assimilationist and pluralist schools, which tend to interpret ethnicity and ethnic organizations as basically imported features of immigrants. The second misconception has to do with the popular myth of the traditional Chinese family, the empirical form of which rarely existed in the modern history of China, and to which the Chinese-Canadian family bears little empirical resemblance.

The development of the Chinese-Canadian family before the Second World War was severely crippled as a result of discriminatory policies and practices towards the Chinese in Canada. Institutional racism and legislative control compelled many Chinese men in Canada to be separated from their wives and children in China. The changes in the immigration laws after the war permitted the immigration of Chinese who had hitherto been excluded from Canada for twenty-four years. These post-war immigrants gradually altered the demographic composition of the Chinese-Canadian community. The once predominantly married-bachelor society began to decline as many Chinese immigrants came to Canada as family units. The increase in family migration also had the effect of restoring the disproportional sex ratio among the Chinese-Canadian community to approach an equillibrium.

When comparisons are made along family types, family size, and fertility rates among married women, the Chinese-Canadian family in 1971 does not appear to be different from the average Canadian family. The similarity reflects more the urban background of the post-war Chinese immigrants to Canada, and not the demise of the alleged traditional familism.

References

Adachi, Ken
  1976 **The Enemy That Never Was: A History of the Japanese Canadians.**
        Toronto: McClelland and Stewart.
Fei, Hsiao-Tung
  1946 "Peasantry and gentry: an interpretation of Chinese social structure and its
        changes". **The American Journal of Sociology** 52:1-17.
Freedman, Maurice
  1961-62 "The family in China, past and present". **Pacific Affairs** 24:323-336.
Ho, Ping-ti
  1965 "A historian's view of the Chinese family system". pp. 15-28, Farber, S.M., P.
        Mustacchi, and R.H.L. Wilson (eds.), **Man and Civilization: The Family's
        Search for Survival.** New York: McGraw-Hill.
Hoe, Ban Seng
  1976 **Structural Changes of Two Chinese Communities in Alberta,** Canada.
        Ottawa: National Museums of Canada.
King, W.L. Mackenzie
  1980 "Report on the losses sustained by the Chinese population of Vancouver, B.C.
        on the occasion of the riots in that city in September 1907". Sessional Paper
        No. 74F.

Lai, Cheun-Yan David
   1975   "Home country and clan origins of overseas Chinese in Canada in the early 1880's". **B.C. Studies** 27:3-29.
Li, Peter S.
   1976   "Ethnic businesses among Chinese in the U.S." **Journal of Ethnic Studies** 4:35-41.
   1979   "A historical approach to ethnic stratification: the case of the Chinese in Canada, 1858-1930". **Canadian Review of Sociology and Anthropology** 16:320-332.
   1980a "Immigration laws and family structure: some demographic changes among Chinese families in Canada, 1885-1971". **Canadian Ethnic Studies** 12:58-73.
   1980b "Income achievement and adaptive capacity: an empirical comparison of Chinese and Japanese in Canada". pp. 363-378 in V. Ujimoto and G. Hirabayashi (eds.), **Visible Minorities and Multiculturalism: Asians in Canada**. Scarborough, Ontario: Butterworths.
Li, Peter S. and B. Singh Bolaria
   1979   "Canada immigration policy and assimilation theories". pp. 411-422 in John Fry (ed.), **Economy, Class and Social Reality**. Scarborough, Ontario: Butterworths.
Morton, James
   1974   **In the Sea of Sterile Mountains**. Vancouver: J.J. Douglas Limited.
Roy, Patricia E.
   1976   "The preservation of the peace in Vancouver: the aftermath of the anti-Chinese riot of 1887". **B.C. Studies** 31:44-59.
Royal Commission
   1902   Report of the Royal Commission on Chinese and Japanese immigration.
Siu, Paul C.P.
   1952   "The sojourner". **American Journal of Sociology**, 58:34-44.
Statutes of Canada
   1885   An Act to restrict and regulate Chinese immigration into Canada. Ch. 71.
   1900   An Act respecting and restricting Chinese immigration. Ch. 32.
   1903   An Act respecting and restricting Chinese immigration. Ch. 8.
   1923   An Act respecting Chinese immigration. Ch. 38.
   1947   An Act to amend the Immigration Act and to repeal the Chinese Immigration Act. Ch. 19.

9

Status Integration and Ethnic Intramarriage in Canada

Thomas J. Abernathy
Director of Research and Development
Calgary Health Services

With the exception of why it is that they marry at all, perhaps no question in family sociology is as intriguing as why people marry the persons they do. Although in this society it is often thought of as a result of personal, irrational infatuation, investigations have suggested the involvement of a number of social factors. Work done in the U.S. (Burgess and Wallin, 1943; Hollingshead, 1950), long ago established that a tendency exists toward endogamy in such variables as age, race, religion, social class, and ethnic background. The importance of these social factors in mate selection is reflected in modern theories of courtship, including Kerchoff and Davis' (1962) "Filter Theory", and Lewis' (1973a, 1973b) "Process of Dyadic Formation".

Social homogamy in mate choices has also been demonstrated to occur among Canadians. With regard to ethnic background in particular, survey research (Anderson 1974; Chimbos, 1971; Wakil, 1973a, 1973b) has found evidence of values and attitudes that reinforce the tendency for adolescents to select marriage partners from within their own ethnic group. The trend toward homogamy is also revealed in Canadian demographic data (Hurd, 1929, 1942, 1964; Kalbach, 1974: Table 1). In 1961 nearly 77%, and in 1971 nearly 76%, of all the existing marriages in the country were between husbands and wives of the same ethnic background. The specific rates of intramarriage, however, vary among different ethnic groups. For example, in 1971 91% of the Jewish males in the country were married to Jewish wives, while in the same year, the rate among other groups was: British, 81%; German, 49%; French, 86%; Asians, 81%; and Scandinavians, 27%.

This variation in rates of endogamy has been explained (Kalbach, 1974) as a consequence of the clustering and distribution of ethnic groups throughout the country—sincea it is logical that in a place where one group makes up a majority of the population, such as Newfoundland that in 1971 was 94% English, or Quebec that was 77% French, a large proportion of these groups would be expected simply by chance to intramarry.

There is considerable evidence to support the notion that the rate of intramarriage for an ethnic group in a particular province is a function of its proportional representation in the provincial population. In 1971 in Newfoundland, where they made up only 3.1% of the population, the intramarriage rate among French-Canadians was 35.3%. In Quebec, which was 77% French, the rate was 94.4%.

On the other hand, there are some other aspects of ethnic intramarriage that are not so easily accounted for in this way. One is that even though the probabilities for intramarriage within groups depend upon their representation in a population, most intramarry at a much higher rate than would be expected by chance. According to probability only 28.6% (Yinger, 1968) of the existing marriages in Canada in 1971 should have been between people of the same ethnic backgrounds, while the actual proportion was nearly 76%.

A second matter is the relationship found in individual provinces between the rates of intramarriage for different ethnic groups and their proportions of the population. If the rates of intramarriage for groups in a province are determined by their percent of the population, then within any province the two ought to be correlated. That is, larger sized groups should intramarry more; and groups of similar size should intramarry about the same. Instead, however, the relationship between them is found to be inconsistent and, in most cases, weak. Correlations for 1971 range from highs of $r = .68$, .64, and .62 for the Territories, Prince Edward Island, and New Brunswick, respectively; to lows of .11, .09, and .05 for Saskatchewan, Manitoba, and Alberta. This results from the tendency for some ethnic groups, notably Native Indians, Jews, Asians, Dutch, and Polish, despite their relatively small proportions of provincial populations, to have high rates of intramarriage; whereas other groups of similar size, Scandinavians and Germans in particular, intramarry at much lower rates.

A third point is that even if various ethnic groups do have different propensities for endogamy, it still would be expected that their individual rates of intramarriage in the various provinces would be related to their proportion of the provincial population. In most instances, a strong relationship is found to exist; but there are exceptions. In 1961 the amount of variation (r^2) in intramarriage rates that can be explained by proportion of the population ranges for different groups from .74 for both the British and "Other and unspecified", to .43 for the Polish ($\bar{x} = .52$). The range in 1971 was from .85 for the British to .0049 for "Other".

These conditions suggest that even though the rate of intramarriage for a particular ethnic group in a particular province is related to its proportion of the population, it cannot entirely be accounted for by it. The purpose of this study is to investigate the possibility that the rate of intramarriage for an ethnic group in a province is a function not only of its own proportion of the population; but of the distribution of other groups as well.

Populations may range, with regard to the distribution of any nominal variable, from being wholly homogeneous to completely heterogeneous. If, for example, a variable has five potential categories, the population can be clustered all into one of the categories, with no observations in the other four; or evenly distributed with 20% of the population in each. A measure of this distribution, termed a "Total Status Integration Measure" was used by Gibbs and Martin (1964:40) to test Durkheim's theory that well-integrated societies should experience lower rates of suicide than poorly-integrated ones. It measures the integration of a population along any variable by using the sum of the squares of the decimal fractions of the population in each of the variable categories. Thus, a population with all of its members in one category would have a number of 1.00; whereas one with its population evenly distributed among five categories would have a number of .20

Methods

The Census of Canada provides an excellent opportunity for the study of ethnic endogamy, since both the 1961 and 1971 editions report the ethnic background of all husbands and wives in the country for those years. Although they report all marriages, not just those of native-born Canadians, the rates of endogamy for the two have been shown (Kalbach, 1974) to be closely correlated. The 1961 Census reported 13 different ethnic categories: British, French, German, Italian, Jewish, Netherlands, Polish, Russian, Scandinavian, Ukranian, Other European, and Other and not stated. In the 1971 edition the categories of Russian, and Other European were dropped, and Native Indian added. For this study the 1961 categories of Russian, and Other European were grouped together with Other and not stated, so as to make the two years more comparable.

Analysis of the relationship among the intramarriage rate of ethnic groups, their proportions of the various provincial populations, and provincial ethnic status integration involved several calculations. These included the rate of intramarriage for each group in each province (and the combined Territories), which was determined by dividing the number of husbands with wives of the same ethnic background by the total number of husbands in that group; and each group's proportion of each province's population—found by dividing the number of males in each group by the total male population. Both the rates of intramarriage and proportions of the provincial populations were also calculated for females, but the differences between the sexes were so slight that for convenience analysis was continued for males alone. The measures of ethnic status integration were determined by summing the squares of each group's decimal fraction of each province's population. These measures ranged, in 1961, from .88 in Newfoundland to .24 in Saskatchewan; and in 1971 from .87 in Newfoundland to .22 in Manitoba. Generally, the measures tend to decrease from East to West across the country (1961: $r_s = .83$, $p.01$; 1971: $r_s = .84$, $p.01$).

Results

The first test of a possible relationship between rates of ethnic intramarriage and status integration was to calculate the degree of correlation between the total proportion of all marriages in each province that were between persons of the same ethnic background and the provincial rates of ethnic integration. In 1961 endogamous marriages accounted for 93.6% of the total in Newfoundland, and only 60.18% of those in Alberta. The range in 1971 was between 92.6% in Newfoundland to 54.5% in Saskatchewan. Results revealed a strong positive relationship between the two. For 1961 the correlation was $r = .90$ (p .001), and for 1971 $r = .89$ (p .001). This clearly demonstrates that total rates of ethnic intramarriage in a province are a function of the ethnic distribution of the population; and that overall rates of endogamy are higher in more homogeneous populations than in more heterogeneous ones.

Because the provincial rates of ethnic intramarriage are known already to be influenced by a group's proportion of the population, the effect of ethnic distribution was measured by calculating, for each group, a multiple linear regression between its proportion of each province's population; the status integration measure for the province; and the percent of males marrying someone of the same ethnic background. As with the simple measures of correlation between rates of intramarriage and proportion of the provincial population, results differ greatly for different groups. The total amount of variation within individual groups explained by this combination of variables ranges from, in 1961, $r^2 = .87$ for the English to $r^2 = .95$ for Poles; and in 1971 from $r^2 = .95$ for the English to $r^2 = .08$ for Poles. Overall, however, significant increase in the total amount of variation explained is achieved by the inclusion of the measure of status integration. In 1961 it upped the average amount of variation accounted for by 19.2%, from $r^2 = .52$ to $r^2 = .62$ (t = 4.83, p .001); and in 1971 by 31.1%, from $r^2 = .45$ to $r^2 = .59$ (t = 2.49, p .01).

Discussion

The marriage choices of Canadians are not random, but instead tend strongly toward ethnic endogamy. Nearly 76% of all the existing marriages in the country in 1971 were between couples of the same ethnic background. The specific rates of intramarriage, however, vary both among different ethnic groups and between members of the same group in different provinces. The variation that occurs within groups has been explained as a consequence of their clustering within the national population. This study has demonstrated that while the rate of endogamy for a group does vary with its proportion of a province's population, it is also influenced by the distribution of other nationalities within that population. Specifically, it has shown that taking the index of ethnic status integration into account can accomplish an increase of as much as 30% in the overall amount of variation that is explained.

It is recognized that the results of this study are subject to many influences, including errors in reporting and the effects of immigration. Nonetheless, the findings seem to suggest that the tendency of an ethnic group toward intramarriage declines, despite its proportion of the provincial population, as that population becomes more ethnically heterogeneous. This, in turn, implies that if geographical mobility in Canada continues to disperse ethnic groups throughout the country, as has already happened in the Western provinces, endogamy will decline.

References

Anderson, Alan B.
  1974   "Intermarriage in Ethnic Bloc Settlements in Saskatchewan: A Cross-cultural Survey of Attitudes and Trends". Paper presented at the Western Association of Sociology and Anthropology, Banff, Alberta.
Burgess, E.W. and P. Wallin
  1943   "Homogamy in Social Characteristics". **American Journal of Sociology**, 49 (September): 109-124.
Chimbos, Peter D.
  1971   "Immigrants Attitudes Towards Their Children's Inter-ethnic Marriages in a Canadian Community". **International Migration Review**, 1 (Spring).
Gibbs, Jack and Walter Martin
  1964   **Status Integration and Suicide.** Eugene, Oregon: University of Oregon Press.
Hurd, W. Burton
  1929   **Origin, Birthplace, Nationality and Languages of the Canadian People.** Ottawa: The King's Printer.
  1931   **Racial Origins and Nativity of the Canadian People,** 1931 Census of Canada, Vol. 8. Ottawa: The King's Printer.
  1941   **Ethnic Origin and Nativity of the Canadian People,** 1941 Census of Canada. Ottawa: Queen's Printer.
Kalbach, Warren
  1974   "Propensities for Intermarriage in Canada as Reflected in the Ethnic Origins of Native-born Husbands and their Wives: 1961 and 1971". Paper presented at the annual meeting of the Canadian Sociology and Anthropology Association, Toronto, Ontario.
Kerchoff, Alan C.
  1962   "Value Concensus and Need Complementarity in Mate Selection". **American Sociological Review** 27 (June): 295-303.
Lewis, Robert A.
  1973a "A Longitudinal Test of a Developmental Framework for Pre-marital Dyadic Formation". **Journal of Marriage and the Family,** 35 (February): 16-27.

  1973b "Social Reaction and the Formation of Dyad: An Interactional Approach to Mate election". **Sociometry,** 36 (September): 409-419.

Wakil, S. Parvez

1973a "Campus Dating: An Exploratory Study of Cross-national Relevance". **Journal of Comparative Family Studies,** 2 (Fall).

1973b "Campus Mate-selection Preference: A Cross-national Comparison". **Social Forces,** 5 (June).

Waller, Willard

1937 "The Rating and Dating Complex". **American Sociological Review,** 2 (October): 727-734.

Winch, Robert F.

1955 "The Theory of Complementary Needs in Mate-selection: Final Results the Test of the General Hypothesis". **American Sociological Review,** 20: 552-555.

Yinger, M.J.

1968 "A Research Note on Interfaith Statistics". **Journal for the Scientific Study of Religion,** 7 (Spring): 89-99.

Part IV
Institutional Control
and Ethnic Organizations

10

Ethnic Organizational Theory: The Chinese Case

Gunter Baureiss
University of Manitoba

Ethnic organizational theory has never been subjected to rigorous systemization, despite the wealth of ethnic relations research. This void has been recognized by many researchers (Sills, 1968; Price, 1979; Smith & Freedman, 1972; Hammond, 1972; Radecki, 1976, 1979; Baureiss, 1982b). Various attempts to typify ethnic organizations (Hausknecht, 1962, Sills, 1957, 1968; Babchuk & Gordon, 1962; Radecki, 1979) have only been partially successful because the typifications have not been integrated into a general comprehensive organizational theory.

In a previous article (Baureiss, 1982b) I have proposed that general organizational theory offers three types of organizations that can be applied also to ethnic organizations, provided the basic distinguishing principle is emphasized and retains primacy over secondary characteristics. In this article, I will apply the above ethnic organizational theory to the Chinese organizations of two cities in Western Canada to demonstrate its utility. Whereas previous publications on the Chinese in Calgary and Winnipeg have either dealt with ecological-demographic issues (Baureiss, 1971b; Baureiss & Driedger, 1982), or used the community approach in historical perspective, in which Chinese organizations were considered as an integral part of community life (Baureiss, 1974; Hoe, 1976; Baureiss, 1980; Baureiss, 1982a), this article takes these organizations as a focal theme.

Ethnic Organizational Theory

Researchers concerned with ethnic organizational theory have stayed away from applying general organizational theory of managerial, business and administrative disciplines. Certainly, general organizational theory is preoccupied with the study of bureaucracy and its variants, since its major focus attempts to explain the structures and functions of large governmental, religious and business enterprises. Following Weber's ideal type of bureaucracy based on formal rationality, organizational theory analyzes the principle of fixed and official areas ordered by laws or adminstrative regulations, the principle of office hierarchy and levels of graded authority, documents of official rules and work procedures which are preserved, office management that presupposes expert training, the demand on office holders of their full working capacity, and dependence on general rules which can be learned (Gerth and Mills, 1964: 196-198). No doubt, when ethnic organizations are analyzed by the above criteria, many fail to be bureaucratic—as Radecki correctly maintains (Babecki, 1979: 13).

However, accepting the premise that most of the bureaucratic criteria mentioned above are derivations of formal rationality and its derived legal authority, the term bureacracy can adequately define certain ethnic organizations. The basis of a bureaucratic organization, then, is the required compliance to what I have termed "optimizing type of decision process" (as exemplified, for instance, in the form of technical rules based on empirical knowledge and specific strategies) resulting in optimizing action. In the bureaucratic organization, those who comply are rewarded by positive sanctions, increased responsibility and positive representation. Negative sanctions, withdrawal of responsibility, and negative representation are applied to non-compliant members who follow the value-rational or the extremizing type of decision process (Baureiss, 1979b).

Organizations emphasizing compliance to extremizing decisions are termed collectivistic. This type has been linked to Weber's value-rationality in contrast to his formal-rational bureaucratic type (Rothschild-Whitt, 1979:509). In such a type of organization, compliance implies the acceptance of the possible oucome as beneficial for a defined collectivity. In the collectivist organization compliance to extremizing action is positively rewarded, whereas optimizing action is negatively sanctioned, responsibility is withdrawn, and negative representation applied.

Adhocracies permit or encourage autonomous decisions, thereby minimizing domination and control. Constrained by their orientation and motivation, members are free to reduce risk by selecting either the extremizing or optimizing type of decision process, resulting in autonomous action. The absence or minimization of compliance produces a very loose structure, and individuals may take responsibility at one time, but not another. Consequently, things may or may not get done. This type of organization is frequently of short duration and is likely to change into a collectivist or bureaucratic type of organization, or to disappear altogether.

Organizations, then, can be typified according to their emphasis of primary type of action and their reflected structure. Thus the major type of decision process they follow—defining how risk can be reduced—allows their typification as bureaucratic, collectivist, or adhocratic (Baureiss, 1982b). Ethnic organizations do not differ in terms of type from other organizations. Nor do they differ in the formal systems of uncertainty reduction. They may assign priority to the pragmatic, ethical, and/or expressive sub-system as any other organization may do. Viewed from the member's action system, these organizations may therefore focus on the technological, institutional and/or communal sub-system of orientation, and within these systemic limits they generate uncertainty and maximally attempt to reduce it.

The uniqueness of ethnic organizations is found in the specific content of the epistemic and evaluative systems of orientation that is "ethnic". Action requires decision processes that limit the range of pssible alternatives (reduce maximum risk). It then follows that ethnic organizations may differ from other organizations in their definition of risk. It is the ethnic content of orientation combined with this difference in defining risk reduction that can be termed as the 'resilience' of ethnic organizations viewed from the perspective of the larger social system.

The analytical distinction between motivation, orientation and decision theory enables the inclusion of various organizations irrespective of their primacy of orientation (as well as their specific area of uncertainty reduction) into the above typology. Thus, bureacracies may generate and then attempt to reduce uncertainty on either the technological, institutional, or communal systems level; or a combination of two; or all three. But so can collectivist or adhocractic structured organizations.

Ethnic organizations, as actors, respond to and interact with the larger social system and cosequently have to be analyzed in this wider context. Their emergence, adaptation and and dissolution can only be understood within the historically-specific context of modern western societies, that of the advanced capitalist system.

Ethnic Structural Discrimination

Structural discrimination is conceptualized as the imposition of constraints, norms and stigmas on specific collectivities that do not apply to other members of the society. Ethnic structural discrimination is but one among several other criteria (gender, age, etc.) that defines differences as significant. Frequently, ethnic structural discrimination is legitimized by the state, supported by religious, racist, or pseudo-scientific ideologies.

Historically-oriented systems analysis treats advanced capitalist systems as one specific type of social system that emphasizes optimizing action directed towards production and consumption, and through this process, maximization of profits for investors. Ethnic discrimination has to be considered as an extension of capitalist expansionism that is facilitated by the cheapest possible wage labour for groups that have unequal power. Since in the advanced capitalist system legitimation from economic organizations has been transferred to the state, it is the state that has to legitimize its policies (Habermas, 1975). Legitimation can be maintained when government policies reduce tension, uncertainty and risk for other interest groups—creating new legitimation crises. Thus, state policies directed towards ethnic collectivities are part of the overall tension-management and risk-reduction in order to avoid legitimation crises in the advanced capitalistic system. Structural legitimate discrimination, then, is applied to those ethnically defined collectivities that have weak or no power bases when the state is assured that its policies are in accord with powerful interest groups. Interest groups or individual citizens may go beyond structural discrimination defined as legitimate. Harassment, verbal and physical; discrimination in hiring and firing; and in the extreme case, riots, expose the state's legitimation crisis. The state may counteract such actions, but more frequently, ignores them.

The explanation of the emergence, adaptation and dissolution of ethnic organizations must take into account the degree of structural discrimination (legitimized or not) and the resilience of ethnic collectivities as two independent variables. Ethnic organizations emerge when ethnic collectivities exhibit resilience. Discrimination accentuates this ethnic resilience, leading towards ethnic community closure. In urban centres, this process is facilitated by ethnic organizations (Baureiss, 1982b).

Adhocratic ethnic organizations frequently emerge from informal gatherings. However, by virtue of the minimal control exercised over their members, they remain peripheral to the community in modern societies. This type does not engage in competition within or outside the ethnic boundaries, as no compliance is required.

By contrast, collectivist organizations requiring compliance can maximize social control under conditions of discrimination, despite their different structure from the general bureaucratic types of organizations found in advanced captilalist societies. It is argued that collectivist organizations can emerge and survive because discrimination forces ethnic individuals to find refuge within ethnic community boundaries. They frequently serve as umbrella organizations dealing with aspects of the technological, institutional, and communal structures of the ethnic commnity. Since discrimination eliminates competition with non-ethnic organization, competition is confined within ethnic boundaries.

Bureaucratic ethnic organizations may also emerge under conditions of discrimination. Ethnic business enterprises fall into this category, but so do ethnic organizations with clear objectives directed towards maintaining or removing discrimination. Compliance to optimizing action can be achieved when such action is positively rewarded within ethnic communities. As a result of community closure, these ethnic organizations are not in competition for membership or on issues with organizations outside their community boundaries.

When socially defined ethnic differences change from being significant to being insignificant, ethnic collectivities gain increasing access to the technological, institutional, and communal structure in the social system. Ethnic resilience can be maintained when segragation is maintained in urban centres; however, the resilience of ethnic collectivities is more difficult to maintain and ethnic organizations need to respond to the changing situation.

It is argued that lack of discrimination forces organizations to compete with other organizations for membership, thereby "aligning" their structure with that of the optimizing principle (i.e. bureaucratic). Consequently, collectivities will dissolve or become bureaucratic, unless ethnic closure can be maintained by new immigrants and/or by reminding members of past discriminatory practices or possible future discrimination. Whereas compliance can be relatively easily enforced under conditions of discrimination, in the absence of them, it can be legitimized by emphasizing a speciality: ethnicity (Baureiss, 1982b). Under a relatively free market system, ethnic organizations compete not only for membership but also with other organizations, whereby their "market value" is determined by their success resulting from optimizing action.

The Chinese in Canada

The Chinese experience in Canada is particularly suited for testing ethnic organizational theory within the larger social system, because two periods, separated by the Chinese immigration prohibition, are clearly distinguishable: discrimination in the first half of this century, and the easing of discriminatory practices after World War II.

The discrimination directed towards the Chinese before and in the first half of this century is well documented (see Basran, Ujimoto, Li). When sentiments towards the Chinese changed during World War II (now defined as Western allies in the war against Japan), the Canadian state successively relaxed Chinese immigration policies. Subsequently, discrimination lessened, though it persisted in disguised stated policies and sporadic illegitimate outbursts. The permission for entry of wives, children, and independent Chinese of various occupational groups not only changed the Chinese cohort that in 1947 was 95 percent older males, but also had a lasting effect on Chinese organizations. Whereas during the first half of this century the Chinese population in Canada was homogeneous—unskilled males from the southern region of China, speaking the same dialect—after World War II it changed to a heterogeneous Chinese population with regard to sex, age, occupational status, religion and dialect.

This changing context provides the background for the analysis of Chinese organizations in Calgary and Winnipeg. Since their records are not entirely complete, the analysis of these organizations and their relation to the larger social system creates certain methodological problems.[2] It relies on ethno-graphic data such as organizational constitutions, the memory of participant members, and newspaper statements made by and about Chinese organizations at that time.

Early Chinese Organizations

The existing discriminatory practices in Canada and the continuous influence from China generated tension, uncertainty and risk among the early Chinese immigrants. This could be dealt with more effectively by formal organizations within the community structure. The Chinese, well known for "organizational genius" (Johnson, 1979:359), created organizations based on their traditions and adapted to the Canadian context. Although the Chinese organizations varied in their structure and the type of action they emphasized, the most important ones were collectivistic.

Collectivist Organizations

Among the early Chinese organizations in Calgary and Winnipeg, the most important ones by far were the political-fraternal organizations, the Chinese Benevolent Association (CBA) in Winnipeg and the clan associations.

As early as the turn of this century, the Freemasons (Chee Kung Tong) operated informally in Calgary, attempting to establish control over Chinese.[3] This philosophy was based on freedom and brotherhood, opposing any government that would interfere with such rights. It was not until the visits of Dr. Sun-Yat-Sen that the Freemasons were formally organized in 1911 in Calgary and Winnipeg.

The second political-fraternal organization, the Chinese Nationalist League (Kuomintang), was formed in Calgary in 1913 and in Winnipeg in 1915. It was an offshoot of the political party in China and therefore supported it financially and symbolically, although it locally emphasized fraternity among its members. Membership of both associations in each city was well over one hundred, and participation occasionally reached several hundred.

The Chinese Benevolent Association was formed in Winnipeg in the early 1920's, as a branch of the national organization founded in Victoria in 1884. Its objectives were to establish goodwill among Chinese immigrants and to promote the social well-being of the Chinese community in general. It was, however, less influential that the political-fraternal associations, and ceased to operate for a number of years towards the end of the mid-century (Baureiss & Kwong, 1979:40).

The clan associations in Calgary and Winnipeg stem from the traditional patrilineal family structure in China. Unable to transfer the traditional kinship system to Canada, they were "fictive" (Johnson, 1979:362) in the sense that all Chinese with one and the same (and sometimes several combined) names could be members. In addition, the district associations were formed for those Chinese whose surname was not common enough in the city to permit a clan association.

It is not within the parameters of this article to list in detail the various activities of these organizations. Emphasis will be placed on how these organizations reduced uncertainty, tension and risk for their members, and on the compliance requested of them.

The Chinese who lived abroad during that period were under strong influence from China, and those in Calgary and Winnipeg were no exceptions. As immigrants, they all had relatives in China. Frequent visits to their home country, and the taking of wives and producing of offspring that remained there, solidified this relationship. Financial remittances were common, but the general well-being of China's future was also of vital interest and it was through their organizations that this concern was expressed. Most importantly, these organizations embraced virtually all Chinese in reducing uncertainty, tension and risk in a discriminatory environment. Participation was expected by all Chinese and non-compliance was occasionally sanctioned with ostracism (Baureiss, 1982a). All organizations had similar patterns of election procedures and methods of financing and were loosely linked with those in other Canadian cities. Their activities followed a typical pattern of what I termed "extremizing action". Embedded in the traditional Chinese culture, their risk reduction was not directed towards optimization of returns but towards collective issues—what Weber called value-rational action (Weber, 1978). Their extremizing action, either directed towards China or local issues, asked for compliance from their members to such a degree that indeed they cannot be called voluntary organizations in the narrow sense.[4]

Collectivist organizations do not necessarily deprive individuals of personal gains. Indeed, in both cities it was the merchant elite that established these organizations, occupied the administrative positions and thereby legitimized their power base. Other Chinese also benefitted from these organizations. But what is of importance is that these organizations made decisions governed by the principles of collective values, and not by the principle of optimizing returns for specific individuals. Individual benefits or deprivations were therefore a by-product of collectivist action.

Risk can only be reduced once alternatives are provided. Alternatives are provided by the orientational sub-systems. Chinese organizations were able to deal with uncertainty reduction in all three sub-systems: they were able to generate and reduce uncertainties on the instrumental, ethical and integrative level of orientation in a diffuse manner. For example, financial contributions for China not only reduced uncertainty on the instrumental level by helping a government that was acceptable to their relatives, but also reduced uncertainty on the expressive level by creating a feeling of solidarity with China. Simultaneously these donations provided an ethical uncertainty reduction in the sense that Chinese away from home felt that "they had done all they could do" under existing circumstances.

For those Chinese who couldn't get help from close relatives, all organizations engaged at one time or another in finding or providing accommodation, mitigating employment, and occasionally in paying for funerals and/or the shipment of bones of deceased Chinese to their home country (Baureiss, 1971:56; Baureiss & Kwong, 1979:12). Overall, these organizations did occasionally assist financially, but more importantly, mitigated between their members to comply to a collective good.

The ethical sub-system specified for the Chinese the systemic limits of norms within which uncertainty could be reduced. These limits placed the Chinese within restraints that were not necessarily in accordance with those of the larger system. Gambling, opium use, certain types of exploitation among Chinese were not necessarily transgressions of the normative boundaries (Baureiss, 1982a). However, conflict between individuals arising out of violation of norms was mediated by organizations and their decision was frequently accepted as final. Since the local authorities preferred not to be involved in internal Chinese matters, they often recognized the organizational leaders as spokesmen for the Chinese, and encouraged these leaders' role in settling internal disputes. This thereby legitimized internal uncertainty reduction (Baureiss, 1982a).

Finally these organizations played an important part in uncertainty reduction on the integrative level. All collectivist organizations provided occasions for expressive activity, informally and formally. Members could drop in to establish contacts with other members, to discuss political, economic and private matters, or just to read the Chinese newspapers and magazines that were usually available. Formally, these organizations were well known for their big celebrations of the Chinese New Year, Moon Festivals, Dragon Boat Festivals and others (Baureiss, 1971a:85-86). These activities provided a strong integrative force among the Chinese, whether it was expressed in solidarity or antagonism. It reinforced the common destiny which they could not escape.

It was this diffuseness of the orientational sub-systems by which uncertainty was reduced, and the type of decision processes that were directed towards community values, that made compliance mandatory; giving these organizations their dominance as collectivist organizations to which some Chinese referred as a "mixed blessing".

Bureaucratic Organizations

Organizations in this early period that can be typified as bureaucracies were the Chinese Missions, the Chinese schools and the Anti-Japanese League.

The missions were under the auspices of the Presbyterian Church and their optimizing action was well established in their proselytizing efforts to convert as many Chinese as possible to Christianity. Their outreach work was an extension of their overseas missionary activities and goes back well into the last century in Calgary and Winnipeg (Baureiss, 1974; Baureiss & Kwong, 1979). When the Methodists, Presbyterian, and Congregational Churches merged under the name United Church in 1925, the Chinese Missions were renamed as the 'Chinese United Church'.

Although the historical-demographic situation of Calgary and Winnipeg differed, the objectives and the structure of the Chinese Missions were the same.

The Calgary Chinese Mission was founded in 1901 and became the centre of the second Chinatown. The Mission was better off than the one in Winnipeg since it had a private sponsor in Thomas Underwood. When the Presbyterian minster was seeking quarters for the Chinese newcomers to teach them English, it was Underwood who provided a two-room buidling for that purpose. When this premise became too small, it was again Underwood who built at his cost and on his property the new Chinese Mission (Baureiss, 1971a:36). By 1911 the Mission acquired its first Chinese minister and services could be conducted in Chinese (Baureiss, 1971a:44).

In Winnipeg the Chinese Mission was founded in 1917, a few blocks away from Chinatown, and remained there until moved to Chinatown in 1947 (Baureiss & Kwong, 1979). Winnipeg's Chinese Mission encountered more financial and leadership difficulties, as it had no generous sponsor. The attitude of the Church bureaucracy can therefore be better analysed.

Records of internal correspondence for the period from 1929 to 1947 between the Winnipeg Mission and the Board of Home Mission in Toronto (United

Church of Canada) highlight not only the hierarchical structure of the Mission, but also its basic principle of optimization. Two related problems evident to the Church leaders were a reflection of their low "success" in attracting Chinese converts: lack of self-financing and lack of local leadership. Funds were raised through small contributions from the Chinese, from the churches, and by occasional fund-raising activities. Although the building in which the Church was housed became titlefree in 1931, funds apparently were not sufficient to maintain it. The second problem was the missing link in the hierarchical chain of the bureaucracy: the minister. Since no full-time minister could be secured, sporadic visits to Winnipeg were made by a minister posted in Moose Jaw (Saskatchewan), his contact being limited to not more than five or six men. Sunday School had been discontinued, and the Chinese Christian population was an estimated dozen out of nearly 1,000 Chinese living in Winnipeg and vicinity (Baureiss & Kwong, 1979:75). Until 1949 the Winnipeg Chinese were sporadically served by three different travelling missionaries.

Since the Missions were part of the bureaucratic church hierarchy, their objectives were clearly directed towards the maximization of returns. The Chinese minister became a link in the church hierarchy necessary to run the Mission effectively and efficiently. Although the main objective was the conversion of Chinese to Christianity, it was soon realized that the language barrier first had to be broken. To achieve this goal, both Missions offered English classes at night for Chinese immigrants, but on weekends the Scripture took precedence. Records show that the Missions attracted more Chinese to the English classes than as church members. English language classes were discontinued when Chinese immigration was halted in 1924. The church's low profile in the two Chinese communities must be seen as related to their orientation, that was in fact in opposition to Chinese resilience. From the Chinese perspective, the Church generated tension, uncertainty and risk through its dogma, and offered salvation as a device to reduce it. Chinese, as non-Christians, accepted this orientation reluctantly, or refused it altogether, and thereby did not comply to the optimizing action of the bureacratic church structure. Optimizing action of course was not strange to Chinese, who were very successful indeed in their overseas business ventures. But here, optimizing actions were applied to the technological sub-system of orientation, whereas the Church required compliance to optimizing actions in the institutional and communal sub-system. As well, the rewards offered by the church for compliance had little meaning to the Chinese. Consequently, being in competition with the Chinese collectivist organizations, church organizations remained at the periphery of Chinese life.[5]

The Chinese schools were created by parents of a small, but rising, number of Chinese children in the 1920's. Classes were held in the evenings, after the children had attended the compulsory school in the city. Both teachers and pupils often lacked enthusiasm. The objective was specifically directed towards the transmission of the Chinese language, traditions, and customs. The Chinese schools were considered supplementary to the informal teaching taking place within the family structure, and were intended to optimize this transmission by a formal curriculum that extended beyond the parents knowledge and ability.

Last in the list of organizations I consider bureaucratic is the Anti-Japanese League. Founded in 1937 purely to raise funds for China's war against Japan, its optimizing action is self-evident. It allied itself not only with other Anti-Japanese organizations across Canada, but also with the Chinese Consulate-General, the Chung King Government, and the local collectivist organizations.

Adhocratic Organizations

In the theoretical exposition I have made reference to adhocratic organizations as being generally shortlived. Indeed, the Chinese Mission, the Freemasons and the clan associations are adhocratic forerunners. One adhocratic organization that survived in both cities for decades was the Chinese Dramatic Society. Its origin goes back in Winnipeg to 1921 and it is one of the earliest Chinese cultural organizations in Canada. In Calgary, a Chinese Dramatic Society was formed around 1930. They never established a formal structure. They depended on the "good will" of other Chinese for a locale to practice, and so members felt little responsibility or long term commitment. Autonomy in decision processes permitted members to make extremizing or optimizing decisions. Although it never exercised community control, it survived by just attracting sufficient interest. These societies would perform at banquets and festivals on a voluntary basis, providing its participants with recognition or small "gifts" in return. Occasionally, however, these organizations would stage Chinese operas and dramas for fund-raising purposes in rented community halls or theaters (Hoe, 1976:90; Baureiss & Kwong, 1979:76). Even though these performances had to be rehearsed and optimization was accepted to achieve a good performance, the volunteers perceived them as an enjoyable, rather than as a serious, activity. An entry fee was never charged, though donations were requested according to ability to pay (Baureiss & Kwong, 1979:46).

Summary of Early Organizations

Chinese organizations—especially those termed collectivistic—focused on keeping the ties with China and making life in Canada tolerable. In so doing they elicited within their communities what I have termed extremizing action. Their reduction of tension, uncertainties and risks in a variety of areas relevant for the Chinese explains the control exercised over members. There was competition among them, expressed in internal conflicts, but none were in competition with organizations outside the community boundaries. Community closure existed until the change in discriminatory practices at the mid-century, when closure was increasingly difficult to maintain. This also affected the Chinese organizations.

Present Chinese Organizations

The change in Western attitudes towards the Chinese after World War II brought about a relaxation in Canadian immigration policies. This allowed unification of families separated for decades and permitted entry of Chinese from different regions, with different dialects, and different occupations. Immigrants entered primarily via Hong Kong, Taiwan and Singapore after the establishment of the Communist regime in 1949. The strong influence from mainland China began to wane, and at the same time Chinese gained increasing access to the technological, institutional and communal Canadian structure. They began to accept Canada as their home country. Present Chinese organizations have to be analyzed within this changed historically-specific situation. Whereas in the past Chinese organizations had established effective instrumental, ethical, and/or expressive definitions of the situation within ethnically defined systemic limits, these were no longer defined as uncertainty to be reduced. Consequently, compliance to extremizing action could no longer be enforced upon the members.

Traditional Chinese Organizations

The lost connection with China and the change in demographic structure of the Chinese population, a result of changing discrimination, presented a challenge to the Chinese organizations. The traditional organizations were confronted not only with the competition of new Chinese organizations, but also with organizations of the larger society. Support for mainland China and the needs of members having lost relevance, some organizations redefined their uncertainty reduction by emphasizing cultural heritage in the term "ethnicity". With their waning community dominance they were reduced to social clubs—a change from collectivistic to bureaucratic organizational optimizing action.

The Chinese Nationalist League encountered its first blow when the Kuomintang lost control over mainland China in 1949. The second came when Canada opened diplomatic relations with the Chinese communist regime in 1970. Today the organization holds banquets, shows the occasional Chinese movie and maintains a musical society (Baureiss, 1971b:52). In 1972, membership in Calgary was about a hundred, and in Winnipeg twenty-four (Hoe, 1976:138). The Freemasons devised new objectives in 1971 (Baureiss & Kwong, 1979:93). At the same time traditional ceremonies were discarded, and whites were accepted within their ranks as associate members in an attempt to increase declining membership and to meet changing times (Baureiss, 1982a:19). The Winnipeg CBA has gradually diminished its assistance program, although in its rhetoric the promotion of the wellbeing of the Chinese and of good relations between Chinese and other citizens is still emphasized. Its paying membership has been drastically reduced, and in fact it cannot be called the spokesman for all Chinese (Baureiss & Kwong, 1979:95).

These organizations have definitely shifted from their previous extremizing actions to optimizing action, and traditional compliance has been lost in an open competitive social system.

The clan associations were limited in their endeavour to attract new members because their fictive nature was without appeal to Chinese originating from various regions of China. Since "clan" had lost its relevance, no uncertainty could be reduced. These Chinese accepted the nuclear kinship structure with its immediate extension, rather than reverting to the traditional lineage. In Calgary the clan associations have been reduced to social clubs organizing banquets, picnics, tea parties and other festive celebrations. Occasionally they still assist oldtimers in minor bureaucratic matters (Baureiss, 1971b:51).

The Chinese Dramatic Societies continue to exist in one form or another as adhocracies, despite the fact that various other organizations have their own musical and theatrical groups. In Calgary the Society had disappeared after World War II, but was reformed as the Wak Kui Musical Society in 1961, providing musical entertainment at Chinese celebrations and for various organizations outside of Chinatown (Baureiss, 1971b:53). The Winnipeg Chinese Dramatic Society remained unaffected by the change, although today it provides primarily "self-entertainment", mostly for a few middle-aged Chinese.

The Chinese Public Schools have encountered different experiences in Calgary and Winnipeg. In Calgary the school continues to flourish as the only Chinese school, attracting about 100 pupils. Accepting also non-Chinese children, its curriculum, taught in Chinese, familiarizes the pupils with Chinese geography, history, historical figures, songs and native dances (Baureiss, 1971b:51). In Winnipeg, however, the school was squeezed out in the 1970's by three other Chinese schools, all offering a somewhat different curriculum and attracting pupils from different socio-economic backgrounds.

The Chinese United Churches were able to maintain their membership and have weathered the competition from other (including Chinese) churches. In Winnipeg, church activity increased with the installation of a full-time pastor in 1949. After a temporary low in church activities in the early 1960's, renewed momentum made the financing of the entire church building possible. It was completed in 1971 (Baureiss & Kwong, 1979:75).

In summary, with the exception of the clan associations in Winnipeg, Chinese traditional organizations have survived the historic change, from a discriminatory to a less discriminatory social system, that brought about a heterogeneity among the Chinese population in Calgary and Winnipeg. Whereas the bureaucratic organizations retained their structure, and optimizing action was in accordance with the larger social system of the advanced capitalist society, collectivist organizations lost community dominance when discriminatory practices changed. Their generation and reduction of uncertainties and risks were increasingly irrelevant to the Chinese. Facing competition not only from within, but also from non-Chinese organizations, most of these organizations underwent a transformation from extremizing compliant action to optimizing compliant action— in the process redefining the content of orientation in which uncertainties could be reduced. Those which did not disappeared.

Nontraditional Organizations

The proliferation of new Chinese organizations in Calgary and Winnipeg gives credibility to the vitality of Chinese communities. However, these organizations were modelled after western organizations—accepting their bureaucratic structure and optimizing action. They have specialized by narrowly defining their systemic limits of orientation, and have consequently attracted a specific clientele within the heterogeneous Chinese population.

Some of these new organizations still restrict membership to individuals befitting specific criteria. Three clan associations (one of which was very short lived), the Chinese Businessmen's Club in Calgary, the Chinese Ladies Club in Winnipeg and the Student Associations in both cities restrict membership, at their name indicates.[6] Other organizations do in general reveal their specific objectives in their name, but an analysis reveals that each of these attract a specific segment of the Chinese population. In general, it was the new Chinese middle class, spearheaded by professionals and businessmen, that were the organizers of these new organizations.

In Winnipeg, besides the Chinese United Church, which draws it membership from the lower middle class around Chinatown, the Alliance Church draws its members from a stable core of members in the suburbs and also from the transient student population. Since an increasing number of its members speak English, it planned to conduct services in that language (Baureiss & Kwong, 1979:102). The Winnipeg Mandarin Church, affiliated with the Mennonite Church, primarily attracts students from overseas (Hong Kong, Taiwan, Singapore and Malaysia); they make up about 60% of its members (Baureiss & Kwong, 1979:98-103). Calgary, with the Chinese United Church, has also seen the emergence of three other Chinese language churches. The Chinese Pentecostal Church provides services in Cantonese only, because it caters to newly arrived immigrants and some students from Hong Kong (Hoe, 1976:174). Membership of the Chinese Alliance Church is comprised about eighty percent of students from Hong Kong. It conducts services in Cantonese and English (Hoe, 1976:175). Finally, the Chinese Gospel Church consists of some thirty-five members who became disenchanted with the Chinese Pentecostal Church in 1973 (Hoe, 1976:176). Despite the fact that they attract members from various segments of the Chinese population, the Chinese churches are no doubt in competition for membership with one another, and also with other churches, since some Chinese have opted for membership in non-Chinese churches as well.

Although the Calgary Chinese Public School was the only one of its kind in that city in 1973, the Winnipeg Chinese Public School could not weather the competition from three other schools and was dissolved.[7] Although they make the same general effort to help Chinese youngsters retain awareness of the Chinese cultural heritage, these schools' curricula differ somewhat, thereby appealing to different sub-populations. The Manitoba Academy of Chinese Studies teaches both Mandarin and Cantonese, and Chinese folk and classical music, and also offers Chinese geography and history in English. The Chinese Institute of Language and Arts offers Cantonese and Mandarin language courses and English classes for adults. The Chinese Alliance Church started its own school using textbooks published in Hong Kong and San Francisco. Chinese geography and history are incorporated in its language program.

The Chinese Cultural Society of Calgary was formed to promote Chinese culture and heritage and to maintain contacts with China. The Sien Lok Society was organized to counteract the proposed destruction of Calgary's Chinatown under the urban renewal scheme. But when the threat had subsided, it changed its objective towards a proposed cultural complex in Chinatown (Baureiss, 1971b:52). The formation of the United Calgary Chinese Association (UCCA) was in response to the lack of a CPA and to counteract the Sien Lok Society. Its office holders came from the business section remaining in Chinatown; they argued that the Sien Lok Society did not represent the interests of all Chinese. Even though it claimed all Chinese automatically as members, it had little influence on the Calgary scene (Baureiss, 1971b:53). Calgary also has three recreational clubs (Chinese Golf, Chinese Bowling, Chinese Curling Club) that attract Chinese businessmen and their wives, and also welcome non-Chinese.

In Winnipeg the Chinese Manitoba Fellowship was formed by professionals and now has accepted businessmen to broaden its base. It is an organization that has interlinking office holders with some other organizations and is influential within these. The Chinese Christian Fellowships in both cities are student-oriented religious organizations, assisting new students to cope in their new environment (Baureiss & Kwong, 1979:100).

In summary, the emergence of so many Chinese organizations, and their duplication in similar areas of uncertainty reduction, reflects the heterogeneity of the historical-cultural experience of the Chinese population in Calgary and Winnipeg. The differences are found in the orientation systems by which uncertainty is generated and reduced, not in the types of decision process. As Chinese organizations have been modelled along the optimizing decision process in order to reduce risks, they have not only emphasized primacy of one of the three orientational sub-systems but have also further narrowed the systemic limits of orientation to functional specificity. Their bureaucratic structure and their optimizing action places both old and new Chinese organizations into the same type, and it is in this context that I have suggested that further typification according to the primacy of the orientational system may have some merit (Baureiss, 1982b).

Conclusion

Analyzing ethnic organizations within the larger historically-specific context is essential for the explanation of their emergence, adaptation and dissolution. Discriminatory practices in the first half of this century against the Chinese in Canada resulted in the formation of Chinese collectivistic, bureaucratic and adhocratic organizations, reflecting respectively their extremizing, optimizing and autonomous primacy of action. The collectivist type of organizations were by far the most significant for community closure, requiring compliance to extremizing action.

Permitting a heterogeneous Chinese population equal access to the technological, institutional and communal systems in which uncertainties can be reduced,

Chinese organizations were confronted with a challenge. The relaxation of immigration laws and the discontinuation of China's influence upon the Chinese abroad affected the resilience of the Chinese in Calgary and Winnipeg. This in turn had a paramount effect on Chinese organizations.

This change cannot be explained simply by assuming that organizations adapt in order to survive as functionalist theorists assume. They take a biased sample of those organizations who have adapted (their present elements must have contributed to systems maintenance), and ignore those which have not.[8] Turner's non-teleological argument of bureaucratic growth—that organizations not making profit either go out of business, divest resources, or split into smaller corporate units—is relevant to any organizational analysis. He continues to argue that there is no grand purpose dictating organizational size in the sense that further growth "decreases survival and thus sets into motion selection against the direction of the trend" (Turner, 1978:107). In this line of thought I argue there is no grand purpose that organizations will always adapt to new situations.

Goal-succession theory follows functionalism, accepting the same teleological principle. This theory maintains that organizations change organizational goals (i.e. areas of uncertainties) when previous goals are reached or become irrelevant. It fails to explain why some organizations change goals (apparently in order to survive) but others do not. More importantly, however, this theory assumes optimizing actions and consequently cannot account for non-bureaucratic organizations, as well as for the transformation from one type to another. Its emphasis on formal-rationality of action allows only for changes in systemic limits of uncertainty reduction (various goals), but not for changes in the type of decision processes.

When the proposed typology as developed by general organizational theory is reduced to its primary principle, and placed into the historically-specific context, it is useful for a better understanding of ethnic organizations. Their emergence, adaptation, and dissolution can be adequately explained in this context. Beyond their typification based on the primary type of decision process they employ, and on which their structure is built, I have suggested that further typification according to orientational sub-systems may be fruitful. Their variability, however, reflects each ethnic group's unique historical-cultural experiences and the discrimination (or lack of it) they encounter in the larger social system.

Footnotes

1. It should be clear that I refer to ethnic organizations and not to ethnic collectivities. Indeed, the latter enter frequently into competition with labour. Ethnic businesses or businesses operated by ethnic individuals also compete on the larger market; these are not included in this analysis.

2. In the subsequent analysis it is not possible to isolate the effects of changes in discriminatory practices directly affecting organization, since the lessening of discrimination permitted entry of a new type of Chinese immigrant that certainly had an

effect on organizational change. New organizations such as the student associations would not otherwise have been formed. Thus I have to accept the change in Chinese population structure as an intervening variable to explain the effect of changing discrimination on organizations. To test the effect between change in discrimination and organizational change, ethnic groups with a stable population would have to be analysed.

3. As one oldtimer reported: "If you didn't join them, they would not help you to look for a job, neither did they allow you in their meetings" (Hoe, 1976:71).

4. Lyman's reference to community dominance by Chinese organizations in the United States through a combination of economic, charitable, judicial and political control addresses the same issue (Lyman, 1974:29-35).

5. Chinese did quite actively get involved in the local YMCA's. As early as 1913 they made use of the facilities for physical fitness and in the 1930's the Calgarian Chinese had formed their own hockey team (Hoe, 1976:90). I consider however the YMCA a different organization apart from the missions. It could be termed as another bureaucratic organization.

6. The Kung Fu Club's members are primarily non-Chinese. Its objective is to impart a correct attitude towards the art of Kung Fu, pride and a competitive spirit (Baureiss & Kwong, 1979:11-112).

7. In 1979 the CPA also claimed to operate a school, but its operation was confined to teaching five to six students Cantonese, while other schools attracted between 70 to 100 students (Baureiss & Kwong, 1979:108).

8. Structural-functionalism takes the worst from biology. "Hair of animals grew longer in the arctic because it was cold in order to survive"—imputation of teleology of adaptation—rather than "Those animals with long hair were able to survive in the arctic".

References

Babchuk, Nicholas and Wayne C. Gordon
  1962 **Voluntary Association in the Slum**. University of Nebraska Studies. No. 27, Lincoln: University of Nebraska Press.
Baureiss, Gunter
  1971a "The City and the Subcommunity: The Chinese of Calgary". Unpublished M.A. Thesis, the University of Calgary.
  1971b "The Chinese Community of Calgary", **Canadian Ethnic Studies**, 3(1):43-45.
  1974 "The Chinese Community in Calgary", **Alberta Historical Review, 2** (Spring):1-8.
Baureiss, G. and J. Kwong
  1979 **The History of the Chinese Community of Winnipeg**. Report to the Chinese Community Committee, Winnipeg.
Baureiss, Gunter
  1980 "Chinese Organizational Development", **Canadian Ethnic Studies,** 12(3):124-130.
  1981 "Institutional Completeness: Its Use and Misuse in Ethnic Relations Research", **The Journal of Ethnic Studies**, 9(2):101-110.
  1982a "Ethnic Resilience and Discrimination: Two Chinese Communities in Canada", **The Journal of Ethnic Studies**, 10(1):67-87.

1982b "Towards a Theory of Ethnic Organizations", **Canadian Ethnic Studies**, Vol. XIV(2):21-42.

Baureiss, G. and I. Driedger
1982c "Winnipeg Chinatown: Demographic, Ecological and Organizational Change, 1900-1980", **Urban History Review**, (Forthcoming).

Gerth, H.H. and C.W. Mills (eds)
1964 **From Max Weber: Essays in Sociology.** New York: Oxford University Press.

Habermas, Jurgen
1975 **Legitimation Crisis.** Boston Beacon Press.

Hammond, Dorothy
1972 **Associations.** Reading, Ma.: Addison-Wesley Publishing Company.

Hausknect, Murray
1962 **The Joiners: A Sociological Description of Voluntary Association Membership in the United States.** Totowa, N.J.: Bedminister.

Hoe, Ban Seng
1976 **Structural Changes to Two Chinese Communities in Alberta, Canada.** Natural Museum of Man: Mercury Series.

Johnson, G.
1979 "Chinese Family and Community in Canada: Tradition and Change", in J.I. Elliot, (ed.), **Two Nations, Many Cultures, Ethnic Groups in Canada.** Scarborough: Prentice-Hall of Canada Ltd.

Jung, Richard
1965 "Systems of Orientation" in Manfred Kochen (ed.) **Some Problems in Information Science.** New York: The Scarecrow Press.

Lyman, S.
1974 **Chinese Americans.** New York: Random House.

Price, John
1979 **Indians in Canada: Cultural Dynamics.** Scarborough, Ontario: Prentice-Hall of Canada Ltd.

Radecki, Henry
1976 "Ethnic Voluntary Organizational Dynamic in Canada: A Report", **International Journal of Comparative Sociology**, 17:276-284.
1979 **Ethnic Organizational Dynamics: The Polish Groups in Canada.** Waterloo: Wilfrid Laurier University Press.

Rothschild-Whitt, Joyce
1979 "The Collectivist Organizations", **American Sociological Review.** 44(4):509-827.

Sills, David
1957 **The Volunteers,** New York: The Free Press.
1968 "Voluntary Associations: Sociological Aspects", D.L. Sills (ed.) **International Encyclopedia of the Social Sciences**, Vol. 16, New York: Macmillan.

Smith, C. and A. Freedman
1972 **Voluntary Associations: Perspectives on the Literature.** Cambridge, Mass.: Harvard University Press.

Turner, Jonathan, H.
  1978   **The Structure of Sociological Theory**. Homewood, Illinois: The Dorsey
          Press.
Weber, Max
  1978   **Economy and Society**. Berkeley: University of California Press.

11

Institutional Controls and Their Impact
On Japanese Canadian Social Relations: 1877-1977

K. Victor Ujimoto
  University of Guelph

According to Dashefsky and Shapiro (1976:5), identity is a concept that is used "to describe the individual's sense of who he is or she is". They argue that there are two major sources of a person's identity: the social roles that constitute the shared definitions of appropriate behaviour, and the individual's life history. As illustrated in Figure 11-1, I will examine the historical aspects of the Japanese Canadian experience in Canada, discuss some of the major components or factors that influenced the ways of feeling, thinking, and behaving of Japanese Canadians, and conclude by discussing implications for the concept of a multicultural Canadian society.

The sense of who we are and how we relate to others in Canadian society obviously depends on whether we occupy the majority or minority position in the Canadian social structure. Another way of looking at this is to see whether a group occupies a dominant or subordinate position in terms of decision making and in influencing others; that is, the amount of power possessed. Usually, at least in terms of political influence, the demographic dimension of a given ethnic group in Canada is very important. The numerical size of the group, where they are located geographically, their role in the economy, their level of overall education, and the occupational positions all tend to influence not only the identity of the ethnic group, but also the attitudes of the dominant groups towards the minority group. Attitudes in turn govern social relationships and the degree to which meaningful social interaction can take place.

Previous studies have been dominated by the overemphasis of the assimilation and acculturation perspectives. Often, the ethnic group's success or failure in the

Figure 11-1

Factors Influencing Interpersonal Relations in the Japanese Canadian Family

	1877-1907	1908-1940	1941-1948	1949-1982
	Issei	Issei Nisei	Issei Nisei Sansei	Issei Nisei Sansei Yonsei Postwar Immigrants

I. Institutional Controls

- legal
- political
- economic
- international events

II. Demographic Factors

- group size
- geographic distribution
- residential segregation
- standard of living

III. Sociological Factors

- traditional cultural elements
- social relations based on a system of obligations
- perceptions based on majority group values
- aspects of social organization within the ethnic community
- behavioural factors (language retention, identity, folklore, folkways, dress etc.)
- socialization

Changing Patterns of Interpersonal Relations

host society was assessed in terms of the degree of conformity with the dominant Anglo-Saxon culture and behaviour. The predominant ideology which eventually developed out of many years of colonial domination was an ideology based on the belief of "White Supremacy" over all other racial groups. In Canada, that the white race was superior to all other races was often a dominant theme perpetuated by the various churches and, in particular, by the missionaries who in their enthusiasm for financial and other support from their home churches over-emphasized the racial and cultural differences between Orientals, the "natives", or the "heathens" and the superior Westerners. Thus, in order to comprehend the anti-Oriental hysteria and the treatment received by the *issei* or first generation Japanese immigrants in Canada between 1877 and 1948, it is essential, as noted by Bolaria (1979:2), "to draw historical connections between international colonialism, treatment of non-white immigrants as colonial subjects, and the pattern of racial domination and exploitation here". Unlike many non-European groups, the Japanese have been successful, until the Meiji Restoration in 1868 at least, in resisting foreign domination and other influences. In this regard, the characteristics of the colonization process may not be directly relevant. Nevertheless, the important point to note is the question of what happens in a society where the dominant ideology of racial superiority is suddenly undermined by the adaptive capacity of a minority previously regarded as being inferior. The study of the social history of the first generation Japanese Canadians provides some insights as to what can happen when the adaptive capacity of a minority group develops into economic competition. The concomitant influence of the various historical factors on the *nisei* or second generation Japanese Canadians can also be discerned.

In examining the social history of the Japanese in Canada, Shimpo (1974:3) suggests four stages or periods into which Japanese Canadian history may be divided. These periods are based on the legal status of the Japanese Canadians in Canada which are as follows:

1. The period of Free Immigration (1877-1907),
2. The period of Controlled Immigration (1908-1941),
3. The period of Deprived Civil Rights (1941-1948),
4. The period of Restored Civil Rights (1949 to present).

Shimpo's categorization scheme is useful in examining historical data because more objective historical data are becoming available today as previously confidential and secret archival materials are gradually released to the public.

The Period of Free Immigration: 1877-1907

The first period may be characterized as one in which problems stemming from cultural and racial differences eventually culminated in the race riots of 1907. However, general hostility and agitation against the Chinese and Japanese immigrants commenced much earlier. As early as 1872 a series of legislative attempts to impose a head tax on the Chinese were proposed. In 1885 the federal government finally bowed to public pressure and passed a bill which imposed the $50 head tax on the Chinese. Although this act was specifically aimed at the

Chinese, it signalled the first of several measures passed by the Dominion parliament to restrict Asian immigration to Canada. It is of some interest to note that prior to this legislation, 15,701 Chinese had entered British Columbia between 1881 and 1884 to work on the construction of the CPR. Woodsworth (1941:35) notes that with the CPR nearing completion, there was evidence that "the federal government consented to check Chinese immigration only when it was assured that sufficient cheap labour was available to complete the railway." This statement aptly describes the colonial mentality and the ideology of racial exploitation prevalent during this period.

There were other legislative attempts to limit Chinese immigration but these attempts had equal consequences for the Japanese. When the 1891 census revealed that 8,910 Chinese out of a total of 9,129 Chinese in Canada were in British Columbia, the provincial legislature requested to the Dominion government that the Chinese head tax be raised to $200. Woodsworth (1941:41) notes that objection to the entry of the Japanese was raised for the first time, and it was also proposed that similar restrictions be applied to the Japanese. This proposal did not receive the required legislative support. Subsequently, in 1892, another attempt was made to increase the Chinese head tax to $500 but this was also defeated.

The provincial legislature continued to press for an increased head tax on the Chinese but their demands were repeatedly refused by the federal government. Consequently, the provincial government took steps within its power and retaliated by disenfranchising the Japanese in 1875. In 1896, provincial disenfranchisement was extended to include municipal elections, and both Chinese and Japanese were "declared ineligible to vote in municipal elections" (Woodsworth, 1941:42). The British Columbia legislature went even further in ensuring that the Chinese and Japanese were prevented from participating in the electoral processes by proposing an amendment to the naturalization laws so that a residency requirement of ten years had to be satisfied prior to naturalization. It was at this juncture that international politics intervened and the federal government rejected the amendment on the grounds that such an amendment would violate the existing treaties between Great Britain, China, and Japan. As expected, the provincial legislasture reverted once more to other means at its disposal and in 1897 passed the Alien Labour Act which "prohibited the employment of Chinese or Japanese on works authorized by the provincial government" (Woodsworth, 1941:42). Once again, recognizing international treaty rights, the Dominion government disallowed the provincial legislation. Subsequently, the provincial legislature attempted to prohibit the Chinese and Japanese from work in coal mines but this was declared unconstitutional. A further attempt to prohibit the employment of Chinese and Japanese was made in 1898 through the Labour Relation Act. The provisions of this act were similar to the Alien Labour Act and thus disallowed by the federal government.

It was becoming quite clear to the provincial legislature that the Dominion government was not about to approve any discriminatory legislation which may have international repercussions. Consequently, it was proposed by the provincial legislature to insert a clause in the Immigration Act of 1900 that "all intending immigrants must make written applications, in some European language, to the provincial secretary" (Woodsworth, 1941:43). This attempt was declared *ultra vires* but it did not prevent the provincial government from proposing another act in 1903 which "stipulated that no person unable to speak English should hold any position of trust in a mine" (Woodsworth, 1943:43). Once again, federal authorities disallowed the act. While the above legislations were being prepared, the provincial government, in 1898 and 1899, attempted to have the Chinese head tax increased to $500 and to have it extended to the Japanese as well, but was not successful.

The various attempts by the British Columbia government to enact discriminatory and racist pieces of legislation were not occurring in a vacuum. Public agitation in the province had been increasing gradually and the Chinese were moving into the urban centers of eastern Canada. Woodsworth (1941:43) has documented some of the public sentiments expressed at this time:

> The Chinese are a people that Canada can afford to exclude. They are producers in no sense of the word. They do not take to farming. They are not needed as scavengers. One Doukhobor is worth a dozen Chinese. In addition to their worthlessness as producers, the Chinese are decidedly a low caste people. They are filthy in their habits and a menace to the public health. The Chinese will not assimilate with the people of any civilized country (**Toronto World**).

As a result of the continued public protests, Prime Minister Wilfrid Laurier was forced in 1900 to amend the Chinese Immigration Act of 1885 by increasing the head tax to $100. An interesting aspect of this amendment was that it did not extend to the Japanese as originally intended by the provincial legislature. The main reason for not including the Japanese derives from the fact that the Japanese consul-generals had protested vigorously to the Governor-General of Canada all aspects of the anti-Japanese legislation. These protests were dispatched eventually to the home government in London, England. The Japanese government had also filed a formal protest and this coincided with a sequence of international events which ultimately influenced Laurier's decision to exclude the Japanese from head tax legislation.

Although the federal authorities were able to satisfy the requests of the Imperial government to enable them to strengthen their Anglo-Japanese alliance, the British Columbia legislature was still faced with mounting public agitation and much resentment. Thus, on August 31, 1900, the provincial legislature passed an immigration act which required a language test for those entering the province. This was disallowed but these several attempts over the years to restrict and control Chinese and Japanese immigration, as well as where they may be employed, do provide us with blatant examples of racial discrimination. As noted earlier, the Chinese and Japanese were prevented from participating in the electoral process of their community. This form of social control which clearly illustrates the racist ideology prevalent at the time and which gave "rise to normative prescriptions designed to prevent the subordinate racial group from

126   *Racial Minorities in Multicultural Canada*

equal participation in association or procedures that are stable, organized, and systematized; has been termed "institutional racism" by Wilson (1973:34). Institutional racism did not end with the Vancouver race riots of 1907 and in order to understand why, it is necessary to examine the demographic and social factors related to Japanese immigration between 1884 and 1907.

One of the reasons for the rapid extension of the anti-Chinese sentiment to the Japanese was the realization that there was a sudden increase in the number of Japanese arriving at Canadian ports. By 1901, 4,578 Japanese were in British Columbia (Woodsworth, 1941:63). The Japanese were engaged in the boat building, fishing, lumbering and mining industries as well as in railway work. Eventually, their control of the boat building and fishing industries provided an economic threat to the white man. The commission appointed to investigate Oriental immigration in British Columbia reported that the Japanese

> find employment where they can, in getting out wood and bolts, in mills, boat building, and other employment, working at a wage upon which a white man cannot decently support himself and his family, and creating a feeling so pronounced and bitter among a large class of whites, as to endanger the peace and be a fruitful source of international irritation.... Almost all witnesses examined by the commission agreed that the Japanese were more independent, energetic, aggressive, and consequently more dangerous, than the Chinese. They were ready and anxious to adopt, in appearance at least, the manners and modes of Western life, but they also fell readily into the vices of the whites. They availed themselves of every opportunity to learn English and often made it a condition of their contracts of hiring that they might do so. They were not so reliable as the Chinese in respect to contracts. They worked for less wages than the Chinese and in some industries drove the Chinese out. With respect to sanitary conditions, their boarding-houses were as crowded as those of the Chinese, but were usually cleaner. As to morality, owing to their different moral standard it was unfair to compare them with the whites. The relative absence of convictions showed them to be law-abiding (Woodsworth, 1941:64-65).

As can be seen from the above quotation, the various social characteristics attributed to the Japanese and perceived by the local residents as threatening rests upon several aspects of cultural differences. The Japanese emphasis on frugality and hard work was reflected in their day-to-day activities and in their daily customs and habits which were all based on the traditional value system. The social organization of the Japanese was centered on shared needs as well as on a sense of group consciousness. Group solidarity within the Japanese community was further strengthened by the fact that they were physically and socially segregated in their residential and work environments. Within this bounded territorial space, it was not difficult to retain the highly systematized and inter-dependent social relations which were based upon the principle of social and moral obligations and traditional Japanese practices of mutual assistance such as the *oyabun-kobun* (parent-child) and *sempai-kohai* (senior-junior) relationship. The *oyabun-kobun* relationship promoted non kin social ties to be formed on the basis of a wide ranging set of obligations. Nakane (1970:42-43) describes the *oyabun-kobun* relationship. He states that "the *kobun* receives benefits or help from his *oyabun*, such as assistance in securing employment or promotion, and advice on the occasion of important decision-making. The *kobun*, in turn, is ready to offer his services whenever the *oyabun* requires them." Similarly, the *sempai-kohai* relationship was based on a sense of responsibility whereby the *sempai or senior member assumed the responsibility of overlooking the social, economic, and religious affairs of the kohai* or junior member. Such a system of social relations provided for a highly cohesive and well unified collectivity which possessed a high degree of competitive power in the economic sphere of daily activities. It was this increasing competitive economic power held by the Japanese which eventually precipitated the 1907 race riots in Vancouver. This external hostility further strengthened the social consciousness of the Japanese community.

Another aspect of traditional Japanese social relations which characterized both the *oyabun-kobun* and *sempai-kohai* systems was the emphasis placed on one's "sense of duty, loyalty, and obligations to employers" (Sugimoto, 1972:92). Out of a sense of unquestioning loyalty, the *kobun* or *kohai* blindly followed the orders by the *oyabun* or *sempai* and as Sugimoto (1972:92) notes, this sometimes led the Japanese workers to "such acts as strikebreaking and the undermining of wage structure". Ironically, this relatively successful adaptation by the Japanese to survive in a new environment, which was only made possible because of their reliance on the traditional values and customs, now became the main reason for the hostile white community to prevent the Japanese from becoming permanent settlers.

The high degree of social organization which characterized the Japanese Canadian community at this time may have been perceived quite differently by the members of the white community who did not fully appreciate the Japanese system of social relations, which emphasized one's strong sense of duty, loyalty, and mutual obligations. Instead, the highly organized Japanese Canadian community was perceived as an economic and political threat and consequently, the traditional colonial ideology of the survival of the fittest at the expense of the inferior became untenable when the dominant white group was suddenly threatened.

The Period of Controlled Immigration: 1908-1940

As noted earlier, the second period of Japanese social history is between 1908 and 1940, representing a period of restricted or controlled immigration. The "Gentlemen's Agreement" of 1908 provided the following conditions which restricted Japanese immigration to the following four classes of people (Woodsworth, 1941:90):

1. returning immigrants and their wives and children,
2. emigrants specially engaged by Japanese residents in Canada for bona fide personal or domestic service,

3. contract emigrants, where the terms of the contract, works to be done, and names and standing of the intended employers were satisfactorily specified, and

4. emigrants brought in under contract by Japanese resident agricultural holders in Canada.

The Japanese consular officials issued the necessary certificates for contract labourers, although final approval of the contract by the Canadian government was required. Furthermore, agricultural labourers were limited in number in direct proportion to the number of acreage held by the Japanese, usually 10 labourers to 100 acres of land held (Woodsworth, 1941:91).

One of the consequences of the "Gentlemen's Agreement" of 1908 was that the demographic composition of the Japanese community changed gradually. The lack of clarification on whether or not the maximum quota of 400 Japanese immigrants was applicable to all four classes of immigrants caused some confusion and anxiety. The Japanese government interpreted the quota restrictions to be applicable only to domestic servants and agricultural labourers and that wives and children of Japanese already in Canada were exempt from the restrictions. The immigration data presented in Table 11-1 indicates that Japanese immigration during the period 1908-1929 exceeded the annual quota of 400 Japanese immigrants except for two years. Another interesting observation to note in Table 11-1 is that the number of Japanese women coming to Canada exceeded that of men nearly every year. Many of the Japanese male immigrants who had arrived in Canada prior to the "Gentlemen's Agreement" of 1908 were unmarried. Not having the means of returning to Japan to get married, they relied upon arranged marriages on the "picture bride" system, a system whereby pictures of the prospective bride and groom were exchanged and the decision to marry made after consultation with relatives and possibly a *nakodo* (go-between). It wasn't very long before natural increases in the Japanese Canadian population became a "problem" in British Columbia as Adachi (1976:85) has noted, "another argument for exclusion or expulsion was ready for exploitation".

The Japanese labourers who came to British Columbia around 1907 were brought in mainly through contractual arrangements between Japanese emigration companies and Canadian importers of labour such as the Canadian Pacific Railway and the Wellington Colliery. Although World War I was on the horizon, the Anglo-Japanese Alliance enabled Japan to be one of Great Britain's allies and consequently, there was very little attempt to restrict Japanese immigration at this time. As a result of World War I, there was a shortage of labour in Canada and this fact also dampened anti-Oriental feelings between 1914 and 1918. Anti-Asian agitations developed once more after the world war because of the general state of economic depression and resulting unemployment which became acute because of the returning soldiers.

The strong control of the fishing industry held by the Japanese by this time once again became a matter of concern for some British Columbia politicians. In 1919 there was an attempt to limit the number of fishing licenses issued to Japanese fishermen. The provincial legislature also tried to prohibit immigration

Table 11-1

Japanese Immigration to Canada 1901 - 1929

Fiscal Years	Male	Female	Children	Total
1901	--	--	--	6
1902	--	--	--	--
1903	--	--	--	--
1904	--	--	--	--
1905	281	62	11	354
1906	1,614	264	44	1,922
1907	1,766	242	34	2,042
1908	6,945	566	90	7,601
1909	312	153	30	495
1910	104	154	33	271
1911	170	217	50	437
1912	322	362	81	765
1913	252	424	48	724
1914	354	447	55	856
1915	191	358	43	592
1916	148	233	20	401
1917	301	310	37	648
1918	450	370	54	883
1919	584	530	64	1,178
1920	280	389	42	711
1921	145	338	49	532
1922	140	300	31	471
1923	141	197	31	369
1924	184	233	31	448
1925	182	269	50	501
1926	126	205	90	421
1927	115	250	110	475
1928	134	258	86	478
1929	121	214	110	445

Source: Charles J. Woodsworth, <u>Canada and the Orient.</u>
Toronto: Macmillan Company of Canada Limited,
1941. p. 289.

from Asia by asking the Dominion government to amend the British North America Act so that the provinces will have the "power to make laws prohibiting Asiatics from acquiring proprietory interest in agricultural, timber and mining lands or in fishing or other industries, and from employment in these industries" (Woodsworth, 1941:107). A further resolution was that "Canada should not adhere to any treaty which would limit provincial authority in legislation pertaining to immigration" (Woodsworth, 1941:107). These attempts by the provincial legislature were unsuccessful because of the original provisions of the BNA Act which defined federal-provincial powers with references to aliens and also because of the provisions of the Anglo-Japanese Treaty of 1913.

In 1922, Mackenzie King and the Japanese government entered negotiations to limit Japanese immigration to Canada. The result of these negotiations was a further reduction in Japanese immigration from the original quota of 400 to 150 for domestic servants and agricultural labourers. No restrictions were placed on wives or children from entering Canada as stipulated in the "Gentlemen's Agreement" of 1908 and as a direct result, 448 Japanese entered Canada in 1924. Because of the continued increases in Japanese immigration in subsequent years (as shown in Table 11-1) the Japanese government was criticized for not living up to its earlier agreement. In 1927, another report was prepared for the British Columbia legislature (Woodsworth, 1941:113) "which drew attention to the high birth rate of the Japanese and to the large number of Orientals employed in the lumbering, fishing, and in the various licensed trades in the province. It showed also that the Orientals owned land and property in British Columbia to the extent of several million dollars". Needless to say, anti-Asian feelings were rekindled and Ottawa was pressured to reconsider Asian exclusion.

The ultimate result of the negotiations undertaken by King and the Japanese government was the revised gentlemen's agreement which went into effect on September 1, 1928. The conditions of this agreement were as follows (Woodsworth, 1941:115).:

> that the total number of Japanese immigrants, including not only domestic servants and agricultural labourers but wives and children of Japanese resident in Canada should not exceed 150 annually. It was also agreed that the "picture bride" system would end; that passports of Japanese immigrants would be visaed by the Canadian Minister in Japan; and that provisions of the Canadian Immigration Act would be applicable to Japanese immigrants, notwithstanding the provisions of the Anglo-Japanese treaty of commerce and navigation.

The immediate impact of the above agreement on Japanese immigration is shown in Table 11-2. The data indicate that Japanese immigration under the terms of the agreement was well below the established quota of 150 immigrants. The terms of the agreement relate only to Japanese nationals and the data for others outside the agreement refer to "Japanese British subjects who have been abroad and have returned, or have gone abroad and married and brought their wives back to Canada, or have had wives and families and brought them back" (Woodsworth, 1941:115).

TABLE 11-2

Japanese Immigration to Canada 1929-1940

Fiscal Years	Under Agreement				Outside Agreement				Total			
	Male	Female	Children	Total	M.	F.	C.	Total	M.	F.	C.	Total
1929	37	43	20	100	4	14	5	23	41	57	25	123
1930	69	46	19	134		37	21	58	69	83	40	192
1931	50	53	24	127		53	24	77	50	106	48	204
1932	57	57	21	135		42	18	60	57	99	39	195
1933	30	47	17	94		16	5	21	30	63	22	115
1934	46	40	13	99		3	3	6	46	43	16	105
1935	38	25	11	74		15	3	18	38	40	14	92
1936	24	34	10	68		15		15	24	49	10	83
1937	24	42	14	80		19	4	23	24	61	18	103
1938	22	44	18	84		24	10	34	22	68	28	118
1939	1	22	6	29		34	4	17	1	35	10	46
1940	1	17	3	21		14	1	15	1	31	4	36

Source: Charles J. Woodsworth, *Canada and the Orient*. Toronto: Macmillan Company of Canada Limited, 1941, p. 2.

Although the annual immigration quota was low, the actual number of Japanese immigrants who entered British Columbia was even lower. Yet, anti-Japanese feelings continued to increase in the province, the basic argument being that there were "too many Orientals already". Charges continued to circulate that the Japanese were entering the country illegally and in 1931, concrete evidence to substantiate these charges was provided by the RCMP when they uncovered an illegal immigrant smuggling scheme. Subsequent investigations revealed that "some 2,500 Japanese were found to have entered the country illegally in the 15 year period up to 1931" (Adachi, 1976:180). Continuing public outcry and charges eventually forced MacKenzie King to appoint a Board of Review in 1938 to investigate the charges that the Japanese were still entering the country illegally. The Board concluded that after 1931, the number of illegal Japanese entrants was negligible. An unannounced "visit" by the RCMP of selected Japanese communities provided a "controlled sample" of 1,862 Japanese who were examined and only 8 were found to have entered the country illegally (Woodsworth, 1941:118).

As noted earlier, external events continued to influence domestic political and social events. The Japanese intrusion into China led to fresh outbursts of anti-Japanese hostility and the conclusions of the Board of Review did not suppress the anti-Japanese feelings. The "Japanese problem" became a political issue and by the time of the federal election in 1935, it was also an election issue. The Japanese were not without friends as the new national political party, the Co-operative Commonwealth Federation (CCF) which was organized in 1932, served notice that if it came into power, legislation would be changed to give minorities of Oriental ancestry equal rights to become citizens by providing "equal treatment before the law of all residents of Canada irrespective of race, nationality or religious or political beliefs" (Adachi, 1976:181).

One of the issues which was still not resolved was the right to vote in elections by persons of Oriental descent. The 1895 act which denied the Japanese the right to a provincial vote had other serious racist implications as Adachi (1976:52) has noted:

> Not only did the 1895 act deny the provincial vote to those who became British subjects by naturalization but, still more important, it was to disqualify—on the basis of race—those children of immigrant parents who were born in Canada. The Japanese were also excluded from voting in municipal elections or for school trustees. Using the voters' list as the basis of qualification, the province effectively barred any Japanese from eligibility for office or from liability to, or privilege of, certain public services. Thus Japanese were excluded from being nominated for municipal office of any sort and for the office of school trustee, and from jury service. And the practice of using the provincial voters' list in compiling the Dominion list prevented Japanese from voting in federal elections; that is, the prior restriction imposed by the provincial authority extended, as a matter of practice, to the federal franchise.

It can be seen from the above that the disenfranchisement of the Japanese prevented them from full participation in several areas of professional employment because of the eligibility requirement of having one's name on the voters' list. For example, to secure hand logging licences required that the applicant be on the voters' list. Provincial legislation applied to "racial groups rather than to aliens" and as Adachi (1976:53) has noted, the denial of basic rights such as the right to vote and employment in professional occupations meant that for the Japanese Canadians, citizenship was meaningless or at best, symbolized the "status of second class citizenship".

In the meantime, Japanese Canadians had volunteered for the Boer War but were rejected. At the outbreak of World War I, the Canadian Japanese Association, which was formed in 1897, attempted to secure permission for Japanese Canadians to enlist in the Canadian Army and Navy but it was not until 1916 that permission was received from Ottawa to commence military training and to organize the Japanese Volunteer Corps. At the end of the three month training period, it was decided in Ottawa that there were insufficient volunteers to form a separate battalion and subsequently, the group was disbanded. Some of the original volunteers managed to enlist in Alberta and as soon as this welcome news reached Vancouver, more volunteers moved to Alberta to join the army. Adachi (1976:103) records that "the first group of Japanese went overseas with the 109th Battalion in the summer of 1916. The 13th Cavalry (the Princess Pats) included 42; the 192nd had 51 and the 175th included 57 Japanese. The 91st Battalion, which left in 1917, took the last of the volunteers".

It was not until the end of the first world war that the campaign to secure the franchise began in earnest. However, public sentiment remained against the granting of the franchise to Japanese Canadians, war veterans included. The hostile public reaction stemmed from the general economic situation at the end of the war and the concomitant unemployment situation faced by many of the returning soldiers. The Japanese control of the fishing industry by then only contributed to the increasing anti-Japanese feelings. The hostile environment reinforced even further the already highly cohesive Japanese community.

The fact that there was a large Japanese population characterized by a common language, religion, and similar occupations, mainly nonprofessional, meant that it was possible to form various social organizations. Friendship groups and prefectural associations numbered approximately 84 units in Vancouver in 1934 (Young, Reid, and Carrothers, 1938:108) and these organizations provided the cohesion to keep both formal and informal social networks intact in the Japanese community. Miyamoto (1972:224) notes that "the *kenjinkai* or prefectural association not only served as a means of drawing workers into particular businesses and training them, but also provided a network of relations that sustained the economy and determined its patterns." Association members were able to secure social and financial assistance from the prefectural associations and this fact, together with the strongly cohesive nature of the Japanese family, enabled the early Japanese immigrants to retain their competitive power in numberous service oriented business enterprises. It was precisely this highly co-operative institutional structure of the early Japanese community which once again resulted in open conflict with the members of the white community.

Because of the continuing economic competition from the Japanese, there were several legislative attempts to reduce Japanese Canadian economic activities. In 1921, the Oriental Orders-in-Council Validation Act provided that "in all contracts, leases and concessions made by the Government, provision should be made that no Chinese or Japanese should be employed in connection therewith" (Adachi, 1976:140). The act was declared *ultra vires*. There were even attempts to amend the BNA Act so that the province could pass a law which prohibited Japanese from owning or leasing land, a law which would have been similar to the Alien Land Law which was already in effect in California. Between 1923 and 1925, The Department of Marine and Fisheries "stripped close to a thousand licences from the Japanese, reducing their control of licenses by nearly half" (Adachi, 1976:142). Such economic harassment continued to plague the Japanese and consequently, many went into farming.

Although the Japanese farmers were given poor land to cultivate, it didn't take too long before hostility was diverted to the Japanese farmers who were too "efficient", a term which "was interpreted as another instance of peaceful penetration" (Adachi, 1976:149). The traditional Japanese practice of mutual assistance greatly aided the newcomers to farming but provided an economic threat to others. For example, the Steveston Japanese Farmers Company purchased land and later rented it out to former fishermen. By 1934, the Japanese farmers dominated the strawberry and other small fruits and vegetable operations in the Fraser Valley. Thus, the competitive problems previously encountered by the white fishermen were now shifted over to those in the farming, forestry, and small business occupations who were unable to compete effectively against the Japanese. The gradual success achieved by the Japanese Canadians in the various occupations and in business ventures obviously aroused some suspicion. One rumour which was transmitted far and wide was that the Japanese Canadian success in various business ventures was directly attributable to the financial support of large business interests in Japan and that capital was channelled into the various ventures in Canada through the Japanese Consulate. Although factual evidence to support the various rumours was completely lacking, public perception of the competitive Japanese Canadian threat in several key industries such as fishing, forestry, and farming heightened to such an extent that the outbreak of World War II provided the anti-Japanese agitators with a valid excuse to take even more severe action against the Japanese Canadians than in the past. Such were the social and economic conditions as the Japanese Canadians entered what we have called the third period in Japanese Canadian social history, the period of deprived civil rights which spanned from 1941 to 1948.

The Period of Deprived Civil Rights: 1941-1948

In terms of civil rights, only the World War I veterans were able to secure the franchise in 1931. However, the supporters of this legislation made certain that the right to vote did not extend to the descendants of the war veterans. Consequently, by 1940, the second generation Japanese born in Canada, the *nisei*, were still struggling to secure their full citizenship rights. In 1936, the *nisei* established an organization called the Japanese Canadian Citizens League (JCCL) "to provide an adequate machinery which would ultimately enable (the nisei) to qualify as an integral part of Canada" (Adachi, 1976:160). In the same year, the JCCL managed to send a delegation of four to Ottawa to appear before the Special Committee on Elections and Franchise Acts of the House of Commons. In spite of the racial discrimination, the Japanese Canadians were willing to prove their loyalty to Canada. When Canada entered the European War in 1939, the JCCL wired Prime Minister King to pledge Japanese Canadian support in the war effort in Europe. Concerning the telegram, Adachi (1976:188) quotes the speech by J.S. Woodsworth of the CCF as follows:

> I would have been almost ashamed, had I been the Prime Minister to read a telegram from the Japanese Candians pledging their loyalty, when we refuse to Canadian-born Japanese the same treatment that we give to other Canadians.

Even the *issei* organizations supported the Victory Loan Drive by sending in unsolicited donations. As it was the case during World War I, it was difficult to enlist in the Armed Services. Although the *nisei* had been medically examined, they were never called for training. The politicians were reluctant to accept the Japanese Canadians because of the franchise issue.

On January 8, 1941, Prime Minister MacKenzie King announced that "a special investigating committee had recommended that citizens of Japanese ancestry be exempted from service" (Adachi, 1976:189). King emphasized that this was because of the anti-Japanese hostility and the dangers it presented. It is of some interest to look back on the committee findings from our present historical vantage point. The committee found "no concrete evidence to support the charges of disloyalty and subversive activity...on the contrary they had an admirable record as law-abiding and decently behaved citizens" (Adachi, 1976:190). These findings did not have any influence on subsequent events, such as the compulsory registration by the RCMP of all persons of Japanese ancestry over the age of 16, and the mass evacuation of Japanese Canadians from the "protected areas" of British Columbia to concentration camps in the interior of the province. Instead of improvements in civil rights and freedom, social controls were enforced even further than before to the extent that Japanese Canadians were now required to carry a registration card at all times.

It is all the more remarkable to note that the registration process took place nearly three months prior to the outbreak of the Pacific War on December 7, 1941. Other restrictions were to follow, but as Adachi (1976:197) has aptly noted,

> To the Nisei, it was not a question of what they would do—as they were so often asked by curious friends—but of what Canada and white Canadians would do. For the past decade, Nisei had asserted their loyalty to Canada in whatever circumstances; they had co-operated in the oner- ous programme of the special registration; they had protested against

their exclusion from military service; they had contributed to the Canadian war effort in all ways open to them. They felt, therefore, that it was not their conduct that was now crucial but the attitude of British Columbians and of Canadians in general. The Nisei felt that the concepts of "fair play" and "British justice" would stand the sternest test.

Following the Japanese attack on Pearl Harbour, Canadian government response was immediate. Fishing boats owned by Japanese Canadians and naturalized citizens were impounded, a total of 1,200 boats. Japanese language schools were ordered closed. The three Japanese language newspapers published in Vancouver were also ordered to cease publication but the English language *The New Canadian* was allowed to continue publishing. By the end of December, 1941, anti-Japanese feelings were extremely volatile and several politicians were demanding "to remove all Japanese 'East of the Rockies'". There was no differentiation between Japanese nationals, naturalized citizens, and the Canadian born *nisei*. Surprisingly, however, the Vice-Chief of General Staff of the Canadian Army was not at all concerned about the "Japanese menace" and reported "fifth column activities". The Canadian Army showed no interest in the proposed evacuation of Japanese Canadians (Adachi, 1976:203).

The initial decision made by Ottawa on January 14, 1942 was not for a complete evacuation but for a compromise or "partial" evacuation which required that "all Japanese male nationals, aged 18 to 45 years, would be removed from the coast by April 1" (Adachi, 1976:208). Other measures announced were that all Japanese be prohibited from "fishing, serving on fishing boats, or holding licenses" and "forbidden to possess or use short-wave radio receiving sets, radio transmitters and cameras" (Adachi, 1976:209). The "partial" evacuation orders did not provide any direction whatsoever on the disposal of private property and the care of families being left behind. Consequently, the government order for "partial" evacuation remained inoperative until its provisions were extended on February 24, 1942 by Order-in-Council P.C. 1486, which provided the Minister of Justice Louis St. Laurent with complete powers "to control the movements of all persons of Japanese origin in certain 'protected areas'" (Adachi, 1976:216). The degree of control in the daily movements of the Japanese Canadians as well as other restrictions is illustrated by the regulations promulgated by the Minsiter of Justice on February 27, 1942.

The rationale for the decision on February 24, 1942 to evacuate all persons of Japanese origin regardless of citizenship from the "protected zone" of British Columbia has been more or less accepted until recently, when access to government documents became possible. Sunahara (1977:65) notes that it has been accepted that the federal position concerning the evacuation orders resulted directly from "the capitulation of the federal government to the demands of public opinion from British Columbia"; she argues however that "several factors undermine the all-encompassing power of public opinion in this instance". She (1977:92) suggests that other considerations may have prompted the federal government to take the action that it did; but, "just how much of this assessment was based in political considerations and how much in a genuine fear of the power of Japan will never by known".

In order to set the machinery of the evacuation order into motion, the British Columbia Security Commission was established on March 4, 1942. The Commission was chaired by Austin Taylor and consisted of the Assistant Commissioner of the RCMP and Assistant Commissioner of the Provincial Police. Order-in-Council P.C. 1665 provided the Commission with extra-ordinary powers (see Canada Gazette, March 11, 1942). For example, the Commission had complete control of one's movements within the protected zone. Section 12(1) outlined the conditions related to securities and properties which the evacuee was "unable to take with him". They were to be placed under the "safety" of the Custodian of Alien Property. Eventually, the Japanese Canadian evacuees were to lose their property through the "government's open breach of trust in later compulsory sale of property" (Adachi, 1976:218).

The first act of the British Columbia Security Commission was to round up some 2,500 persons of Japanese origin, mainly fishermen, who lived along the coast from Vancouver to Prince Rupert and on Vancouver Island. They were detained in the Hastings Park Exhibition Grounds in Vancouver which became the initial "assembly centre" prior to the relocation of the evacuees to the interior of the province. Adachi (1976:218) describes the assembly area and the handling of the evacuees as follows:

> The use of former stables and cattle stalls of the Livestock Building, only perfunctorily and hastily improvised for human habitation, was perhaps symbolic of the entire evacuation movement as the RCMP, with the assistance of the army, transported the first group of coastal Japanese to the Park beginning March 16, there to be "herded together like a bunch of cattle" as many complained. By March 25, as the RCMP accelerated the process of removal, 1,593 persons had been shipped to the Park. At the same time, men were being moved directly to road camps in the interior and in Ontario.

[handwritten marginal note: parallel to Nazi]

As noted by Adachi (1976:220), the authority of the Security Commission "to restrict, control, evacuate and detain—and even deport—Japanese without bringing charges against them derived from the encompassing powers of the War Measures Act of 1914, the same act which was invoked in Montreal, Quebec as recently as October 1970 during the Front de Liberation du Quebec situation. Aspects of social control imposed on the "members of the Japanese race" and now strictly enforced were the impoundment of automobiles, censorship of mails, and curfew from sunset to sunrise.

The distribution of the Japanese Canadian Evacuees to various interior locations and projects is shown in Table 11-3. The idea of having the Japanese Canadians build roads stemmed simply from the fact that British Columbia was in need of better transportation networks. Thus, having the evacuees working on road construction projects provided some means of controlling them as well. In addition to the British Columbia and Alberta road construction projects, there were several projects in Ontario.

At the same time, a number of evacuees were assigned to sugarbeet projects in Alberta, Manitoba, and in Ontario. Because housing had to be constructed for the evacuees at these internment camps, to label them "housing projects" seems to be somewhat misleading. Former mining towns or "ghost towns" in British Columbia which were renovated to house the evacuees included Greenwood (1,177 evacuees), Kaslo (964), Sandon (933), New Denver (1,505), and Slocan and the Slocan area (4,814). Descriptive accounts of life at these various camps are provided by La Violette (1948), Adachi (1976), Takashima (1971), and Nakano (1977).

The task of the Security Commission proceeded relatively easily because of the lack of serious resistance by the Japanese Canadians to the evacuation order. The sociological explanation for this behaviour stems from the traditional inculcation of certain cultural norms which emphasized unquestioning obedience to higher authority. Included in this notion of obedience were the concepts of duty and obligation. Also, the traditional emphasis on the group, conformity, and consensus decision-making was strongly reinforced in Canada during the earlier

Table 11-3

Distribution of Japanese Canadian Evacuees to Various Projects

Road Camp Projects	986
Sugar-Beet Projects	
Alberta	2,585
Manitoba	1,053
Ontario (males only)	350
Interior Housing	11,694
Self-Supporting Projects	1,161
Independent and Industrial Projects	431
Special Permits	1,337
Repatriation to Japan	42
Evacuated voluntarily prior to March, 1942	579
Internment Camps	669
In Detention, Vancouver	57
Hastings Park Hospital	105
TOTAL	21,079

Source: Forrest la Violette, **The Japanese Canadians and World War II**. Toronto: University of Toronto Press, p. 96.

periods of immigrant adjustment, because community leadership was provided mainly by the first generation Japanese or *issei*. The transfer of community leadership to the Canadian born *nisei* was invevitable and this gradual change commenced with the evacuation process. From the *nisei* point of view, Adachi (1976:226) notes that "they wished to prove that they were 'Canadian' by co-operating fully with the authorities". However, recognition as full-fledged Canadians did not materialize until June 15, 1948 when the last of the restrictive controls were removed and the Japanese Canadians finally secured the right to vote.

The Period of Restored Civil Rights: 1949-1982

The legislative controls imposed upon the Japanese Canadians through the War Measures Act and subsequent Order-in-Council were relaxed gradually. The freedom of geographic mobility was eased somewhat by Order-in-Council P.C. 946 on February 5, 1943, which provided Labour Minister Humphrey Mitchell with the power "to require, by order, any person of the Japanese race in any place in Canada to proceed to any other place in Canada at such times and in such manner as he many prescribe" (Adachi, 1976:261). This same Order-in-Council enabled Mitchell "to determine from time to time the localities in which persons of the Japanese race may reside". Although at the outset it may appear that Japanese Canadians were now free to move out of the internment camps just by applying for permission to do so to the Minister of Labour, such was not the case. The ulterior motive for passing the Order-in-Council appears to have been the acute shortage of labour in Eastern Canada and the fact that the government was attempting to apply the rules of National Selective Service to Canadian citizens. In this instance, the compulsory job placement regulations were applicable to Canadian citizens, and this condition placed the *nisei* in an awkward position, as it now seemed that they were considered as Canadian citizens just because it was convenient for the government to do so.

On August 1, 1943, travel restrictions became "less stringent" and as noted by Adachi (1976:257), the Japanese Canadian evacuees were now able to secure permission from the RCMP or the Security Commission for "temporary visits within certain limits... such as (1) entering a "protected area" of Canada; (2) crossing any provincial boundary; (3) changing residence; and (4) travelling, 'for any purpose whatsoever', a distance of more than 50 miles in British Columbia from a place of residence or for a period of 30 days or more". Several other restrictions were also gradually relaxed. In December 1943, the Department of Labour permitted single Japanese Canadian males to take jobs in the province. In April 1944, the use of cameras was permitted in the camps. It was not until the fall of 1945, however, that McGill University accepted a *nisei*. This latter example illustrates one of the more important consequences for the *nisei* in terms of future occupational mobility because of delayed access to higher education. McGill University's excuse for not admitting the *nisei* until this time was based on the excuse that it was involved in "vital war research".

One of the outstanding issues still to be resolved at the end of World War II concerned the deportation orders which affected many Japanese Canadians. Order-in-Council P.C. 7355 of December 15, 1945, provided the major categories of deportable people. These were as follows (Adachi, 1976:308):

1. Every person of 16 years of age or over, other than a Canadian national, who is a national of Japan resident in Canada and who has, since December 8, 1941, made a request for repatriation or has been interned for any reason as of midnight of September 1, 1945.

2. Every person who is a naturalized British subject, 16 years of age or over, who made a written request for repatriation which was not revoked in writing prior to September 1, 1945, the day before the unconditional surrender of Japan.

3. Every Canadian-born person of Japanese origin, 16 years of age or over, who has not revoked his request prior to the making of the labour Minister of an order for his deportation.

4. The wife and children under 16 years of age of any person against whom an order for deportation is made.

Labour Minister Mitchell had made arrangements for 800 deportees to leave from Vancouver on January 6, 1946, but opposition to the deportation orders was voiced by the Co-operative Committee on Japanese Canadians (CCJC) and also by other organizations such as the Civil Rights Defence Committee which was formed in Winnipeg. Many prominent Canadians opposed the deportation orders. As a result, Prime Minister King asked the Supreme Court of Canada to determine whether the deportation orders were *ultra vires*. According to Adachi (1976:315), "Five of Canada's Supreme Court Justices gave an almost complete approval of Cabinet's deportation program without inquiring into the character of citizenship, its sources, rights and terminability, and sustained a drastic act without inquiring into its factual justification". Strong public protest forced King to take the deportation matter to the Privy Council in London. There, it was ruled that the deportation orders were valid. The Cabinet was now faced with three choices (Adachi, 1976:313) as follows: "to proceed with deportation as originally planned; to limit deportation to those categories unanimously approved by the Supreme Court; to rescind its orders". On January 24, 1947, King announced "that the deportation orders had been repealed".

Another issue to be settled after the war was the property claims issue. A Commission was set up on July 18, 1947, to determine the extent of property losses suffered by the evacuees. The hearings took 2½ years to hear 1,434 claims. Details of these hearings to assess the property losses are documented by Adachi (1976:328). Although most of the claims were "settled" in one way or another, the larger property claims issues continued to be fought in the courts until 1968. As previously secret documents were released for public perusal at the Public Archives in Ottawa, many Canadians, including the *sansei* and *younsei* (third and fourth generation Japanese Canadians) began to learn about the "unique and distinct" history of the first 100 years of Japanese Canadian history.

Summary and Conclusion

A very brief overview of the social history of Japanese Canadians has been provided. By examining the various events as they impinged upon them, we have been able to indicate the institutional controls which were imposed on the Japanese Canadians from the period of free immigration to the postwar period of restored civil rights. It can be seen from Figure 11-1 that each of the factors that may have influenced the formation of a Japanese Canadian identity will have had different effects on each generation of Japanese Canadians. The institutional controls imposed upon the *issei* also contributed to the formation of a much more cohesively organized community in which the *issei* were able to establish their own ethnic institutions. The formation of a social organization which drew its strengths from traditional customs and values enabled the early *issei* to survive in a hostile environment. Both the environmental factors and the emphasis on a traditional system of social relations strengthened the sense of identity as a group. Demographic factors such as the high concentraion of Japanese Canadians in a given territory, in terms of both geographic distribution and residential segregation greatly facilitated the formation of a cohesive collectivity based on a common language.

The fact that the *issei* and their offspring, the *nisei*, were able to share the various experiences of hardship based on racial prejudice and discrimination meant that the *issei* were able to control and influence the *nisei* in terms of inculcating certain traditional Japanese values. Thus, for the *nisei*, their earlier childhood socialization processes were basically those based on group conformity, emphasis on hard work and filial piety, and *gaman* or the will to perservere. Unquestioning obedience and blind faith for those in authority were other traditionally Japanese characteristics which the *nisei* learned very well. This aspect alone will account for the relatively smooth "evacuation" process of the Japanese Canadians from the coastal areas of British Columbia to the interior of the province. In order to understand the Japanese Canadian experience in terms of minority-majority Kitano (1970:5) may be helpful. By the "two category" system, they mean "a system of stratification that is divided into two broad categories: the white and nonwhite". In this system of analysis, it is assumed that the white group is superior to the other group. Although it is recognized that there are other systems of stratification, our analysis of Japanese Canadian historical data indicates that the prejudice, discrimination, and concommitant segregation in internment camps inflicted on the Japanese Canadians can be adequately assessed in terms of the simple two category system. From what we have described, it becomes evident how the social and political structures were manipulated, often by legislative means, in order to perpetuate the two category system of stratification.

In order to maintain a particular set of beliefs or attitudes, reinforcement is required and this reinforcement can often be provided by various socialization agents, institutions, and contrived mechanisms. Daniels and Kitano (1970:11) hypothesize that there are four basic stages of racial separation. These stages are illustrated in Table 11-4. They have called the first three stages "ordinary" stages as the responses to prejudice, discrimination, and segregation are not "unusual" responses to these characteristics of racial problems. In contrast, the fourth stage is labelled "extraordinary" as the response or solution such as apartheid, concentration camps, expulsion or deportation, or extermination are indeed extreme reactions. It is useful to keep these four stages in mind as we review the various events which affected the lives of the early Japanese immigrants in Canada and their children, the Japanese Canadians. Particular attention should be given to the sequencing of the various stages and how each stage can gradually develop into the following stage depending on internal or external political events. A given event may act as a trigger or even as an excuse to push a given situation to deteriorate into an extraordinary stage.

As illustrated in Table 11-4, prejudice can be maintained by stereotypical attitudes. Some of the views held concerning the early Japanese immigrants were that they were a "menace to health" because of their lower standard of living as compared to that of white Canadians. The fact that the Japanese immigrants were able to support themselves on much lower wages than a white person created some irritation. The employers were quite content to have Japanese workers, for they worked long hours without complaining; only their fellow white workers complained because of the competitive threat. Other views on the Japanese were that they were too energetic, and more aggressive and consequently more of a dangerous threat than the Chinese. The perceived threat was amply demonstrated by the adaptive capacity and economic success of the Japanese immigrants in various occupations such as in fishing, lumbering, and farming. The lack of understanding of traditional Japanese social relations such as the *oyabun-kobun* (parent-child) relationship also contributed to some of the misperceptions of the early Japanese in Canada.

An important misunderstanding in this regard concerned the role of the Consul-Generals of Japan in Canada before World War II. To the Canadians, the constant motherly role of the Consul-Generals was an indication of unnecessary interference into domestic affairs. However, from the Consul-Generals' point of view, they were the *oyabun* and thus they had the moral obligation of seeing to the welfare of the Japanese immigrants. This concern apparently extended to the *nisei* or the children of the first generation Japanese immigrants. As one Consul-General expressed it, "after all, they are the children of former Japanese citizens". In retrospect, the paternalistic role of the Consul-Generals enabled the early Japanese immigrants to have some protection and security, more than was the case for the early Chinese immigrants to Canada.

In analyzing historical data in relation to a general framework of race relations such as the one illustrated in Table 11-4, there is always the danger of overgeneralizations. The degree of prejudice concerning the early Japanese settlers can not be determined accurately from historical data. We can, however, obtain some insight concerning this question by examining the extent to which some anti-Japanese organizations were successful in securing public support. Roy (1980:82) notes that the failure of the White Canada Association to secure the support of

Figure 11-2

The Four Stages of Maintaining the Two Category System of Stratification

	Stages	Beliefs	Action-Effects	Primary Mechanisms
Ordinary solutions	1	Prejudice	Avoidance	Stereotyping, informally patterned rules governing interaction
	2	Discrimination	Deprivation	More formal rules, norms, agreements; laws
	3	Segregation	Insulation	If the out-group is perceived as stepping over the line, there may be lynchings and other warnings.
Extraordinary solutions	4	A. Apartheid, concentration	Isolation	A major trigger such as war is necessary; out-group perceived as a real threat or danger to the existence of the host culture. Ordinary mechanisms (e.g., Stages 1, 2 and 3) have failed.
		B. Expulsion, exile	Exclusion	
		C. Extermination	Genocide	

Source: Roger Daniels and Harry H.L. Kitano, American Racism: Exploration of the Nature of Prejudice. Englewood Cliffs: Prentice-Hall, Inc. p. 12.

either the provincial government or the public at large and the relative absence of public discussion of the "Oriental Question" during the early 1930's... "tend to confirm a hypotheses that when British Columbians faced other unrelated crises racial agitators had difficulty in attracting widespread attention... and it indicates that white British Columbians were beginning to tolerate their Asian neighbours". These are important aspects to examine more carefully from several different perspectives in order to obtain a much better appreciation of the overall context in which certain events took place and which may have influenced later personality and identity developments.

The anti-Japanese feelings and the eventual culmination of those feelings in the Vancouver Race Riots of 1907 probably best characterize the first stage of the two category system of stratification illustrated in Table 11-4. The introduction of formal rules, laws, or legislation characterizes the second stage of the two category system of stratification. The belief that Japanese immigrants would eventually take away employment opportunities contributed to the increased anti-Japanese political activities. As Baar (1978:336) notes, "The Japanese were believed to constitute a threat to the economic and cultural supremacy of British Protestants and thus a significant threat to the existing distribution of power". Subsequently, the "Gentlemen's Agreement" of 1908 limited Japanese immigration to four classes of people.

The third stage of the two category system of stratification is characterized by segregation and isolation. The mass evacuation of the Japanese Canadians from the "protected areas" of British Columbia to the interior camps and work projects provides a good example of this stage. Complete insulation from the rest of society was maintained by confiscating radios, camers, and automobiles. Freedom of movement was restricted. All letters were censored. These restrictions were enforced legally and applied to all persons of Japanese ancestry regardless of Canadian citizenship. . Institutionalized discrimination applied completely and limited access to higher education during the internment years meant that future occupational mobility would also be limited for several decades.

The final stage of the two category system of stratification is the extraordinary solutions stage. In the case of the Japanese Canadians, segregation into internment and concentration camps did occur. Another aspect is expulsion or deportation. In the Japanese Canadian case, it was called "repatriation". These various aspects of social control, ranging from informal rules to legislative acts, illustrate what may happen to an ethnic minority group when their adaptive capacity to adjust to the new environment becomes so successful that they become a competitive threat. Social control mechanisms were gradually put into place and in the case of the extraordinary solutions, it only required the excuse of certain political events to enforce them. By reviewing the circumstances behind the various means of social control described above, it is hoped that "extraordinary solutions" to racial problems can be prevented in the future.

With the gradual decline in external constraints imposed on the Japanese Canadian, the *sansei* and *yonsei* (third and fourth) were able to gain access to higher education and into certain professional occupations closed to the *issei* and *nisei*. For the study of Japanese Canadian identity, (and for that matter of any ethnic group in Canada), we must take into account the international differences. As argued by Baar (1978:335) a generational approach enables one to see the important changes over time in relation to the social, economic, and political environments. Thus, for the *sansei* and *yonsei*, we would expect to see a different pattern of participation in ethnic institutions, in ethnic identity formation, as well as in patterns of intermarriage, family cohesion, and socialization. Indeed, Makabe (1978:107) has shown that the assimilation of the *sansei* into Canadian society is almost complete and that the *sansei* "are not characterized by anything meaningfully Japanese other than their physical appearance". Makabe's study may be slightly biased because of the sampling procedure she employed in her original study, and therefore may be nonrepresentative of the Japanese Canadian community in Toronto. Nevertheless, her hypotheses on social mobility and retention of ethnic identity are worth further empirical investigation.

In the study of ethnic identities, we should attempt to evaluate the significance of retaining one's ethnic identity. The various aspects of Japanese Canadian history reveal that external constraints can very well reinforce ethnic group solidarity. However, in terms of contemporary social realities, do we necessarily have to be always conscious of our ethnic identity? In terms of our multicultural society, perhaps we have been too preoccupied with ethnic identity retention and not enough with Canadian identity. If we continue to stress the importance of one's ethnic identity, then it is quite possible that the political aspects of retaining one's own ethnic group identity will eventually create a situation of conflict in Canadian society which originates along both ethnic and racial dimensions. In the ideal situation, a multicultural society should be able to incorporate all those aspects of culture from diverse sources into something distinctly suited to Canadian society. That is the ideal sitatuion. The reality is that many newcomers to Canadian society are actually far more attached to their original home country than they are to Canadian society. The reason for this is that family cohesion for many ethnic groups is quite strong and consequently interaction with relatives left behind is a reasonable response. The institutions available today to encourage traditional culture and language should be such as to facilitate all Canadians' awareness of the diversity of Canadian society and not just to create pockets of ethnic communities. If this gap between the "reality" and the "ideal" is left to widen in Canadian society, then we can expect to experience severe conflict situations based along ethnic and racial lines, as have been occurring in some other countries recently.

References

Adachi, Ken
1976   **The Enemy That Never Was**, McClelland and Stewart.

Baar, Ellen
    1978   "Issei, Nisei, and Sansei." In Daniel Glenday, Hubert Guidon, and Alan Turowetz (eds.) **Modernization and the Canadian State**. Toronto: Macmillan of Canada, pp. 335-355.

Blauner, Robert
    1972   **Racial Oppression in America**. New York: Harper and Row.

Bolaria, B. Singh
    1979   "Cultural Assimilation or Colonial Domination: East Indians in Canada." Paper presented at the annual meeting of the Canadian Sociology and Anthropology Association, University of Saskatchewan, Saskatoon, June, 1979.

British Columbia Security Commission
    1942   **Removal of Japanese from Protected Areas**. A Report of the British Columbia Security Commission, March 4, 1942 to October 31, 1942. Vancouver: British Columbia Security Commission.

Broadfoot, Barry
    1977   **Years of Sorrow, Years of Shame**. Toronto: Doubleday Canada Limited.

Daniels, Roger and Harry H.L. Kitano
    1970   **American Racism: Exploration of the Nature of Prejudice**. Englewood Cliffs: Prentice-Hall Inc.

Daniels, Roger
    1971   **Concentration Camps USA: Japanese Americans and World War II**. Toronto: Holt, Rinehart and Winston Inc.

Driedger, Leo
    1978   **The Canadian Ethnic Mosaic**. Toronto: McClelland and Stewart.

Ferguson, Ted
    1975   **A White Man's Country**. Toronto: Doubleday Canada Limited.

Hughes, David R. and Evelyn Kallan
    1974   **The Anatomy of Racism: Canadian Dimensions**. Montreal: Harvest House.

Ishino, Iwao
    1953   "The Oyabun-Kobun: A Japanese Ritual Kinship Institution," **American Anthropologist** 55(5), pp. 695-707.

Kinloch, Graham G.
    1979   **The Sociology of Minority Group Relations**. Englewood Cliffs, N.J.: Prentice-Hall Inc.

Fukutake, Tadashi
    1962   **Man and Society in Japan**. The University of Tokyo Press.

La Violette, Forrest E.
    1946   **The Japanese Canadians**. Toronto: Canadian Institute of International Affairs.
    1948   **The Canadian Japanese and World War II**. Toronto: University of Toronto Press.

Makabe, Tomoko
    1978   "Ethnic Identity and Social Mobility: The Case of the Second Generation Japanese in Metropolitan Toronto." **Canadian Ethnic Studies**, Vol. X, No. 1, pp. 106-123.

Miyamoto, S. Frank
1972 "An Immigrant Community in America." In Hilary Conroy and T. Scott Miyakawa (eds.) **East Across the Pacific**. Santa Barbara: American Bibliographical Centre, pp. 217-243.

Nakane, Chie
1970 **Japanese Society**. Berkeley: University of California Press.

Nakano, Takeo Ujo
1977 "An Issei in Internment Camp." **The New Canadian**, Vol. 41, No. 82 (November 1, 1977) to Vol. 42, No. 16 (February 28, 1978).

Needham, Richard
1979 "A Writer's Notebook." **The Globe and Mail**, June 8, 1979.

Roy, Patricia E.
1980 "The Illusion of Toleration: White Opinion of Asians in British Columbia, 1929-37." In K. Victor Ujimoto and Gordon Hirabayashi (eds.) **Visible Minorities and Multiculturalism: Asians in Canada**. Scarborough: Butterworth and Company.

Shimpo, Mitsuru
1974 "Social History of the Japanese in Canada." **Rikka**, Vol. 1, No. 1 (Fall), pp. 2-3.

Sugimoto, Howard H.
1972 "The Vancouver Riots of 1907: A Canadian Episode." In Hilary Conroy and T. Scott Miyakawa (eds.) **East Across the Pacific**. Santa Barbara: American Bibliographical Centre, pp. 92-126.

Sunahara, Ann
1977 "Federal Policy and the Japanese Canadians: The Decision to Evacuate, 1942." In K. Victor Ujimoto and Gordon Hirabayashi (eds.) **Proceedings of the Asian Canadian Symposium**. Ottawa: Multiculturalism Directorate, Secretary of State. Also, in K. Victor Ujimoto and Gordon Hirabayashi (eds.) **Visible Minorities and Multiculturalism: Asians in Canada**. Scarborough: Butterworth and Company, 1980.
1979 "Historical Leadership Trends Among Japanese Canadians: 1940-1950." **Canadian Ethnic Studies**, Vol. XI, No. 1.
1980 **The Politics of Racism**. Toronto: James Lorimer and Co.

Takashima, Shizuye
1971 **A Child in Prison Camp**. Montreal: Tundra.

Ujimoto, Koji Victor
1976 "Contrasts in the Prewar and Postwar Japanese Community in British Columbia: Conflict and Change." **Canadian Review of Sociology and Anthropology**, 13(1), pp. 80-90.
1979 "Postwar Japanese Immigrants in British Columbia: Japanese Culture and Job Transferability." In Jean Leonard Elliot (ed.) **Two Nations, Many Cultures: Ethnic Groups in Canada**. Scarborough: Prentice-Hall of Canada Ltd.

Weglyn, Michi
1976 **Years of Infamy: The Untold Story of America's Concentration Camps**. New York: William Morrow and Company, Inc.

Wilson, William J.
1973 **Power, Racism, and Privilege**. London: Collier Macmillian Publishers.

Woodsworth, Charles J.
1941 **Canada and the Orient**. Toronto: Macmillan.

Part V
Theoretical Perspectives
of Race Relations

12

Emancipatory Social Psychology as a Paradigm For the Study of Minority Groups

Henry L. Minton
University of Windsor

The purpose of this paper is to consider how paradigms or models of science can affect the way in which knowledge is acquired about minority groups. A paradigm is defined here in terms of Kuhn's (1970) broad sense of the term: that is a constellation of beliefs, assumptions, and values that are shared by the members of a given scientific community—in other words, a "disciplinary matrix." These fundamental sets of assumptions are generally unstated and form the basis for deriving theories, hypotheses, and specific models of problem solving.[1] It should be pointed out that Kuhn's notion of a paradigm as a general system of beliefs underlying scientific inquiry is consistent with a number of other concepts that have been presented, including "world hypotheses" (Pepper, 1942), "world views" (Bunge, 1963), "presuppositions" (Pap, 1949), and "metaphysical models" (Reese & Overton, 1970).

In the biological and social sciences two major paradigms can be identified as sources of influence—the mechanistic model and the organismic model (Brown, 1936; Reese & Overton, 1970; Wheeler, 1929). Each of these models, based on cosmologies which are incompatable with one another, has led to the development of a distinct family of systems, schools, and theories within given disciplines. The mechanistic model is based on the metaphor of the machine. According to Overton and Reese (1973) when this world view is applied to psychology:

> The resulting model is the *reactive organism model of man.* In its ideal form the reactive organism model characterizes the organism, like other parts of the universal machine, as inherently at rest, and active only as a result of external forces (p. 69).

Historically, this model derives from the British empiricist philosophy of Locke, Berkeley, and Hume and it can be traced through the subsequent development of Comtean positivism, logical positivism, behaviorism and neobehaviorism.

In contrast to the metaphor of the machine, the organismic model is based on the living organism which is conceived of as an organized whole. When applied to psychology Overton and Reese (1973) state:

> The organismic model is reflected in the *active organism model of man*. In this model, the organism is inherently and spontaneously active; the organism is the source of acts, rather than being activated by external or peripheral forces. Man is represented as an organized entity, whose parts gain their meaning and function from the whole (p. 70).

Historically, this model stems from the Continental rationalist philosophy of Leibniz and Kant and can be traced through the subsequent development of Hegel's idealist philosophy, the various phenomonological schools, Gestalt psychology, field theory, and general systems theory.

Paradigms in Social Psychology

With respect to social psychology, at least in North America, it is not surprising in view of the British-North American empiricist tradition that the sub-discipline has been dominated by a mechanistically-based positivist paradigm. It has only been during the past decade that a significant countermovement has emerged.

The challenge currently being waged against positivist social psychology has developed out of the so-called "crisis of confidence" that has characterized the field during the past decade (Elms, 1975). Beginning in the late sixties a literature of self-criticism began to emerge in social psychology.[2] This crisis literature falls into three general categories (Pepitone, 1976; Rosnow, 1981). First, there is the extensive consideration of issues in experimental methodology, such as experimenter effects, demand characteristics, and the artificiality of the experimental situation (Orne, 1969; Rosenthal, 1969). A second area deals with alleged ethical abuses of social psychological research, which include the deceptions inherent in experimental manipulations and the exploitation against powerless subjects (Kelman, 1972; Ring, 1967). The third category involves meta-theoretical issues, and a common theme among these criticisms is social psychology's failure to address itself to the political, ideological, and historical context of social behavior (Gergen, 1973; Moscovici, 1972; Sampson, 1978).

In essence this crisis literature represents an assault on the underlying assumptions of the positivist paradigm in social psychology. Such positivist notions as experimental objectivity, theoretical verification, and temporal irrelevance are called into question (Gergen, 1978; Rosnow, 1981). Within the past few years the crisis literature has moved beyond a criticism of the positivist model. What has emerged has been the advocacy of alternative paradigms which would provide the basis for a reconstruction of social psychology. The particular paradigm that I will focus on has been labeled in various ways, including Rappoport's (1977)

"Dialectical Social Psychology", Buss' (1979) "Hermeneutic-Dialectic" model, Sampson's (1978) "Historical" model, and Gergen's (1979) "Socio-rationalism". These proposed alternative models share a common set of assumptions which are basically consistent with an organismic model.

At this point it would be useful to delineate the major differences between positivist social psychology and this alternative model. These distinctions are drawn from a number of analyses of paradigms in social psychology (Baumrind, 1980; Buss, 1979; Gergen, 1978, 1980; Rappaport, 1977; Rommetveit, 1976; Rosnow, 1981; Sampson, 1978). It should be noted that the alternative model, while based on the organismic principle of the active organism functioning as an organized whole, adds a social perspective that is derived from the ideas of neo-Marxist philosophers of science, most notable Apel (1967; see also Radnitzky, 1970 and Habermas 1971).

The two paradigms can be contrasted in terms of four assumptions. First, with respect to the nature of reality the positivist model assumes that it is independent of the observer and consequently there should be consensual agreement regarding reality, while the alternative model assumes that reality is socially derived and therefore people do not necessarily share similar views. Second, with respect to the nature of knowledge the positivist model assumes that facts and principles of psychological functioning are universal and transhistorical, while the alternative model assumes that these facts and principles are contextually embedded in a particular culture and history. Third, regarding the function of theory the positivist model assumes that theory is a guide to gathering facts with the goal of verifying hypotheseized causal relationships, while the alternative model assumes that theory is a guide to critically evaluating cultural ideology and patterns of social life with the goal of fostering human emancipation. Fourth, regarding the role of the scientist the positivist model assumes that the scientist should describe reality as it is and not as it ought to be because knowledge is value free, while the alternative model assumes that the scientiest should prescribe what ought to be because knowledge is value-laden and should serve an emancipatory interest or function.

It seems most appropriate to label the alternative model "emancipatory social psychology" (Rommetveit, 1976) because it is based on the notion that social psychology should be prescriptive and committed to human liberation. Now that the two contrasting world views in social psychology have been sketched out they can be considered in relation to the study of minority groups.

Social Psychology Paradigms and the Study of Minority Groups

The study of minority groups in social psychology emerged from the numerous and varied attempts to measure social attitudes which characterized the field during the 1920's and 1930's. As Samelson (1978) has noted it was during this period that psychological thought regarding racial and ethnic minorities underwent a dramatic shift. The dominant view in psychology that racial and ethnic groups were genetically inferior to the Anglo-Saxon-based American stock—a view which was used to explain the group differences found in the army intelligence-testing program during World War One—was replaced by the view that racial-ethnic minorities, as a consequence of their cultural differences from mainstream American society, were targets for irrational, negative, and over-generalized attitudes—in other words, targets for racial prejudice. Samelson points to several factors underlying this conceptual shift, including the ascendancy of behaviorism, with its environmentalist focus as the dominant school of American psychology; the rise of fascism in Europe; the Great Depression of the 1930's, which pushed many psychologists towards the left; and the increasing number of psychologists of Jewish origin, who entered the field which had virtually no previous representation from racial and ethnic minorities.

The investigation of racial prejudice continued to be a major area of concern within social psychology during the 1940's and 1950's (Allport, 1954). It should be noted that from its inception the study of prejudice was primarily undertaken from the white gentile perspective. Citing Gordon Allport's (1954) work as an example, Brewster Smith (1978) comments:

> From the standpoint of white experience, prejudice seemed more central than the discrimination and injustice encountered by Jews and blacks... We need to remember also that Allport was writing at a time when Gunnar Myrdal... could call the "Negro problem" really a white problem (p. 197).

It was not until the impact of the civil rights movement in the early 1960's that social psychologists began to shift their focus away from the liberal white concern with prejudice to such minority concerns as racism, oppression, and protest.[3] An excellent example of this new genre was Kenneth B. Clark's (1965) analysis of the oppressive effects of black ghettos. The extent to which the black experience of racism could be misinterpreted was compellingly illustrated in the 1968 book, *Black Rage*, written by two black psychiatrists, Grier and Cobbs (1968). Addressing themselves to the apparent psychiatric symptoms often displayed by blacks, such as paranoia and depression, Grier and Cobbs (1968) state:

> These and related traits are simple adaptive devices developed in response to a peculiar environment... They represent normal devices for "making it" in America and clinicians who are interested in the psychological functioning of black people must get acquainted with this body of character traits which we call the Black Norm... To regard the *Black Norm* as pathological and attempt to remove such traits by treatment would be akin to analyzing away a hunter's cunning or a banker's prudence. This is a body of characteristics essential to life for black men in America and woe be unto that therapist who does not recognize it (pp. 178, 179).

The concern with racism in social psychology soon spread to an interest in sexism. The women's movement appeared to act as a catalyst in drawing attention to the masculine bias that characterized not only social psychology, but social science in general. For example, Sampson (1978) referring to positivist social science points out that it:

Emerged within the male subculture, expressing male values (e.g.,
individualism, achievement, mastery, detachment)...Such science reflects and reaffirms agentic values and thereby has a greater congruence
with masculine sex role values and ideals (p. 1338).

During the 1970's another minority issue began to appear in the social
psychological literature, namely sexual orientation. As Morin (1977) points out
in his review of psychological research on lesbianism and male homosexuality,
psychology inherited a marked "heterosexual bias" from the earlier interests of the
medical discipline. In the case of homosexuality the traditional religious values
that all non-procreative sexuality was pathological were initially incorporated into
medical beliefs and eventually as part of psychological thinking (Altman, 1971;
Morin, 1977). Homosexuality as sexual pathology therefore became subject
matter more relevant for abnormal psychology than for social psychology. Consequently homosexuals, unlike other minorities, were until recently ignored for the
most part in social psychological theory and research. Consistent with the impact
of other minority protest movements the gay rights movement has served as a
significant stimulus for new directions in psychological research on homosexuality (Morin, 1977, 1978). These new directions are social psychological in nature
because lesbianism and male homosexuality are now being viewed from the
perspective of sexual minority rather than sexual deviation. Furthermore, the
guidelines advocated for theory and research on homosexuality stress the need to
incorporate both the minority point of view, that is the issues and experiences that
lesbians and gay men consider to be significant, and the social action dimension of
changing pejorative attitudes toward homosexuality which are held by the majority (Morin, 1977).

Conclusions

The point of this brief excursion into the history of social psychology's analysis
of minority groups is to demonstrate that the field's commitment to a
mechanistic, positivist paradigm has resulted in an ideological bias of interpreting
minority experiences from the perspective of the dominant class in North American society, that is white, gentile, male, and heterosexist. Such an ideological bias
is inherent in the underlying assumptions of positivist social psychology. For
example, if reality is independent of the observer, then consensual agreement
regarding reality from the perspective of a dominant majority in society should be
sufficient to account for the experiences of minority group members. If facts and
principles of psychological functioning are universal and transhistorical, then the
unique and concrete cultural and historical experiences of minorities are irrelevant. If the role of the theorist is to predict value-free causal relationships and
describe reality as it is, the unquestioned cultural assumptions of the dominant
class continue to define social reality and consequently act as obstacles to the
emancipatory interests of minorities.[4] It has only been during the past decade that
the positivist hegemony in North American social psychology has been significantly challenged. The alternative organismically-derived emancipatory paradigm

is based on understanding reality in terms of cultural and historical context, as well as prescribing how reality ought to be, so that it is consistent with human values such as liberation. It is therefore not surprising that the minority protests of the 1960's appear to have served as an impetus in the attempts during the 1970's and 1980's to restructure social psychology in terms of an emancipatory paradigm.

The conclusion to be drawn from the consideration of paradigms in social psychology is that the study of minority groups should be based on an organismic, emancipatory model rather than on the traditional mechanistic, positivist model. The relevance of the emancipatory paradigm to the analysis of minority groups is suggested by Gergen (1980), who argues that social psychology is an interpretative enterprise in which theories function to make experience intelligible, or to give meaning to such experience. Theories can therefore be used to generate challenges to the guiding assumptions of the culture. With respect to minority groups such "generative theories" may serve as a challenge to the dominant beliefs of an oppressive society, thereby freeing or emancipating those who are victimized by these beliefs. Speaking to the role of the social scientist Gergen (1980) comments:

> An investigator may act on behalf of minority groups that do not share majority group perspectives or assumptions, and that simultaneously appear to be exploited by these perspectives. Frequently those who believe themselves to be oppressed by majority views share interpretive modes that have neither been fully articulated nor understood by members of the majority. By attempting to articulate these views, the social scientist may first galvanize the minority group by enabling it to achieve common understanding, and second, undermine or re-order the views of the majority (p. 263).

In conclusion, the purpose of this paper has been to consider how paradigms can affect the way in which knowledge is acquired about minority groups. In this regard, mainstream positivist social psychology has been found to be deficient. This conclusion raises questions about positivist social psychology in general, and suggests that it may indeed be necessary to restructure the entire sub-discipline (Gergen, 1980; Sampson, 1978).

Footnotes

1. Kuhn (1970) also uses the term "paradigm" to refer to the particular models or examples of how to solve problems ("shared examplars").
2. This literature has not been confined to North America. There have been important European counterparts (See Israel & Tajfel, 1972).
3. The classic research by the Clarks (Clark & Clark, 1947) on black children's racial identification was a notable exception to the pre-1960 trend to focus on the white perspective of prejudice.
4. An analysis of the effects of ideological domination on minorities is provided by Adam (1978).

References

Adam, B.D.
  1978   The Survival of Domination: Inferiorization and Everyday Life, New York: Elseviet.
Allport, G.W.
  1954   The Nature of Prejudice, Cambridge, MA: Addison-Wesley.
Altman, D.
  1971   Homosexual: Oppression and Liberation, New York: Outerbridge and Dienstfrey.
Apel, K.O.
  1967   Analytic Philosophy of Language and the Geisteswissenschaften, Dodrecht, Holland: D. Reidel.
Baumrind, D.
  1980   "New Directions in Socialization Research", American Psychologist, 35: 639-652.
Brown, J.F.
  1936   Psychology and the Social Order: An Introduction to the Dynamic Study of Social Fields, New York: McGraw-Hill.
Bunge, M.
  1963   Causality: The Place of the Causal Principle in Modern Science, New York: World.
Buss, A.R.
  1979   "A Metascience Critique of Attribution Theory", in A.R. Buss (ed.) A Dialectical Psychology, New York: Irvington.
Clark, K.B.
  1965   Dark Ghetto: Dilemmas of Social Power, New York: Harper and Row.
Clark, K.B. and M.P. Clark
  1947   "Racial Identification and Preference in Negro Children", in T.M. Newcomb and E.L. Hartley (eds.) Readings in Social Psychology, New York: Holt.
Elms, A.C.
  1975   "The Crisis of Confidence in Social Psychology", American Psychologist, 30:967-976.
Gergen, K.J.
  1973   "Social Psychology as History", Journal of Personality and Social Psychology, 26:309-320.
  1978   "Toward Generative Theory", Journal of Personality and Social Psychology, 36:1344-1360.
  1979   Social Psychology and the Phoenix of Unreality, a paper presented at the American Psychological Association, New York, September.
  1980   "Toward Intellectual Audacity in Social Psychology", in R. Gilmour and S. Duck (eds.) The Development of Social Psychology, London: Academic Press.
Grier, W.H. and P.M. Cobbs
  1968   Black Rage, New York: Basic Books.

Habermas, J.
1971 **Knowledge and Human Interests,** Boston: Beacon Press.
Israel, J. and H. Tajfel (eds.)
1972 **The Context of Social Psychology: A Critical Assessment,** New York: Academic Press.
Kelman, H.C.
1972 "The Rights of Subjects in Social Research: An Analysis in Terms of Relative Power and Legitimacy", **American Psychologist,** 27:989-1016.
Kuhn, T.S.
1970 **The Structure of Scientific Revolutions,** Chicago: University of Chicago Press.
Morin, S.F.
1977 "Heterosexual Bias in Psychological Research on Lesbianism and Male Homosexuality", **American Psychologist,** 32:629-637.
1978 "Psychology and the Gay Community: An Overview", **Journal of Social Issues,** 34(3):1-6.
Moscovici, S.
1972 "Society and Theory in Social Psychology", in J. Israel and H. Tajfel (eds.) **The Context of Social Psychology: A Critical Assessment,** New York: Academic Press.
Orne, M.T.
1969 "Demand Characteristics and the Concept of Design Controls", in R. Rosenthal and R.L. Rosnow (eds.) **Artifact in Behavioral Research,** New York: Academic Press.
Overton, W.F. and H.W. Reese
1973 "Models of Development: Methodological Implications", in J.R. Nesselroade and H.W. Reese (eds.) **Life-Span Developmental Psychology: Methodological Issues,** New York: Academic Press.
Pap, A.
1949 **Elements of Analytic Philosophy,** New York: Macmillan.
Pipitone, A.
1976 "Toward a Normative and Comparative Biocultural Social Psychology", **Journal of Personality and Social Psychology,** 34:641-653.
Pepper, S.C.
1942 **World Hypotheses,** Berkeley, CA: University of California Press.
Rodnitzky, G.
1970 **Contemporary Schools of Metascience,** Goteborg, Sweden: Scandinavian University Books.
Rappoport, L.
1977 "Symposium: Towards a Dialectical Social Psychology", **Personality and Social Psychology Bulletin,** 3:678-680.
Reese, H.W. and W.F. Overton
1970 "Models of Development and Theories of Development", in L.R. Goulet and P.B. Baltes (eds.) **Life-Span Developmental Psychology: Research and Theory,** New York: Academic Press.

Ring, K.
  1967   "Experimental Social Psychology: Some Sober Questions About Some Frivol-
           ous Values", **Journal of Experimental Social Psychology**, 3:113-123.
Rommetveit, R.
  1976   "On 'Emancipatory' Social Psychology", in L.H. Strickland, F.E. Aboud, and
           K.J. Gergen (eds.) **Social Psychology in Transition**, New York: Plenum.
Rosenthal, R.
  1969   "Interpersonal Expectations: Effects of the Experimenter's Hypothesis", in R.
           Rosenthal and R.L. Rosnow (eds.) **Artifact in Bahavioral Research**, New
           York: Academic Press.
Rosnow, R.L.
  1981   **Paradigms in Transition: The Methodology of Social Inquiry**, New York:
           Oxford University Press.
Samelson, F.
  1978   "From 'Race Psychology' to 'Studies in Prejudice': Some Observations on the
           Thematic Reversal in Social Psychology", **Journal of the History of the
           Behavioral Sciences**, 14:265-278.
Sampson, E.E.
  1978   "Scientific Paradigms and Social Values: Wanted—A Scientific Revolution",
           Journal of Personality and Social Psychology, 36:1332-1343.
Smith, M.B.
  1978   "Psychology and Values", **Journal of Social Issues**, 34(4):181-199.
Wheeler, R.H.
  1929   **The Science of Psychology**, New York: Crowell.

13

Dominant Perspectives and Non-White Minorities

B. Singh Bolaria
University of Saskatchewan

Introduction

With few exceptions, the sociological studies of non-whites in this country are guided by the traditional "race relations cycle" perspective and its many present day variations of assimilation theory. One can hardly escape the literature dealing with cultural distinctiveness, cultural patterns and orientations, adaptation, integration, accommodation, identity, assimilation and so forth (Li and Bolaria, 1979; Bolaria, 1980, 1982). In addition, the tendency has been to examine the "problems" of non-whites. In this regard, studies of non-whites, for the most part, tend to degenerate into more or less social-psychological examination of "ethnic problems" or "identity crises" or "cultural marginality" or "adaptation problems" or "assimilation problems" or "race problems" or "colour problems" or "family problems". In short, personal and social "pathologies" of immigrants and their institutions are highlighted.

This paper, therefore, presents a critical evaluation of the dominant perspectives in the study of "race relations". Shortcomings and ideological and policy implications of these perspectives are outlined. Finally, alternative theoretical models and research directions are proposed.

The Assimilationist Bias and Immigrant Analogy: A Critique

Park's notion of the "race relations cycle" has had a dominant influence within the sociological studies of immigrant groups. In his pioneer formulation Park (1950:150) observed that "in the relations of races there is a cycle of events which tends everywhere to repeat itself... which takes the form, to state it abstractly, of contact, competition, accommodation and eventual assimilation." His assumption that assimilation and integration are in the long run the most probable and even desirable outcomes of racial and ethnic heterogeneity has been a dominant theme in the study of race relations (Blauner, 1972).

In Canada, notwithstanding the official rhetoric of multiculturalism, pluralism and ethnic mosaic, the academic studies of the non-white immigrants are dominated by the assimilationist perspective. In this scheme of things white immigrants, because of their alleged assimilability, are considered more desirable than non-white immigrants. This perspective provided rationalization for restrictive entry of non-white immigrants to this country (Li and Bolaria, 1979; Bolaria, 1980). In practice then the assimilationist perspective, to the extent that it was used to justify the Canadian immigration policy which was based upon differential selection on the basis of racial origins, became a substitute for more crude theories of racism based on biological inferiority of various racial groups. In other words, non-whites were (are) subject to an exclusionist policy not because of some innate racial inferiority, but because of their inability to assimilate in Canadian society.

The assimilationist perspective has also been used to explain ethnic and racial inequality. For instance, the frequent explanation of ethnic and racial inequality is to interpret it as differential degrees of assimilation or non-assimilation, depending upon one's position within the assimilation school. In either case, it becomes important to identify those factors which are seemingly unique to a particular cultural origin as explanations of that group's economic success or failure. This particular theme is evident in the writings of Oscar Lewis (1959, 1966), Herberg (1960), Wagley and Harris (1958), Hsu (1972), and Light (1972). Wagley and Harris (1958:264), for instance, attribute adaptive capacity and subsequent success or failure to cultural heritage. They view adaptive capacity as:

> Those elements of a minority's cultural heritage which provide it with a basis for competing more or less effectively with the dominant group, which afford protection against exploitation, which stimulate or retard its adaptation to the total social environment, and which facilitate or hinder its upward advance through the socio-economic hierarchy.

In the mobility literature, the assimilation perspective is expressed in various motivational hypotheses which stress value orientation differences among ethnic groups (Rosen, 1956, 1959). These explanations of ethnic stratification have been challenged both on theoretical and empirical grounds (Li and Bolaria, 1979).

As noted earlier, Park's basic assumption that assimilation and integration are in the long run the most probable and desirable outcomes of racial and ethnic heterogeneity has been a dominant theme in the study of race relations. Assimilation and integration and becoming absorbed in the "melting pot" were considered the only viable paths for various racial and ethnic groups. This type of argument did not take into account the aspirations of the minority groups in developing their own culture and institutions. Implicit in this view is also the assumption that the cultural traditions of minority groups are either nonexistent or inferior to those of the dominant society (Blauner, 1972).

A corollary of this perspective which has become widely accepted is the "immigrant analogy" (Blauner, 1972). This posits an alleged similarity between the historical experience of European immigrants and the contemporary situation of non-whites (Blauner, 1972; Grove, 1974). A comparison is made between the racial minorities and white ethnic groups and it is suggested that Blacks, East Indians, and Chinese will follow the pattern of white ethnic groups with regard to assimilation and social and economic mobility. The most common folk version of this type of thinking is somewhat like this. Historically, every new immigrant group has successively improved their social and economic position in the society. It is assumed that the same destiny awaits the groups who are presently the object of prejudice and discrimination. Some groups may have to endure this for a somewhat longer period than others, but their incorporation into the mainstream and the inevitability of upward mobility for every group is assumed. In the case of non-white groups the process of assimilation has been somewhat slower than the European ethnics. The proponents of this view tend to discount or minimize the special impact of racism and in Blauner's view the immigrant analogy "in a contemporary version of the myth of progress and opportunity" (Blauner, 1972:10).

This tendency to use ethnic analogy on racial minorities has been under attack. First of all many authors do not make a distinction between ethnicity and race. Grove (1974) argues that the difference between ethnicity is more substantive than more error in measures of ethnicity and race. Different political mechanisms are used to sustain ethnic and racial cleavages. According to Grove (1974:320-321) "ethnic cleavages are politically manipulated by intense negotiations... Racial cleavages tend to merge into class differences and are rigidly stabilized by political coercion. Apartheid is not a function of ethnicity, but of race." The distinction between ethnicity and race also has important implications in terms of immigration policy differences in government policies toward ethnic and racial groups. Immigration policies are governed by racial rather than ethnic considerations. As Grove (1974:321) states: "Although not often stated, these policies are racial, not ethnic. They exclude racial groups that are different from the racial composition of the host nation. They do not exclude ethnic groups that are culturally different from receiving countries." Blauner (1972) points out that it is a mistake to equate present day racism against third world groups with the ethnic prejudice and persecution faced by European immigrants. There was obviously intolerance and discrimination in the sphere of religion, for example. The orthodox religious practices of some immigrant ethnic groups were mocked and scorned, but they never lost the freedom to practice their own religion. However, in the case of Native Indians, there was an all-out attack on their way of life, cultural genocide, and legal proscription against tribal rituals and beliefs. The third world groups experienced similar attacks on their cultural institutions (Blauner, 1972:68).

Differences in entry status of whites and non-whites must also be noted. White immigrants entered the country and the labour force under considerably more favourable conditions than did the racial minorities (Bolaria, 1980).

Additionally, the assimilationist perspective is also criticized for its ideological support of the notion of equality of opportunity and its "blaming the victim" approach. Equality of opportunity is assumed, and racial inequality is attributed to different degrees of assimilation or inadequate socialization into the value system of the host society (Geshwender, 1978; Glazer and Moynihan, 1970). Success or failure of a particular racial group is attributed to their transplanted cultural values. This perspective is also criticized for its inadequacy in explaining racial conflict. It is based upon a framework of "order" rather than "conflict". Conflict is attributed to the "pathological behaviour of the minority group" rather than its location in the structure of the society (Horton, 1966).

In summary, a review of the assimilationist perspective shows that it entails obvious theoretical flaws and ideological biases. The main points of critique may be summarized. Assimilationist perspective is criticized for its ahistorical approach as it, for the most part, does not take into account the initial entry status of racial groups. It is noted that many authors do not make a distinction between ethnicity and race in their application of ethnic analogy to racial minorities. In their preoccupation with integration and assimilation the assimilationists show a consistent disregard for the cultural traditions and cultural consciousness of the non-white minorities. Also, this perspective is criticized for ideological support for the "myth of equality of opportunity" and its "blaming the victim" orientation. It does not explain racial conflict because it is based upon a framework of "order" rather than "conflict".

One important implication of assimilation theories has been to justify Canadian immigration which has been based upon differential selection on the basis of racial origins.

Alternative Perspectives

It is apparent that there are many shortcomings associated with the assimilationist perspective. The situation of non-white minorities cannot be fully appreciated in the context of immigration and assimilation models applied to European immigrants. As in many areas of academic sociology the pressure of events has forced sociologists to re-examine old definitions and concepts and long accepted frameworks. The inadequacy of the present theories of race relations challenges sociologists to provide alternative theoretical perspectives. To fully comprehend the situation of non-white minorities, it is essential to draw historical connections between international colonialism, treatment of non-white immigrants as colonial subjects, and patterns of racial domination and exploitation in Canada.

In the context of the international situation it has been argued that concomitant with colonialism a racial ideology flourished to justify the exploitation of colonized people. The origins and functions of racialism, then, is to be understood in terms of ideological needs of the European colonialism. Racial ideology justified the exploitation of the coloured people all the world over (Cox, 1959; Baran & Sweezy, 1966; Braverman, 1974; Leggett, 1968).

Other writers have proposed an internal colonial model (Blauner, 1972;

Carmichael and Hamilton, 1967; Tabb, 1970, 1971; Moore, 1975). The basic argument here is that non-white minorities in ghettos are living in a colonial relationship to the larger society and that this racial subordination leads to political and economic exploitation. It is argued that the situation of non-whites, for instance blacks, is qualitatively different from that experienced by other ethnic groups. Blacks are certainly not just another immigrant group that will assimilate and move up in American society (Geshwender, 1978).

Germane to the colonial expansion model or the internal colonial model is the capitalist class/race exploitation thesis. Due to colonial expansion and domination non-whites came to be exploited by whites. In fact all workers are exploited as a class, but non-white workers more intensively than whites. As Cox (33) states:

> But the fact of crucial significance is that racial exploitation is merely one aspect of the problem of the proletarianization of labor, regardless of the color of the labor. Hence, racial antagonism is essentially political-class conflict. The capitalist exploiter, being opportunistic and practical, will utilize any convenience to keep his labor and other resources freely exploitable. He will devise and employ race prejudice where that becomes convenient. As a matter of fact, the white proletariat of early capitalism had to endure burdens of exploitation quite similar to those which colored peoples must bear today.

Adoption of the colonial models or capitalist class/race exploitation model allows fresh insights into areas of race relations. In this context, for instance, blacks in the United States are kept as a reserve army of labour or as subproletariat (Geshwender, 1978; Leggett, 1968). According to Tabb (1971) blacks in ghettos are living in a colonial relationship to the larger society and its basic export is unskilled labour power. Tabb (1971:101) states:

> From the time black slaves were freed to sell their labor as a commodity they came to serve both as a reserve army and as a pool of labor, ready and willing to do the "dirty work" of the society at low wages. In the first role they served as an equilibrating factor in the economy. In periods of labor shortage blacks have made important gains, but with economic downturns they have been systematically displaced... In the second role they were restricted to the most menial, physically exhausting and alienating labor which the white society offered.

Kellough (1980) and Adams (1975) point out the similarities between the colonization of native people in Canada and the colonial domination of people living in Africa, Latin America and Asia.

The similarity between the employment patterns of the "guest workers" and the blacks in the United States is pointed out. As Baron (1975:209) states:

> An amazing similarity exists between the employment pattern of the 'guest workers' and Black Americans in regard to industries, job classifications, and concentration in particular urban centers. Although both groups are subject to a great deal of fluctuation in employment, they occupy permanent niches in the economy.

The class/race exploitation model also suggests an alternative approach to the study of historical and contemporary situations of immigrants and migrants. Rather than focusing on the "problems" of immigrants and migrants (adaptability, lack of assimilation, and so forth) attention is on the role of the colonized countries and colonial labour in capital accumulation and management of capitalist crises.

The migration of labour across national boundaries has been part of the global relationships between the colonial and advanced capitalist and the colonized or neo-colonial underdevelopment countries. Historically, it took the form of slave trade from Africa (Williams, 1964); indentured and 'Coolie' labour from India and China (Tinker, 1974; Hutternback, 1976; Gangulee, 1947; Saha, 1970). At the present time, the Western European countries are importing a large part of their labour force across national lines—Britain from the old empire, France from their old colonies and other Western European Countries import their labour from Southern Europe (Castles and Kosack, 1973; Gorz, 1970; Bohning, 1972). In North America, particularly since the sixties in the United States, there has been a considerable influx of migrant workers (Piore, 1979). Rather than bringing in more landed immigrants, Canada since the mid-sixties is importing workers to supplement the supply of Canadian seasonal agricultural workers, and domestic and other workers since the 1970's on short-term work permits (Arnopoulos, 1970; Bolaria, 1982).

The objective of the Canadian immigration policy remains the importation of foreign labour to meet the labour force needs in this country (Cappon, 1975). However, more recently the Canadian State has also entered in to the business of converting immigrant settler labour into migrant contract labour.

Migration involves the transfer of valuable human resources from one country to the other and this transfer represents a very large economic cost for the countries of emigration. As Bohning (1970:410) notes, "international migration is an inequitable and unrequired resource transfer" and it "contributes to the widening gap between poor and rich countries". In the present international economic order of things, the poorest countries are most exploited. As Moore (1977:141) states: "There is something of a chain exploitation in that America recruits British doctors whilst Britain recruits doctors from the Indian sub-continent. Thus each nation received 'cheap' doctors and the poorest countries experienced a net loss." It has been noted by Elston (1977) in the case of England that many of the overseas doctors and women physicians end up in low grade posts and unpopular specialties. In any event, this labour-power is lost to the countries of emigration.

The crucial element is the existence of an industrial resesrve army in the underdeveloped areas of the world. To the extent that the advanced capitalist countries have access to this reserve, the workers either are vulnerable to exploitation in their own countries by capital export or subject to exploitation when they migrate to the advanced capitalist countries. The point is that the capitalists benefit either way, by capital export or labour import. The decision will be dictated by the political climate in underdeveloped areas, profit motive, resource availability, market consideration, among others.

For instance, historically, Britain's dominant position as a colonial power made it possible to exploit cheap labour in many areas through capital export as well as export of indentured labour from India to many other British Colonies (Tinker, 1974, 1976). Britain was also the first industrial power to have recourse to migrant labour from another country (Berger and Mohr, 1975:108).

> After the famine of 1845-7 hundreds of thousands of Irish peasants, their agriculture destroyed by English policies, their families dispersed and decimated by starvation, crossed the sea to Liverpool and Glasgow. In their new situation they were without a trade. They had to accept low wages. They were mobile. They were disorganized. They were seen by English working class as inferiors, and were accused by them of cutting wages. They lived in the worst slums, which became Irish ghettos. They worked as navvies, dockers, steel-workers, and they were indispensable to the building of the physical installations necessary for the expansion of British industry after the invention of the steam engine.

The present day inheritors of the work of the Irish in the "dirty" trades are Indians, Pakistanians and West Indians (Oppenheimer, 1974:12).

If today many of the workers from the underdeveloped economies are brought to the advanced capitalist countries because it is convenient for the capitalists to use them here rather than in their own countries, this does not alter the basic situation of their exploitation. Migrant workers in particular find themselves not even in the same labour market as the indigenous workers. Non-white migrant workers additionally find themselves "branded with the stigma of colour and racial inferiority" (Moore, 1977:146). Migrant workers do share some common characteristics with the non-unionized poorly paid worker, especially with wo-men workers. As Moore (1977:145) points out

> They are poorly paid in insecure jobs, their employment is regarded as temporary, they suffer discrimination in wages, training and promotion, they are victims of prejudice. But the poorest and most defenceless non-unionized woman worker is a formally—and compared with the migrant, actually—free labourer. By virtue of his terms of employment the migrant worker appears to be not even in the same labour market as the indigenous worker. His political deprivation keeps him in this separate labour market.

Many descendants of colonial people find themselves that migration from their countries has not changed their colonial status. Non-white immigrants to Canada have had experiences similar to the colonial situation. This is reflected in the immigration legislation in the form of restricted entry and quotas for non-whites. Historically, it is also evident in the denial of political rights and racial labour policy (Bolaria, 1980, 1982). For instance the Chinese residing in British Colum-bia were denied the right to vote as early as 1875 and twenty years later this was extended to other Asians living in British Columbia. The defranchisement had a wider impact in terms of occupations and employment opportunities. Chinese and Japanese were denied practice of law and pharmacy because eligibility to these fields was limited to those on the voters' list. East Indians could not enter certain occupations because they were disfranchised (Krauter and Davis, 1978).

Asians were also exploited even when they were employed. As Ward (1978:81) notes: "generally East Indian workers, like other Asians, earned one half to two-thirds of the wages paid whites for similar sort of work."

Justification for exploitation was provided by racial stereotypes and colonial heritage. It was noted earlier that concomitant with colonialism a racial ideology was developed to justify the exploitation of subjugated people. In this process, negative stereotypes were developed about the native population. India, a colony of the British Empire, was no exception. These negative stereotypes were popularized in Canada as well. As Ward (1978:82) notes:

> Popular conceptions of India preceded Indian immigrants to North American shores just as those of China had once arrived in advance of the Chinese. The India which they depicted was a land of teeming millions, of filth and squalor, of exotic, peculiar customs. The Indians seemed a lesser breed of men, given to weakness, servility, and in some cases villainy.

Many of these stereotypes are still prevalent in Canada.

The labour-power transfer is only one aspect of the unequal and exploitative relation between advanced capitalist countries and the countries with underdeveloped economies. These include international trade agreements involving raw material and resources transfer of goods and services, most, if not all, to the advantage of the advanced countries. This perpetuates underdevelopment of the economies of poor countries (Frank, 1969:21). This situation creates high unemployment, surplus labour force and forces many to migrate. In the words of Moore (1977:145), "he is either a skilled worker drawn from his own country by the metropolitan economy or a worker forced into the metropolis by the underdevelopment of his own country by the very neo-colonial powers on whose production lines or refuse disposal he now works. Exploitation at home forces him into exploitation abroad."

The writer has pointed out elsewhere (Bolaria, 1982) that the use of immigrant labour and migrant workers is not only economically profitable, but also politically useful. In this context we noted that the use of labour, already produced and paid for elsewhere, means a considerable saving for the receiving country. It was also pointed out that in the case of migrant workers, the host country saves most of the social cost of welfare benefits—unemployment benefits, retirement benefits, and so forth. It is the very disposability of these workers which makes them so useful. An additional factor in this cost may be considered in case of the non-white worker, that is, the social cost of management of race-relations. In the case of migrant workers, as they are recruited when needed and sent back when they are no longer required, the capitalist state not only "exports unemployment" and passes on other social costs to the countries of immigrants, but also exports "race problems" and saves social costs of "race relations" management.

Racism is used to create divisions among the working class. For example, Reich (1971) shows that one of the effects of racism in capitalist society is to divide the solidarity of the working class, and weaken union organization, thus strengthening the positions of employers. Bonacich (1972, 1976) indicates that a split labour market operates in advanced capitalism, in which the price of labour for blacks is cheaper than that for whites. Szymanski (1976) argues that capitalist society requires a group of oppressed workers to perform its menial tasks, and demonstrates that racism and sexism serve similar functions in producing such oppression. These studies clearly suggest the importance of understanding racism in the context of capitalism.

Labour market segmentation at the structural level is a major obstacle in the way of working class unity on a political level (Oppenheimer, 1974). Workers are divided ethnically, racially and sexually as well as occupationally. According to Oppenheimer (1974) there is an equally serious segmentation of the working class due to the existence at the bottom of the blue collar life in the form of a permanent group of 'subproletarians' whose working conditions are so markedly different from that of even many unskilled manual workers. In the Western World this "subproletariat correlates closely with the populations that are dark-skinned, and that the work engaged in by the subproletariat is regarded by that particular society at that particular moment as the least desirable, the 'dirtiest'" (Oppenheimer, 1974:7-8).

Whatever the fine distinction between Leggett's (1968) 'marginal working class' and Oppenheimer's (1974) 'dirty worker', these workers share some common characteristics, such as subordinate racial and ethnic status, job insecurity, and high unemployment.

Oppenheimer (1974: 10) defines subproletarian labour:

> unskilled, physically exhausting and uncomfortable (as, in a hot kitchen, or stoop labour) work utilizing a minimum of machinery (that is, labour-intensive); where unionization tends not to exist, hence there is a low level of job, wage, and safety protection; in a situation where it is unlikely that the work will become capital-intensive in the near future either because of the small scale of the enterprise (a local restaurant or small construction company) and/or because of the competitive picture, domestically or internationally (profits would deteriorate if machinery were to replace labour)

The work which many of the "illegals" or "legal guest" workers perform in many Western countries place them into the subproletariats. Seasonal agricultural workers and domestic workers in Canada would particularly fall into the category of subproletariat (Bolaria, 1982).

To be sure, there are certain differences in the overall patterns of labour force segmentation in various countries. There are also certain similarities whether one looks at North America or Europe. According to Oppenheimer (1974: 12) "lower-income and lesser-skilled groups tend to be dark-skinned. That is, racism is superimposed upon technological differentiation in virtually every national case."

Racism is then to be understood in this broader context. Racism is not a "mental quirk" or personality disorder on an individual's part (Fanon, 1967), neither is it solely a matter of overt discriminatory attitudes and acts of the individuals and their personal tasks and preferences.

In summary, adoption of colonial models and capitalist class/race exploitation model suggests alternative approaches to the study of historical and contemporary situations of migrants, immigrants and non-white minorities. The workers enter into a structured labour market over which they have little or no control. An analysis of the labour market segmentation and the location of the various "types" of workers in different segments of the labour market directs our attention to the role of labour (indigenous or otherwise) in capital accumulation and management of capitalist crises. These studies also suggest the importance of understanding racism in the context of capitalism, capitalist labour market and class/race exploitation.

Concluding Remarks

A review of the assimilationist perspective shows that it entails obvious theoretical flaws and ideological biases. The main points of critique may be summarized. Assimilationist perspective is criticized for its ahistorical approach as it, for the most part, does not take into account the initial entry status of racial groups. It is noted that many authors do not make a distinction between ethnicity and race in their application of ethnic analogy to racial minorities. In their preoccupation with integration and assimilation, the assimilationists show a consistent disregard for the cultural traditions and cultural consciousness of the non-white minorities. Also, this perspective is criticized for ideological support for the "myth of equality of opportunity" and its "blaming the victim" orientation. It does not explain racial conflict because it is based upon a framework of "order" rather than "conflict".

One important implication of assimilation theories has been to justify Canadian immigration which has been based upon differential selection on the basis of racial origins.

Adoption of class and colonial models suggest alternative approaches to the study of historical and contemporary situations of migrants, immigrants and non-white minorities. An analysis of the labour market segmentation and the location of the various "types" of workers in different segments of the labour market directs our attention to the role of white, black, brown, yellow labour in capital accumulation and management of capitalist contradictions. These studies also point out the importance of racism in the context of capitalism and class/race exploitation.

References

Adams, Howard
  1975   **Prison of Grass**. Toronto: General Publishing.
Arnopoulos, Sheila McLeod
  1979   "Problems of Immigrant Women in the Canadian Labour Force." Ottawa: Canadian Advisory Council on the Status of Women.

Baran, Paul and Paul Sweezy
  1966   **Monopoly Capital: An Essay on the American Economic and Social Order**. New York: Monthly Review Press.
Baron, Harold M.
  1975   "Racial Domination in Advanced Capitalism: A Theory of Nationalism and Division in the Labor Market." pp. 173-215, in Richard C. Edwards et al. (eds.) **Labor Market Segmentation**. Toronto: D.C. Heath and Company.
Berger, John and Jean Mohr
  1975   **A Seventh Man: Migrant Workers in Europe**. New York: The Viking Press.
Blauner, Robert
  1972   **Racial Oppression in America**. New York: Harper and Row Publishers.
Bohning, W.R.
  1979   "International Migration in Western Europe: Reflections on the Past Five Years." **International Labour Review**. 118:4, pp. 401-414.
  1972   **The Migration of Workers in the United Kingdom and European Community**. London: Oxford University Press.
Bonacich, Edna
  1972   "A Theory of Ethnic Antagonism: The Split Labour Market". **American Sociological Review**, 37:547-559.
  1976   "Advanced Capitalism and Black/White Race Relations in the United States: A Split Labour Market Interpretation." **American Sociological Review**, 41:34-51.
Bolaria, B. Singh
  1980   "Cultural Assimilation or Colonial Subordination" pp. 107-126 in K. Victor Ujimoto and Gordon Hirabayashi (eds.) **Asian Canadians and Multiculturalism**. University of Guelph. (Selections from the Proceedings Asian Canadian Symposium IV University of Montreal, Montreal, Quebec, May 25-28, 1980).
  1982   "Migrant Workers in the Canadian Labour Force" pp. 116-138 in K. Victor Ujimoto and Gordon Hirabayashi (eds.), **Asian Canadians Regional Perspectives**. University of Guelph. (Selections from Proceedings of the Asian Canadian Symposium V, Mount Saint Vincent University, Halifax, Nova Scotia, May 23-26, 1981).
Braverman, Harry
  1974   **Labour and Monopoly Capital: The Degradation of Work in the Twentieth Century**. New York: Monthly Review Press.
Cappon, Paul
  1975   "The Green Paper: Immigration as a Tool of Profit" **Canadian Ethnic Studies**, Vol. VIII, No. 1, pp. 50-54.
Carmichael, Stokeley and Charles W. Hamilton
  1967   **Black Power: The Politics of Liberation in America**. New York: Vintage.
Castles, Stephen and Godula Kosack
  1973   **Immigrant Workers and Class Structure in Western Europe**. Oxford: Oxford University Press.
Cox, Oliver C.
  1959   **Caste, Class and Race: A Study in Social Dynamics**. New York: Monthly Review Press.

Elston, Mary Ann
    1977   "Women in the Medical Profession: Whose Problem?" pp. 115-138, in
            Margaret Stacey, et al. (eds.) **Health and the Division of Labour**, London:
            Croom Helm.
Fanon, Frantz
    1967   "Racism and Culture" in **Toward the African Revolution**. New York:
            Monthly Review Press.
Frank, A.G.
    1969   **Latin America: Underdevelopment or Revolution**. New York: Monthly
            Review Press.
Gangulee, N.
    1947   **Indians in the Empire Overseas**. London: The New India Publishing House
            Limited.
Geshwender, James
    1978   **Racial Stratification in America**. Dubuque, Iowa: William C. Brown.
Glazer, Nathan and Daniel Moynihan
    1970   **Beyond the Melting Pot**. Cambridge: The M.I.T. Press.
Gorz, Andre
    1970   "Immigrant Labour" **The New Left Review**. 61 May/June. pp. 18-31.
Grove, John
    1974   "Differential Political and Economic Patterns of Ethnic and Race Relations: A
            Cross National Analysis". **Race**, 15:3, pp. 303-329.
Herberg, Will
    1960   **Protestant, Catholic, Jew**. New York: Doubleday.
Horton, John
    1966   "Order and Conflict Theories of Social Problems as Competing Ideologies".
            American Journal of Sociology, 71:701-13.
Hsu, Frances L.K.
    1971   **Challenges of the American Dream. The Chinese in the United States**.
            San Francisco: Wadsworth.
Huttenback, Robert A.
    1976   **Racism and Empire**. Ithaca: Cornell University Press.
Kellough, Gail
    1980   "From Colonialism to Economic Imperialism: The Experience of the Cana-
            dian" pp. 343-737, in John Harp and John Hoffley (eds.) **Structured In-
            equality in Canada**. Scarborough, Ontario: Prentice Hall of Canada, Ltd.
Krauter, Joseph F. and Morris Davis
    1978   **Minority Canadians: Ethnic Groups**. Toronto: Methuen.
Leggett, John
    1968   **Class, Race and Labour: Working Class Consciousness in Detroit**. New
            York: Oxford University Press.
Lewis, Oscar
    1959   **Five Families: Mexican Case Studies in the Culture of Poverty**. New
            York: Basic Books.
    1966   **La Vida: A Puerto Rican Family in the Culture of Poverty**. San Juan and
            New York: Random House.

Li, Peter S. and B. Singh Bolaria
　1979　"Canadian Immigration Policy and Assimilation Theories" pp. 411-422 in John A. Fry (ed.) **Economy, Class and Social Reality**. Toronto: Butterworths.
Light, Ivan H.
　1972　**Ethnic Enterprise in America: Business and Welfare Among Chinese, Japanese and Blacks**. Berkeley, California: University of California Press.
Moore, Joan W.
　1975　"Colonialism: The Case of Mexican Americans". in Norman R. Yetman and C. Hoy Steel (eds.) **Majority and Minority**. Toronto: Allyn and Bacon, Inc.
Moore, Robert
　1977　"Migration and the Class Structure of Western Europe" pp. 136-149 in Richard Scase, (ed.) **Industrial Society: Class, Cleavage and Control**. London: George Allen and Unwin Ltd.
Oppenheimer, Martin
　1974　"The Sub-Proletariat: Dark Skins and Dirty Work." **Insurgent Sociologist**, Vol. 4, pp. 7-20.
Park, Robert E.
　1950　**Race and Culture**. Glencoe, Illinois: Free Press.
Piore, Michael J.
　1979　**Birds of Passage**. Cambridge: Cambridge University Press.
Reich, Michael
　1971　"The Economics of Racism" pp. 107-113 in David Gordon (ed.) **Problems in Political Economy**. Lexington, Mass.: Heath.
Rosen, Bernard C.
　1956　"The Achievement Syndrome: A Psychological Dimension of Social Stratification." **American Sociological Review**. 21.
　1959　"Race, Ethnicity, and the Achievement Syndrome." **American Sociological Review**. 24:47-60.
Saha, Panchanan
　1970　**Emigration of Indian Labor (1834-1900)**. Delhi: People's Publishing House.
Szymanski, Albert
　1976　"Racism and Sexism as Functional Substitutes in the Labour Market." **Sociological Quarterly**. 17:65-73.
Tabb, William
　1970　**The Political Economy of Black Ghetto**. New York: Norton.
　1971　"Capitalism, Colonialism, and Racism". **Review of Radical Political Economics**, Vol. 3, No. 3, pp. 90-106.
Tinker, Hugh
　1974　**A New System of Slavery**. Oxford: Oxford University Press.
　1976　**Separate and Unequal**. Vancouver: University of British Columbia Press.
Wagley, Charles and Marvin Harris
　1958　**Minorities in the New World**. New York: Columbia University Press.
Ward, Peter
　1978　**White Canada Forever**. Montreal: McGill-Queen's University Press.
Williams, Andre
　1964　**Capitalism and Slavery**. London: Andre Deutsch Ltd.